SHANNON MILLER

Also by Krista Quiner

Dominique Moceanu: A Gymnastics Sensation

Kim Zmeskal: Determination to Win

SHANNON MILLER
America's Most Decorated Gymnast

A Biography by Krista Quiner

THE BRADFORD BOOK COMPANY
East Hanover, New Jersey

Printed in the United States of America
Second Edition
10 9 8 7 6 5 4 3 2 1

Photo Credits:
All photographs and artwork were produced by Steve Lange, unless otherwise noted.

Library of Congress Cataloging-in-Publication Data

Quiner, Krista, 1970-
    Shannon Miller : America's most decorated gymnast :
a biography / by Krista Quiner. — 2nd ed.
        p.   cm.
    Includesbibliographical references (p. 238).
    1. Miller, Shannon, 1977-   2. Gymnasts—United
States—Biography.   I. Title.
GV460.2.M55Q55   1997
796.44'092—dc20
[B]   96-36316
                                                      CIP

ISBN: 0-9643460-5-2

To my parents, Keith and Judy Bailey,
who have been very supportive of all my endeavors
I love you both

To Shannon Miller,
whose attitude and discipline are an example to us all

ACKNOWLEDGMENTS

To Barry Quiner, who sacrificed many evenings and weekends to shape this book into what it is today;

To Cara Bailey, who made time to carefully proofread and correct the manuscript;

To Steve Lange, who has again proven to be one of the biggest assets to the project;

To Shannon Miller, who found time to patiently answer all my many questions despite her busy schedule;

To Steve Nunno, who took the time to share his thoughts and allowed me to watch him coach;

To Ron and Claudia Miller, who provided delightful stories about their daughter;

To Peggy Liddick, who candidly talked with me about coaching Shannon from a young trickster to a polished athlete;

To Terri Thomas, who honestly shared her views;

To Rob Klein, Matt McCann, and the rest of the Team USA staff, who opened up the camp to me;

To Paul Quiner, whose counsel, despite his own enormous work load, was invaluable;

To Mark Quiner, for his advice and willingness to help;

To Brian Bailey, whose shipping services could not go without mention;

To Sherry Davis, for her assistance and distinguished signature;

I owe sincere *thanks*.

Krista Quiner

FOREWORD

—————————•○●●○•—————————

Ironically, here I was in Moscow, Russia, 1986, when the Soviet Union was still the ever-so-powerful communist country that literally dominated women's gymnastics. In fact, dominate was a bit of an understatement. I was crouched in the corner of a chalkless training gym, where few, if any, Americans had ever been previously, searching for the secret to coaching an Olympic Champion. But rather than watching the top gymnasts train, my eyes were fixed on a pixie-like, almost fragile-looking young girl from our own U.S. tour group scowling after each attempt to learn a simple double twist into a foam pit. As a former competitor myself, I somehow shared her frustration and knew right away how to help her channel her negative energy, though we had never even been formally introduced.

About one month later, I found myself coaching this little diamond in the rough as a budding, young, eight-year-old gymnast at my newly formed Dynamo Gymnastics Club in Oklahoma. Little did I know that later she would become the most decorated American gymnast ever. Shannon Miller was her name. An energetic youngster with a tremendous drive for perfection. She lived just forty-five minutes away, almost in my own back yard as far as elite gymnasts go, although she was far from an elite at the time. In fact, she had barely even reached competition level when we met.

Most people who do not know her well describe her as shy and introverted, especially due to her lack of words just after her stellar performance at the 1992 Olympic Games in Barcelona, Spain. But how many fifteen-year-old girls have ever done what Shannon Miller had just done, let alone realize the impact of such a feat at such a young age? A record five medals at a single non-boycotted Olympic Games. It seems unbelievable even now. Yet Shannon's modesty has always been her trademark, courteous to the feelings of those whom she has defeated, and respectful of those whom she has not. Shannon always had more to *do* than she had to *say*, and in a world of so much hype and super sport figures, one must find this quality somewhat refreshing.

Shannon Miller is the most dedicated individual that I have ever met in or out of the gym. Throughout the ten years that I have coached her, she has never missed one scheduled practice. She is usually the first one finished with her assignments no matter which event it is, and the most eager to develop new skills. Shannon is also a straight A student who attended regular public high school and graduated with honors with her class.

But the one thing that I respect most about Shannon Miller is her perseverance. She continually proves to get better and better when almost everyone, including history, tells her it just can't be done. Shannon has won consecutive world all-around titles, many world event titles, and scores of medals from numerous international competitions. Internationally, she has brought a new level of respect to USA Gymnastics. Shannon's goal was to help the USA team win the team gold medal on home turf at the Olympic Games in Atlanta. But now that the Atlanta Olympics are over, you can bet that Shannon Miller's results will always speak louder than she does as she continues her quest to be her best. A feat that only she understands.

Truly, I can't help but think that it was fate that brought us together in Moscow as we were both chasing our Olympic dreams. Yet I must say that Shannon's success came not only from her unshakable trust in her coaches and devotion to her family, but mostly from her belief in herself. Shannon is an incredible, unique individual, a true believer. She is a living legend and an inspiration to thousands of people around the world, young and old.

I hope that this book will bring all of you closer to the wonderful person that I have been so fortunate to coach.

—Steve Nunno
Shannon Miller's Coach; Owner, Dynamo Gymnastics

CONTENTS

Chapter 1

Moscow Sensation

"And voted this year's best female gymnast . . . Shannon Miller from Dynamo Gymnastics."

An elegant young woman approaches the microphone and graciously accepts her award—one of many she has received from her tremendous success in the sport of gymnastics. Now there are too many to count. Ribbons, medals, trophies, and plaques fill her house; there is hardly room for them all.

People recognize her face in grocery stores. Autograph seekers rush toward her in shopping malls. Adoring fans scream out her name at competitions and paper their bedroom walls with her likeness. Wherever there are girls striving for gymnastic glory, there are dreams of becoming like Shannon Miller. Generations past looked to heroes named Olga, named Nadia, named Mary Lou. Now the name is Shannon.

SHANNON MILLER

She has endorsed several products, her own workout line of clothing, a step aerobics video, and even a fan club. Letters from admirers pack an entire room in her house, and the phone rings constantly with offers and requests to attend dinners and benefits. Her face appears in many places, from television commercials and magazine covers to small-town billboards.

She is America's most celebrated gymnast. She has been the U.S. Champion and the World Champion—twice. At the 1992 Olympic Games she won more medals than any other U.S. athlete. No gymnast has ever amassed more major victories than this young woman.

She has won every prize imaginable, except one: Olympic gold. The most coveted and prestigious medal in all of gymnastics. The medal that slipped from her grasp twice in 1992 by mere *thousandths* of a point. The medal for which she still hungers, for which she will defy conventional wisdom and continue training until the "old" age of nineteen.

Some say she is past her prime. Some mock a string of second-place finishes. Others point to a competition she left without finishing as proof of the end of her reign.

But this young fighter will not be stopped by criticism. She is committed to going all out for the 1996 Summer Olympic Games. She has tasted the sweetness of victory and the bitterness of defeat. She has spent her childhood in a chalky gym, and she knows the price that must be paid in sweat and tears to become a champion. She will endure the frustration, the pain, and the exhaustion—all for one last chance at Olympic glory.

She is America's Queen of Gymnastics, and she is not ready to relinquish her crown.

★　★　★

Shannon Lee Miller was born Thursday, March 10, 1977.

Her entrance into this world was not spectacular. She almost emerged without a name.

The Millers lived in Rolla, Missouri. They had been tossing around a few names but could not settle on one, even in the delivery room. Shannon's mother, Claudia, liked unique names while her father, Ron, liked more common ones. Claudia had been working at a bookstore when someone suggested the name Shannon. When she told her husband the name, he said he liked it well enough but was not sure one way or the other. Finally, on the delivery table, they agreed to name the baby Shannon. Her middle name came from her paternal grandmother, Mabel Lee.

Shannon's parents met in college. Both attended Trinity University in San Antonio, Texas. During their junior year they started meeting in the parking lot; they parked near each other frequently. They began walking to class together and a short time later started dating, which continued throughout their senior year.

Upon graduating, both continued their education at separate schools in Missouri. Ron went to graduate school and Claudia went to law school. For a year they were separated by one hundred miles which Ron drove on Sundays to spend time with Claudia. The next year they were married.

Four years afterward, Tessa was born. "Tessa was a terror," Claudia joked, "it's amazing we ever had another child after her."

Then Shannon came along. "When Shannon was born, I did not believe the nurse when she told me her birth weight," Claudia remembered. "Her sister had been small at six pounds five ounces, but she was two weeks early, so I thought that must partly explain her small size. But Shannon came exactly on her due date and weighed only five pounds six ounces; I was concerned and questioned the doctor, but she assured me she was a very healthy baby, and so it proved to be."

Shannon was a good baby, very different from Tessa. She did not cry or fuss too much. This was a relief to her parents.

3

Even as an infant, Shannon had a lot of energy. She liked to skip her morning nap, which made it difficult for her mom to keep up with her.

When Shannon was brought to the hospital for a routine four-month checkup, the pediatrician noticed that Shannon's legs were not growing properly. She did not think it was anything serious and told the Millers to do certain exercises with Shannon's legs and to come back in a month. But at the next visit it was apparent that additional corrective measures needed to be taken.

Shannon was referred to a specialist, Dr. Rick Beller, who determined that she would need to wear special shoes attached to a heavy metal bar that would turn her legs outward. Her feet had been turning in. Dr. Beller thought Shannon should wear this gear for a full year if necessary, even in bed, and only take it off for a bath.

"Shannon vigorously protested her new equipment for a week or two and then decided to make the best of it," Claudia recalled. "In no time she was crawling, dragging the brace with her, and then pulling up, balancing expertly on the bar. With the bar as her constant companion, her legs responded quickly, and in only six months, Dr. Beller decided the bar could come off. In less than two weeks she was walking, at the same age that her sister had begun!"

When Shannon was six months old, she and her family moved to Edmond, Oklahoma, a quiet little town of about 60,000 people, where Ron began to work as a physics professor at the University of Central Oklahoma. Claudia took a job as vice president of a local bank.

Claudia looked forward to hearing her little daughter's first word. One day Shannon was playing in the bathtub with her sister when Tessa stole her toy. Shannon was not happy, so she reached over and grabbed the toy and said, "Mine."

Her mom was thrilled. "Oh my gosh! Her first word!" she

remembered thinking.

Claudia took Tessa and Shannon to a shopping mall to look for some new clothes. She set them both on the floor in a narrow aisle for just a second as she browsed through the rack of baby clothes. But when she looked down they were both gone. She was not worried since only a few seconds had passed and she did not think they could have gone very far. She went to the next aisle, and sure enough, there was Tessa. She thought Shannon would be nearby, but there was no sign of her anywhere.

"Where's Shannon?" she asked Tessa.

Tessa responded with an innocent "I don't know."

Claudia recalled what happened next: "Now I'm starting to get a little nervous, so I start looking up and down around the aisles and I can't find her. I'm calling her, 'Shannon! Shannon!' After about five minutes of looking, which seemed like a half hour, I was really getting terrified. By now I'm telling every single clerk I can find about my child: 'She's this little (indicating Shannon's height with her hand) and she has curly blond hair.' By ten minutes I'm crying. I'm carrying Tessa and we're both going through the store crying. I'm scared to death she's gone out into the mall. They brought me two other kids that they found, and I'm like, 'No, no, that's not my kid!' It's kind of scary to think this many kids are lost.

"By now about twenty minutes have gone by and I'm really hysterical. I've gone through that entire store ten times. About that time an older man comes to me and says, 'I think I might have found your child.' I said, 'Where? Where is she?' He says, 'Come over here, I think you need to see.' So he takes me over and she's in the shoe department. She's sitting on the floor behind a big rack and she's trying on these big men's shoes. It was so funny because she had these little, tiny, baby feet inside these big shoes."

While she developed an early interest in shopping, Shannon

was not too interested in food. She was very finicky. At her first Thanksgiving dinner she fell asleep, and her face fell in her food.

Shannon was a small but active toddler. She was so tiny that she did not even make it to the bottom of the growth chart during her first year. Her size did not seem to hold her back, however.

Like many little sisters, Shannon wanted to do everything that her older sister did. Tessa would climb to the top of the jungle gym in the back yard, and Shannon would try to tag along.

"Shannon was this little, tiny, short thing standing on the ground trying to climb up," Claudia said. "One day I looked out—she was barely walking—and she was halfway up that jungle gym." Her parents were amazed. They ran outside and took pictures. They were a bit nervous for Shannon, but she looked like she was in control so they did not stop her.

At the age of four, Shannon decided she wanted to do ballet and jazz dancing because Tessa was doing it. Her mother thought she was too young, but Shannon convinced her grandmother otherwise.

"My mother said 'No, if she wants to go with her big sister, I'll pay,' " Claudia remembered. "I said, 'Okay, if you want to throw your money away.' "

"We started in dance," Shannon said. "But after a year we were getting a little bored." She wanted an activity that was more exciting, so she told her parents she wanted Santa to bring her a trampoline for Christmas.

Her dad was apprehensive. "Uh-uh," he said. "No. We're not having a trampoline. Those are dangerous." Besides, the Millers could not afford a brand new one since trampolines were so expensive. But Shannon kept asking, and she finally got her wish. Her parents found a used one and Shannon's grandmother chipped in some money since Shannon desperately wanted it.

"Dad, put it up, please," she begged on Christmas morning. "Put it up!" She was eager to start jumping, but the trampoline was outside and it was a cold morning, around nine degrees. Shannon convinced her dad and uncle to set it up despite the frigid temperature.

Shannon liked to bounce all day on her new trampoline. She and her sister were very daring.

"We would egg each other on," Shannon laughed.

They fell a lot, but within two weeks Shannon could do a front flip. She also liked to bounce around the living room. Her parents were impressed with her acrobatic skills, but they worried she might get hurt or tear up the furniture, so a few months later on her fifth birthday they signed her up at a local gymnastics center called Adventures in Gymnastics. They picked this gym because it was the only one that returned Claudia's phone calls.

"My mom put my sister and me in gym because we bounced so much on our trampoline," Shannon remembered. "She thought we needed some instruction. My sister later went on to other sports, but I loved gymnastics."[1]

At the age of five, Shannon was becoming more independent, holding her own with Tessa. "She rules the roost at home," her mom said, "and she really always has." While Tessa excelled at many sports and frequently liked to try new ones, Shannon was more focused and capable of concentrating on one sport.

Shannon did try other sports, however. She went snow skiing with her family at Keystone, Colorado, and easily glided down the slopes. Members of the ski resort staff were so impressed that they took a picture of her and hung the 8" x 10" photograph inside the lodge. This was one of her favorite family vacations.

Shannon also learned to ride a horse. One day while she was learning to ride from her mother, Claudia had to step inside the stable to get a whip. She figured Shannon would be okay because the horse was walking and Shannon had ridden before. When she returned, she noticed a lot of people standing around and pointing at Shannon, who had made the horse canter.

Claudia asked, "How did you get him to canter?"

"I just kicked and kicked," Shannon replied.

When Shannon was nine, a high school diver saw her flipping off the diving board at her neighborhood pool and told the diving coach about her. The coach began calling to ask Shannon to try diving, so one day she practiced with the diving team. The coach really wanted her on the team, but she was not interested.

Shannon felt that her natural athletic ability came from her mom. "She does about every sport that there is, or at least tries it," Shannon said. "My dad, he isn't quite as athletic but he plays tennis, racquetball, and golf."

Though she had talents in other areas, Shannon liked nothing more than gymnastics. She had not watched much gymnastics on television, so she did not have a favorite gymnast that she wanted to emulate. She participated for the pure joy and excitement that the sport had to offer.

The first skill Shannon learned was a back walkover. Upon mastering the trick, she was eager to demonstrate her new ability. When her hometown had a Fourth of July parade, she performed back walkovers all over the streets of Edmond.

Shannon's coach, Jerry Clavier, saw potential in his tiny pupil and asked her to increase her involvement by taking classes every day for an hour.

Claudia was surprised. "*Every* day! That's crazy!" she exclaimed. But Ron agreed to take Shannon on his lunch hour. Both of them thought she would get tired of going at that pace, but they were willing to support her for as long as she wanted to do gymnastics.

Shannon's interest in the sport kept growing and growing. One time she was misbehaving and her father refused to take her to gymnastics class that day. This really upset her.

"She wanted to go that badly," her mom remembered, "that

we could use it as leverage."

After about a year, Shannon's coach suggested that she get tested for the junior elite program. To make the team she needed to learn a press to handstand. She was having a little trouble with it so her coach told her to practice at home. It was not very fun for her to practice the skill at home, but her parents came up with an incentive.

"She wanted a Cabbage Patch doll really bad, but you couldn't even get them here," Claudia recalled. "So we finally told her, 'Look, if you work your press to handstand at home and get your press to handstand, we'll buy you a Cabbage Patch doll.' We figured it would be a couple months before she got it, and by then they would have the doll. She got [the skill] in a couple of days."

Claudia tried to explain to Shannon that the dolls were not yet available locally. Finally, about a month later, a shipment of dolls came into a nearby Target store.

"It was a limited number," Claudia said. "First-come, first-served. Her dad got up at five in the morning to stand in line to get a ticket to be able to come back later when the store opened and try to get the doll. He gave it to me. I took my lunch hour, only at ten o'clock in the morning, so I could be there when the store opened." Shannon was elated when her parents handed her the new doll.

On her first attempt to make junior elite, Shannon did not qualify. She went back in the gym and worked very hard. The next time she did much better, easily making the United States Association of Independent Gymnastics Clubs' (USAIGC) junior elite team. The members of this team did not compete but went to clinics and camps to improve their skills so that one day, when they were old enough, they could represent the United States in international competitions.

Shannon's family didn't know what a lifetime commitment they were making to gymnastics. "It was a gradual process," Ron said about his daughter's early involvement in the sport. "It went pretty quick, though. But it was a gradual process of being sucked into it. In other words, she was just going locally to the club for a year or so and then we went into hock for two years to send her and Claudia to Russia."[2]

Shannon's first big trip outside the United States was to the Mecca of gymnastics, Moscow, in the Soviet Union. As part of the junior elite program, she went to train in Russia for two weeks in the summer of 1986. This was hard on her parents because she was so young and the trip was very expensive.

Shannon just missed seeing the Goodwill Games in Moscow, which were held a couple days after the tour ended. She thought the Games seemed exciting and hoped she could compete in them someday. The Goodwill Games were held every four years and were next scheduled to be in Seattle in 1990.

During the training camp in Moscow, Shannon's extraordinary ability was immediately noticed by the Russian coaches. Of the forty girls at the training camp, the Russians picked two who had elite potential, and Shannon was one of them. An American coach who was on the tour and interested in improving his training methods also spotted this petite girl. Coincidentally, this coach was also from Oklahoma.

"Shannon came from a small club nearby in Oklahoma City," the American coach recalled. "There was some kind of a trip that was going on in the Soviet Union. And their club happened to be going the same time as I was going for a professional tour, and we just happened to see each other in the gym. I saw this little girl training hard and I said, 'Boy, that one looks like a good one for me.' "

Shannon tried very hard to do her best and became quite upset with herself whenever she messed up. This quality endeared her to the American coach.

"There's a girl I can help," he remembered thinking. "If I can help that girl channel her frustration into some positive energy, I believe I can get her to perform at a much higher level than she's at now." This instructor, Steve Nunno, happened to coach at a gymnastics club about forty-five minutes away from the Millers' house.

When Shannon returned home from Moscow, she was eager to learn the tricks she had seen the Russians trying. However, her coach, Jerry, had the opposite reaction after attending the camp. He realized how much more advanced the Russians were and said that neither his program nor Shannon could ever compete with them.

"He stood right in the doorway, I remember," Claudia said, "and told me, 'Forget it. There's no way she's ever going to be an elite.' At that time I'm not thinking in terms of Olympics, but I'm thinking at least the national team. So that's when we decided, 'Wait a minute, if that's the attitude you have, we need to find ourselves another gym.'

"So we talked to her about it. Well, she was hot to compete. I think she might have stayed except that he told her, 'You're not ready to compete.' He had told her all the year before that 'When you turn nine you'll be able to compete,' and now he told her, 'No, you're not ready. There's no way.' We could see we were going to lose her because you don't spend that many hours just training year after year and never get anything back out of it."

So Shannon switched gyms and began training with Steve Nunno, the head coach of a team called the Dynamos. Steve was planning to move into his own gymnastics facility, but while he saved money and looked for a location he rented space at the Gymnastic Chalet, a gym owned by Bart Conner, a 1984 Olympic gold medalist, and his coach, Paul Ziert.

Up to this point, Shannon had always done gymnastics for

fun. But after returning from Moscow, she became more serious about her sport. Steve applied the strict training he had learned in Russia.

"The turning point was when I went to the Soviet Union," Shannon remembered, "and I realized that it takes a lot of hard work. We worked out there a lot harder than we did at home, and I saw how good the Soviets were, and I realized then that I wanted to be that good."

Steve was initially hesitant to coach Shannon. "When she first came I wasn't entirely sure I wanted to take her," he said. "I saw her in Russia. I saw her petite size and her determination, but she cried all the time. Every time she'd take a turn, she'd cry. I knew that I was going to have to put my foot down on the crying part. In our gym, only if you're hurt are you allowed to cry."

In the fall of 1986, Shannon began competing in local class II competitions at the age of nine. She skipped the first two classes because of her high ability level.

The gymnastics class system has changed, but at that time class IV was the lowest and class I was the highest. Beyond class I was a special group called elite, the ultimate ranking possible. Nowadays, there are ten levels and elite, with level 1 the lowest. Many gymnasts do not aspire to be an elite; a level 9 or 10 gymnast may be capable of receiving a college scholarship. Only if an athlete's goal is to be on the national team or compete internationally does she seek the highest ranking.

In her very first competition in Dallas, Shannon fell off the beam and bars, but she made all of her tumbling passes, so she ended on a good note.

"My first competitive season was rocky, to say the least," Shannon remembered. "It seemed that I fell at least once in every meet."

Steve agreed. "Most of the competitions Shannon had early

on in her career were very unsteady," he said. "She'd always have a fall on something. When she fell, it wasn't a wipeout. It was usually on a trick that was something fairly risky."

Shannon had to get used to competing in different gyms and on different equipment. She also had to adjust to wearing grips on bars, which was very hard. Steve told her she needed to start wearing them because they would protect her hands and make swinging easier. But swinging on the bars still caused the skin on her hands to tear sometimes. When she did get rips, she put ointment on her hands and covered them with socks while she slept at night. This kept her hands moist and prevented the fresh skin from cracking.

Competitions were a lot different from practice because there were judges, fans, and nerves with which to contend. Shannon saw some athletes who looked sharp in practice but fell apart under pressure. She had to become familiar enough with competitions to transfer her performance in practice to the meet. It took much of her first season to make that adjustment.

"By the end of the season, through hard work and determination, I had my act together and won the class II state championship," Shannon said, "and our team won the first-place trophy."

"I remember a meet in Bartlesville," Shannon's dad recalled, "which is fairly close to here—a three-hour drive—and we were driving back from it and I thought, 'Wow, this is a real trip, a real experience.' And then I saw some vapor trails (from a jet) up above Route 66 and I said, 'Wow, Shannon's gonna be going to Reno here in a couple of weeks. Wow, one of those big airplanes will have her on it.' I can remember thinking that." He laughed. "Little did I know that that was just the start. I mean, I thought a trip to *Bartlesville* was something."[3]

Steve was impressed with Shannon's natural ability, so he decided to have her skip class I and try to compete as an elite. He placed her in a group with his top gymnasts.

Shannon did not stand out right away. "Early on, she was not one of my best kids," Steve said. "In fact, she was one of the worst kids. And she had to play catch up for a couple of years. But she easily surpassed a number of athletes at a very rapid rate because of her determination."

Shannon's parents were not sure how good their daughter was, either. "We thought she was pretty good, but we had nothing to go by," her dad said. "So you can do a flip better than the next girl—big deal!"[4]

Shannon looked up to her teammates and wanted to be as good as they. "Shannon always wanted to be like Tracey Cole," Steve said. "She always wanted to be like somebody better than her in the gym."

Shannon and her teammates progressed very rapidly under the direction of Steve, a former gymnast himself. He was born and raised in the western part of New York state in a town called Canandaigua, and his parents divorced when he was nine. Because money was tight, Steve paid his own way through college by receiving a gymnastics scholarship. He was the captain of the team his junior year. He used his education to receive a bachelor's degree in business and a master's degree in sports administration from the University of Massachusetts and began coaching at the Gymnastics Junction in 1979.

Steve believed that gymnastics could help children in all aspects of life. He loved his work and was as driven as his students. He rarely, if ever, took vacations. His tenacity also meant that he was not easily intimidated.

"Anybody who knows me, knows that I'm not the shy character or the person who's going to back down from anyone," Steve once said. "I've been a competitor all my life, and when my back's against the wall, I'm at my best."

His own determination combined with Shannon's ability to work started paying off, and people began to notice her.

When Shannon was in the fourth grade, Bart Conner took note of her talent. "One of the great things about Shannon Miller is that . . . she's doing all the big difficulty at a very early age. When she matures, she will be a really top notch competitor. . . . She really does have a tremendous amount of skill going for her. She's quick. She has that fast-twitch muscle fiber which you need to have to be a very explosive gymnast."

Steve and Shannon experimented in practice with many difficult skills. "She was a trickster and I was a trickster," he stated. "I made sure that she was doing the big skills from day one, skills that were way beyond what she thought she could do. But she was willing to try them, so I was willing to go with it."

Shannon's first national competition was the 1987 USAIGC National Gymnastics Championship at the University of Delaware in Newark. This was a team competition, and her team, the Dynamos, was in third place after the preliminaries.

With her naturally curly hair tied in two pigtails—braided and looped on the side—tiny Shannon captivated the audience. On balance beam she was steady on a side aerial but came a bit unglued on her back handspring layout and fell. She climbed back onto the beam, went through the rest of the routine, and dismounted with a high double twist. She saluted the judges then burst into tears. Steve gave her a hug and tried to console his still-developing pupil, who was disappointed and mad at herself for falling.

This was Shannon's first television appearance, and she received much attention, especially from the commentators, who praised her talents and declared that she would be one to watch in the future. Bart Conner, one of the television announcers, was flattered when Shannon listed him as her favorite television star on her press sheet.

On floor exercise, ten-year-old Shannon started with a difficult double pike somersault. A medley from the Broadway musical *Cats* accompanied her as she played to the crowd and executed two whip backs to a double twist. She had plenty of endurance for her young age and ended with another high double twist. She scored a 9.25.

Shannon and her youthful teammates placed third among some of the best clubs in the United States. This meet really changed Shannon's perspective. Although her teammates were older, she felt, for the first time, like an important part of the team.

Shortly after this competition, Steve decided to fulfill a dream and open his own facility. He named it Dynamo Gymnastics after a famous Russian gymnastics center he had visited during his trip to Moscow.

"I wanted to go see the main training facility; there were two of them at the time in Moscow," Steve said. "So I broke off from the traveling group and snuck into the Dynamo gym there. They called it 'Dinamo' (dee-NAHM-o). [It] was a government-run facility and they didn't allow people with video cameras in there. I was in there videotaping and watching, and I really liked the atmosphere. I had heard all these secrets that the Russians beat up [their athletes]. Baloney. They were having a great time with the kids but they were training hard. I liked the energy in it and I said, 'I'm going to call my gym Dynamo.' "

Shannon made the switch from the gym in Norman to the one in the capital, Oklahoma City, to continue training with Steve. She trained four hours a day, Monday through Saturday. Sunday was a day to relax and spend time with the family, although sometimes her mom, a level 10 gymnastics judge, would be off scoring meets.

In her free time, Shannon liked to play with her older sister, Tessa, her younger brother, Troy, and the many family pets. The Millers had a thoroughbred horse named Bruce, a chubby gray cat named Gizmo, a dog named Ebony, gerbils, hermit crabs, and fish. They had a big yard, but the horse, which belonged to Shannon's mother, was not kept at their house, so Shannon did not ride him very much. Besides all the real animals, Shannon collected lots of stuffed animals, which filled her room.

"I *love* stuffed animals," Shannon said. "I have a lot of bears."

One time Shannon brought home a little kitten without asking her parents. A lady was giving away kittens, and Shannon thought one was particularly cute. She called the kitty Gym T. Her parents decided to let her keep the pet, although they got stuck taking care of it whenever Shannon traveled.

One of Shannon's favorite hobbies was sewing. "I started sewing in seventh or eighth grade for home economics class," she said. "We had to learn how to sew. When I did, I decided I'd sew myself a leotard. A friend's mom gave me a pattern for a leotard, and I just started making my own."

Shannon made about ten leotards. "I won't say that I didn't ever screw any up," she laughed, "but I think they got better the more I did."

Shannon did not watch a lot of television, but when she did her favorite programs were *The Cosby Show*, *Cheers*, and *Full House*. She liked to watch television before practice, but she was allowed to watch only after her homework was done.

During family meals, Shannon was so small that she had to sit on a telephone book to reach the dinner table. She did not eat very much; sometimes she only had a baked potato for dinner. Shannon was a very picky eater by nature, but she liked to indulge every so often in her favorite foods: pizza, Chinese, and frozen yogurt.

Steve did not like her to eat much junk food. Ice cream was a definite no-no. Sometimes she would crave fast food, which Steve said was okay as long as it was not fried in fat. That eliminated french fries from McDonald's, but a roast beef sandwich from Arby's was allowed.

Shannon was weighed in periodically, about once a week. Her coaches monitored the girls' weight to make sure no one was gaining or losing too many pounds.

"She's always been a very particular eater," Steve said. "And I don't feel she's ever really had too much of a problem with eating. She's seen kids with eating disorders and what happens to them. She certainly didn't want to be like them. But there have been times where I think she's tried to lose weight or tried to eat not so much and she ends up with not much of an energy level. So we've had to try to keep an eye on that."

Shannon's normal diet consisted of a good breakfast and lunch with a small snack before gym and another small snack afterward. Most of her meals were small, so her intake of calories was spread evenly over the course of the day.

At her first major elite-level meet, the 1988 American Classic, Shannon placed second in the children's division (or junior B division). Participation in this event marked her passage to the highest level in gymnastics.

An athlete had to qualify as an elite by receiving certain scores in special qualifying meets. Most of the girls competing on television were elites. Not many gymnasts attained this level; it required many hours of intense and expensive training.

A month after the American Classic, Shannon traveled to Athens, Georgia, for the 1988 U.S. Classic. She performed superbly, winning vault and balance beam. She captured her first major victory in the all-around as well. By winning the meet, Shannon established herself as the best gymnast in the country in the children's division.

During her stay in Georgia, Shannon and her teammates were invited to country music legend Kenny Rogers' house for lunch. Steve thought his gymnasts would really enjoy this, so he agreed to go.

Steve recalled a funny incident that happened before they left for lunch: "I had all the girls dressed up to go. All the kids get in the van and I'm ready to drive them out there, and I look down and Shannon's got a dress on and a pair of tennis shoes. And I mean an old, *beat up* pair of tennis shoes. That's all she's got and she's in a dress. I just happened to mention it; you don't want to hurt somebody's feelings. But she didn't think anything of it."

Steve said, "Shannon, do you have another pair of shoes? Do you have a pair of dress shoes?"

"No, I don't have a pair," Shannon replied.

"Well, I'm sure you have some at home, right?"

"Yeah, but this is what I'm going to wear."

"I don't think so," Steve declared firmly.

Steve drove to a discount shoe store and Shannon ran in to get a pair of shoes that would match her dress.

"She was actually just gonna go over to Kenny Rogers' house with a pair of high-top tennis shoes that were all beat up and ugly," Steve remembered with a smile. "She likes to wear her tennis shoes until they're just ready to fall off her feet. It was pretty funny. Ever since then we always rag her about it. Now she is so very stylish that she would never think of that. But she laughs every time we talk about it."

Shannon's high placement at the U.S. Classic allowed her to travel to the Junior Pan American Games in Puerto Rico. One of Shannon's favorite things about gymnastics was the traveling. This was her first competition abroad, and she finished second overall and third on bars.

Shannon was steadily improving and quietly making a name for herself. Even at the age of eleven, she was tough and persistent. At the Dragon Invitational she had a bad uneven bar fall during warmups, but the spill did not rattle her confidence. She finished eighth overall, even with members of the senior national team, like Christy Henrich, competing.

At the 1989 American Classic in May, Shannon won the junior division. Her achievement qualified her to the Olympic Sports Festival, where she would battle against the toughest juniors in the country.

In the event finals at the American Classic, Shannon wowed the crowd in Oakland, California, winning bars, beam, and floor. While capturing first place on three events, Shannon also captured the hearts of the fans, especially on floor with her dramatic routine to *"Jesus Christ Superstar."*

Shannon was outstanding on bars, beam, and floor, but she sometimes had problems on vault. "I was so little and it just seemed like the vault was so high and so far away from the board," she said. "I was scared I wasn't going to get to the horse."

A month after the American Classic, Shannon went to San Antonio, Texas, for the 1989 U.S. Classic. Unfortunately, she sustained a pulled hamstring in her right leg shortly before the competition. This hampered her performance, and she placed sixth overall.

Shannon's success as a junior was due to her spectacular routines, which were packed with tricks. Her style was a product of Steve's instruction. He did not bring the typical conservative attitude to his coaching.

"I was a breed apart," Steve said. "I didn't care whether I stuck my beam dismount. I was going to do a full-in off the beam and if I stuck it, great; if I didn't, take the tenth. I was willing to sacrifice the tenth for the difficulty and later on I'd polish it up. And it paid off in flying colors. That was always my philosophy. If I couldn't win with the difficulty, knowing that it was going to be high-level gymnastics—and not politics—that was going to win, then I didn't want to win. I wanted to win because I had the best gymnastics and not because I was the best politician."

While Steve was able to teach Shannon many difficult skills, he realized that he needed a good assistant coach to help with the dance movements, so he hired Peggy Liddick, a coach from the University of Nebraska. Peggy also recognized Shannon's ability, but she saw a few shortcomings.

"She was always a talent, but she was far from what she needed to be dance-wise," Peggy said. She worked with Shannon for hours at a time in front of a mirror, getting her legs straight and her toes turned out. She concentrated the most on compulsory beam and floor routines since she thought those were Shannon's weakest areas.

During the summer, Shannon participated in a major national meet, the 1989 Junior Nationals, held at the United States Olympic Sports Festival in her home state of Oklahoma. There were many other Olympic sports at the Festival, like track and field, swimming, diving, basketball, volleyball, and tennis. Of all the athletes at the Festival, Shannon was the tiniest, weighing only fifty-five pounds.

Shannon began on vault with a beautiful full-twisting layout Yurchenko (roundoff entry), but she took a step on the landing for a 9.475. Steve put his arm around her then patted her on the back; he was happy with her vault. As Steve and Shannon walked back to the starting marker, he told her how to improve on her next attempt, and she nodded eagerly.

Four-foot-two-inch Shannon ran hard down the runway and exploded off the springboard. Unfortunately, her hands touched the floor as she landed.

Shannon made up for her mistake on vault with a phenomenal uneven bar routine. She did two release moves, a Tkatchev (or reverse hecht) and a Gienger, then capped it off with an extremely difficult full-twisting double back flyaway that she nailed. She scored a 9.65.

"She [does it] every time in practice," Steve said of the stuck landing on her complicated dismount, "but I have yet to see that in competition. In competition she's always a bit conservative. Tonight, the crowd was really helping her out."[5]

Going to balance beam, Shannon was in third place. For a twelve-year-old, her difficulty was incredible! She threw almost every trick imaginable. The thrilling set inched her even closer to the leader. With one rotation to go, Shannon was in second place behind Kim Zmeskal, another rising star from legendary coach Bela Karolyi's gym in Houston, Texas.

Shannon's final event was floor—her best apparatus—while Kim's was the most difficult, the balance beam. Shannon fidgeted her toes nervously on the edge of the mat as she waited for the judges to signal her to begin. The local fans called out encouragingly, "Come on Shannon!"

Shannon took her position in the corner then turned to the beat of her music and faced the diagonal. She opened with a high full-twisting double pike somersault and smiled at the crowd in the Myriad Convention Center. Her two whip backs to a double twist punch front brought many cheers. She was on her way to becoming the champion until she ran out of gas on her last tumbling pass, a double pike, and landed far short of completion. She received only a 9.10.

Kim was steady on balance beam and finished first. Shannon placed third, which assured her a spot on the junior national team.

"I was really excited," Shannon remembered, "because it made me realize that I might be able to keep up with the other athletes and make the Olympic team if I kept working hard."

In the event finals, Shannon won the uneven bars and shyly admitted that she had done a good routine. She placed fifth on beam and sixth, with another fall, on floor. Her hamstring injury held her back from challenging the other competitors for the top spots, but she did not use it as an excuse.

After the meet, Shannon casually revealed to Steve that she and her teammates were going to stay up all night to celebrate.

Steve was amused. "Oh, you're staying up all night?" he asked with a smile.

After this competition, the people of Oklahoma City could not help but notice their home-grown celebrity. During the Festival, Shannon's accomplishments were reported ahead of the national news in the local newspaper.

Near the end of the summer, Shannon took advantage of an opportunity to go to the Far East for Japan's Junior International. Her pulled hamstring was still bothering her. In fact, she almost did not make the trip to Yokohama, Japan, because of it. But Steve really wanted to compete, so they went despite the injury. He told her to gut it out. Against a talented field, Shannon placed sixth overall and fourth on bars.

Shannon returned home looking forward to resting her leg during the off season. However, Steve decided to have her perform in an exhibition, the 1989 Tour of Champions, on November 8 in Oklahoma City. Her balance beam routine was extremely taxing on her leg, and Shannon became very upset with Steve for putting her in this exhibition.

"As soon as that was over, she threw a fit," her mom recalled. "That was the first time she came in and said, 'This is it. I'm not doing this anymore. I wanna quit.' And we said, 'What? What?!' She goes, 'I can't take this any longer. If this is what it means to compete, to just constantly have pain, I don't want to do this. I don't want to quit gymnastics. I want to take classes. I want to enjoy tumbling. But I'm not going to have this constant pain and never have any relief.' "

Chapter 2

In the Shadow

At the age of twelve, just when her career was beginning to blossom, Shannon felt burned out and considered quitting gymnastics.

Steve kept telling her, "One more meet, and then you can rest your pulled hamstring." Only the rest never came. Her leg injury had first occurred in the spring of 1989, and six months later it had not gotten any better. Finally, Shannon and her parents went to talk with Steve about the situation.

"She'd never had an injury before, not anything," Claudia said. "[Steve] just hadn't dealt with injuries. I don't think he understood what pain she was going through."

Steve called Bart Conner for advice. Bart invited Steve and Shannon to visit his trainer in Nevada, so they flew out and spent the night at Bart's home. The next day the trainer told Shannon she had a severe pull and needed to be off the leg for *four* months.

"Steve almost had a heart attack," Shannon's mom remarked. "He said, 'No way. You don't understand. A gymnast doesn't take four months off!' "

The trainer told Steve he would see improvement within three months if Shannon rested her leg. Steve reluctantly agreed. For two-and-a-half months Shannon did not tumble, vault, or try any skills that would irritate her injury. But Steve became impatient by mid-January and told Shannon she needed to begin preparing for the upcoming season. She had an exciting schedule ahead. She was the first junior to have ever been invited to the prestigious American Cup, and it was only a few weeks away.

Shannon quickly put together her routines and trained as well as she could under the circumstances. Her first meet of the new season was the Peachtree Classic in Marietta, Georgia, on February 17, 1990. Despite her lack of preparation, she placed fourth overall.

A few weeks later at the McDonald's American Cup in Fairfax, Virginia—Shannon's biggest international competition yet—she finished a respectable sixth overall in the preliminaries. This meet was significant because it showcased the best gymnasts from many different countries, such as the United States, the Soviet Union, Romania, and China. It was a well-known international competition. Former American Cup Champions included Nadia Comaneci, Mary Lou Retton, Kristie Phillips, Phoebe Mills, and Brandy Johnson.

The top eight finishers in the preliminaries advanced to the finals, but only two gymnasts per country were permitted to continue. Sandy Woolsey of the Desert Devils in Tempe, Arizona, and Kim Zmeskal finished ahead of Shannon.

A few days later on March 7, Shannon participated in the 1990 McDonald's International Mixed Pairs competition at Villanova University in Philadelphia. In this competition, one female and one male gymnast formed a team, and the pair with the highest combined total after three rounds won. Shannon was paired with Tom Schlesinger, a member of the U.S. men's national team.

Shannon chose to begin on the treacherous balance beam. She mounted with a nice press to a handstand into a planche, followed by a roundoff back handspring. She next executed a back handspring to two layouts, but she unfortunately lost her balance and fell off the beam. Still, she finished on a good note with a difficult full-twisting double back dismount.

Steve patted her on the back and encouraged, "You finished strong at the end." She scored a 9.15.

Her partner, Tom, did a good parallel bars routine, but it was not enough to make up for Shannon's fall. Only eight pairs could advance to the next round, and their total score was not high enough.

Next on Shannon's busy schedule was the 1990 Canadian Cup in Toronto, Ontario, where she placed ninth in the all-around. The Canadian meet was followed by the 1990 Pyramid Challenge: USA versus Germany held April 28-29.

Shannon had a fall on her balance beam tumbling series in the preliminaries but still managed to qualify for the team. Hoping to improve her beam set in the team finals, Shannon mounted confidently and hit her aerial front walkover. She stuck her two layouts in a row—the skill on which she had fallen the day before—but she sat down on her dismount, which counted as a fall. She scored a disappointing 9.20. Floor also did not go as planned, with another fall and a 9.225.

The errors were costly, and she ended up seventh in the all-around. Still, the U.S. team soundly beat Germany.

Although Shannon was not yet in the spotlight, Steve was confident that she would succeed. He knew she had the natural talent necessary to become great. Steve described her as "dainty, daring, and deceptively strong." He thought these attributes would eventually work to her advantage.

Shannon decided to enter the 1990 U.S. Championships as a senior even though she was only thirteen. This was an important meet because it ranked athletes for the upcoming year. The higher a gymnast placed, the greater her chance to attend major international meets of her choice.

The competition was held June 7-10 in the beautiful Rocky Mountain state of Colorado. After the compulsories, Shannon was in seventh place.

The compulsories are prescribed routines that must be performed by each athlete on every event to demonstrate technical competence. They are similar to the figures in ice skating.

Shannon started the optionals on her favorite event, the balance beam. Although only a little taller than the beam, she was undaunted. She threw all of her complex skills and managed to land a full-twisting double back dismount on her feet. Shannon had been the first American to compete this difficult dismount off beam. Steve picked her up and gave her a warm hug. The judges posted a 9.675.

Shannon turned in another good performance, this time on the floor exercise, to move up to sixth place. Her vault was equally strong.

Steve pumped Shannon up for her last event, uneven bars. He went over each move, using hand gestures to demonstrate how the skills should be performed. Unfortunately, Shannon was unable to hang onto the bar during her routine and scored only a 9.0, which dropped her to eighth. Still, being the youngest competitor ever to make the senior national team was quite a feat in itself.

The U.S. Championships awarded prize money to the winners, but by accepting the money an athlete had to forfeit her college eligibility. Shannon opted to accept the money she had won.

Shannon qualified to two event finals, balance beam and floor exercise. On beam she went through a near-perfect set until the dismount, during which she fell backwards and sat down. She tried to fight back the tears as she walked over to Steve, who put his arm around her and assured her that it was okay.

On floor, Shannon performed a decent routine and scored a 9.75, but against an experienced group of competitors she only placed fifth. All in all, the meet was a good experience for Shannon, as she gained the recognition of some national judges.

Shannon sometimes fell on balance beam or uneven bars, but her routines were packed with difficult skills. Steve's strategy was to let Shannon practice and get used to competing these intricate routines at an early age. He believed the skills would eventually become second nature to her and not result in falls. Some gymnasts updated their routines slowly to remain consistent, but they did so at the expense of difficulty. At the age of thirteen, Shannon already had all the difficulty she needed, and Steve knew this would prove to be an advantage when she had perfected her routines.

"Everybody always thought that she was a hot shot because she was always throwing the big skills," Steve explained. "My philosophy was I never really cared about who we beat in this country. I had a goal that I wanted Shannon to win at the world level. And if she was going to win at the world level she had to get these skills under her belt early on and not be afraid of them."

Shannon was willing to try any skill that Steve suggested, and she was not very fearful. "I don't remember Shannon ever really being afraid," Steve said. "I think I did enough progressions with her on every event so that she never really had a fear factor that stood out."

The top four competitors in the optional portion of the U.S. Championships qualified for the Goodwill Games team. Shannon had hoped to be part of this group, but the fall on uneven bars prevented her from making the team. She was an alternate, however, and would have been used if someone on the team had become injured.

Although Shannon did not compete at the Goodwill Games, she got a chance to compete against the top Soviet gymnasts at the USA versus USSR McDonald's Challenge. This was her first duel against the Soviet Union. "Mighty-mite Miller"—a nickname given Shannon by several magazines—held her own, placing sixth overall with the second highest score on the American team.

The Soviets brought some of their new hopefuls, including a thirteen-year-old trickster named Tatiana Gutsu. She was the Soviets' equivalent of Shannon. Tatiana wowed the crowd with her high level of difficulty on all the events, proving that she might be a top contender in the years to come. Both Shannon and Tatiana had great skills; they just needed to mature in their dance and expression. That would come in time.

Shannon took the remainder of the summer to concentrate on some new moves. While Steve was away at a meet, Shannon came up with an idea for a new skill to put in her beam routine: a back handspring with a quarter twist. She showed Steve when he returned, but at first he was indifferent about the trick. However, when he later began to piece together her beam routine, he realized that Shannon needed another skill, so he asked her to do the back handspring with a quarter twist. Steve looked in the Code of Points, which determined the value of each skill, and found that it was rated high in terms of difficulty. He had Shannon try it again. Steve decided he liked it better than he had the first time he had seen it, especially since it was worth a lot, and he added it to her routine.

Shannon learned new tricks on beam by first practicing them on the floor, then on the low beam, and eventually on the high beam. Once she mastered it, the back handspring with a quarter twist added a unique quality to her beam routine.

In the fall, Shannon went to Tempe, Arizona, for the American Classic. Unfortunately, she had a fall on compulsory bars. She came back with a vengeance in optionals, however. She hit her two release moves on bars and a full pirouette to an immediate full-twisting double back flyaway.

During the touch warmups on beam, Shannon crashed on her second layout. Her coaches ran over to make sure she was okay. But Shannon was unhurt, and she jumped back on the beam to complete her full-twisting double back dismount.

The frightening fall did not seem to faze her at all. She nailed her beam set during the meet, including her layouts and her back handspring with a quarter twist. Shannon finished the meet in second place and qualified to the 1991 U.S. Championships. In the event finals, she showed true grit by conquering the beam and floor for first place on each.

Never slowing down, Shannon traveled to Sicily, Italy, for the Catania Cup. She was spectacular, triumphing in the all-around and dominating in event finals. She won vault, beam, and floor, and she placed second on bars.

"Everywhere we went, we were mobbed by autograph seekers," Steve remembered. "It was great." The Italians loved Shannon, calling her "Queen Yankee." They really enjoyed her floor routine performed to the *"Hungarian Rhapsody."*

"We were on TV quite a bit doing promotions," Steve said. "Because I'm Italian they thought I was one of them, so they called me the Italian-American coach Nunno. They put me on a wireless microphone. I got out on the floor and about halfway through the meet they came up to me and said, 'How come you're not speaking Italian?' They thought I was going to be speaking Italian to Shannon [while] trying to coach her. I said, 'Because she doesn't understand Italian first of all, and half of it I don't understand.' So then they took the microphone away from me. They thought I was going to be part of their show."

Shannon returned from Italy with several large marble trophies for her four first-place finishes and one second-place finish. Since she had won so many, she could not fit them all in her luggage to bring home. The Italians did not exclude Steve, either; he was given a guitar and some other gifts.

After this meet, Shannon went home to train for a few months and improve her routines for the next season. The 1992 Olympics were looming on the horizon. Shannon intended to make *that* team, and she was willing to work hard for it.

"The most important characteristic that she has is her work ethic," Steve remarked. "I mean, she is just a meticulous worker, that everything that she does, she does to perfection and she does over and over and over to get it perfect without any qualms about it."

Shannon's hard work was paying off. "She became the best in the gym the year before the Olympic Games," Steve recalled. "[At first] she was always chasing somebody. She started off as the worst kid in the gym. . . . But she was the youngest kid that got accepted to the program, so that's one of the reasons I took her and I challenged her in all the big competitions. I put her with the big dogs and put her right off the porch to begin with, so she had to run with the big dogs or not at all. It was always a challenge for her."

With the start of 1991, Shannon found herself on the cover of the January/February issue of *USA Gymnastics* magazine. She was hoping to make a big splash in the gymnastics scene this year and entered the 1991 American Cup with the intent of making the finals. She had a solid meet and placed third in the preliminaries, but Betty Okino and Kim Zmeskal were the two in front of her, and only two Americans could advance to the finals.

Days later, Shannon paired up with Patrick Kirksey for the International Mixed Pairs competition. Shannon elected to do uneven bars and scored a 9.725. Patrick did well on the pommel horse for a 9.65, but in a familiar scenario, Kim Zmeskal and Betty Okino along with their partners finished ahead of Shannon and Patrick. Only two U.S. couples were allowed to continue. Shannon would have to wait for yet another meet to shine.

Shannon did not let these incidents intimidate her, because she knew her time would come. "I knew that as long as I kept working hard that it would pay off," she said, "whether I came in first, second, or third, as long as I did my job I could feel good about myself. I didn't really look at myself as being the underdog to Kim even though that's probably a position I'm comfortable with."

The next meet in which Shannon participated was the 1991 USA versus Romania competition held in the U.S. gymnastics haven of Houston, Texas. Although Kim Zmeskal won the meet, Shannon managed to turn more than a few heads with her third-place performance in the all-around. She tied with Cristina Bontas of Romania for the highest beam score of the day, a 9.95. Shannon again increased her difficulty on beam, adding a back handspring after her two consecutive layouts, and on floor she ended with a full-twisting double back, serving notice that her routines were harder than most anyone's.

Shannon also excelled in the classroom. She was an eighth grader at Summit Middle School, where she was a 4.0 student. Her favorite subject was algebra. Shannon's parents encouraged her to do well in school. Education was an important priority in the Miller household. Besides, a good day in school could balance a bad day in the gym. If gymnastics was the only thing on which she concentrated, it would be hard to break a slump.

Inside the gym, Shannon practiced roughly thirty-five hours a week. Usually five hours were spent each day after school and on Saturday, with an hour and a half before school three days a week.

Practice was very serious. Shannon did not fool around. She had a reputation for being all business. She rarely spoke, and when she did, her soft voice barely rose above a whisper.

Shannon was sweet and friendly to her teammates. She was quite strict with her herself, though, and became visibly frustrated when a move was not going right. She looked as if she might burst into tears at any given moment during practice.

Workouts were the hardest about three weeks before a meet. Shannon did about fifteen beam routines, ten bar sets, one or two full floor routines, and some dance-throughs. A dance-through is a floor routine with minimal tumbling; most of the emphasis is on the dance elements. In addition, Shannon did ten of each tumbling pass and countless vaults. As the day of the meet drew nearer, the number of repetitions decreased slightly, but the routines were expected to be perfect down to the smallest detail.

Shortly before the school year ended, fourteen-year-old Shannon entered the 1991 U.S. Championships as one of the favorites to win. She had come off a solid second-place finish at the U.S. Classic and was raring to go.

Unfortunately, things did not go her way. Shannon was in tears several times during the competition. She had some stumbles on floor and missed, of all things, a simple maneuver on bars called a jam. She did not perform a jam consistently because she had just learned it. Usually a jam is one of the first moves learned on bars, but her pulled hamstring had prevented her from learning it sooner.

Shannon finished a disappointing seventh. Steve was not happy; he had wanted her to challenge for the top positions.

After the meet and the press interviews, Shannon had to undergo a routine drug test. By the time she left the arena it was after midnight. She had not eaten for many hours, and her dad had to search for a restaurant that was still open for dinner. The competition had seemed to last forever, and the length of the meet concerned Shannon's parents.

"They used to not bring the kids food or water or anything," Shannon's mom said.

A doctor who worked with Claudia on a committee that looked into changing the system had once told her, "You can't expect those kids to be out there for that many hours. You don't feed them or give them any liquids and they start getting dehydrated. They start burning too many calories, and then they can't function properly. It truly becomes the survival of the fittest."

At about 2:00 A.M. Shannon finally got to bed. She still had to get up early for a team meeting and a workout before the next round of competition, but with the start of a new day, Shannon was determined to redeem herself in the event finals. She had qualified to the vault, beam, and floor.

Shannon's first vault was extremely high, but she took a big hop on the landing. She smiled at the judges then looked to Steve for some advice.

"The pike down caused the hop; you gotta keep it open," he said with one hand on her shoulder as they walked back. "We're gonna do the handspring front now. Make sure you're running hard and blocking it up there." Shannon nodded in agreement. The judges flashed a 9.70 for her first vault.

Shannon began her second vault poised at the edge of the blue carpet, intending to use the full length of the runway to build speed. She stood on her right leg with her left outstretched and her toes sharply pointed. She raised her arms, then lowered them to her side. The few seconds it took to perform this vaulting ritual helped Shannon gather her thoughts, calm her nerves, and focus her mind. She breathed deeply, then she was off. She sprinted toward the horse, hit the springboard, and performed a handspring front, landing with only a slight step forward.

"All right, just a step," Steve commented as he patted her on the head. "Very good block coming off the horse. Good distance, too." She scored a 9.625 to win the bronze medal.

On balance beam, Shannon was rock steady; she did not miss a beat. Tim Daggett, the NBC television announcer and 1984 Olympic gold medalist, raved about her high skill level and world-class routine. Shannon took one tiny step on the dismount, but the routine was good enough for a 9.887 and the gold. She was met by a warm embrace from Steve, who told her what a good job she had done.

In winning the gold, Shannon edged out Bela Karolyi's gymnasts Kim Zmeskal and Kerri Strug. Bela congratulated Shannon with a pat on the back. He also complimented Steve for his fine coaching.

Steve smiled and said, "A better day today." Bela nodded in agreement. Although Shannon fell in the floor finals and finished sixth, she was pleased with her successes on vault and beam.

Shannon returned to Oklahoma for some fervent training in the summer. She then traveled to Indiana for the World Championship Team Trials which she hoped would lead to the 1991 World Championships. This would be only the second time since 1903 that the World Championships were held on American soil. The other time had been in 1979 in Fort Worth, Texas.

The team selection meet was held before a private audience on August 24. Shannon was determined to make the team and place higher than she had at the U.S. Championships. She performed admirably and finished third, sandwiched between several Karolyi gymnasts. Kim Zmeskal and Betty Okino placed ahead of Shannon, and Kerri Strug and Hilary Grivich placed behind.

Shannon was the only U.S. gymnast on the final team to have never been coached by Bela Karolyi, but this did not influence her to consider switching clubs. She was loyal to Steve and Oklahoma.

"For the most part she respected Steve," Claudia said, "and she was living at home. She had no desire to move away from her brother and sister. She may fight with them from time to time, but she sure liked having them around."

"I've been with Steve for almost six years now and I've never wanted to leave—or go to Karolyi's or anything—because I know he's going to be able to get me to the Olympics and train me hard," Shannon stated firmly.

But Shannon's dad knew the frustration of being from a lesser-known club. "That's when I get in my depression, sort of, saying, 'Why aren't we recognized?' " he mused. "But it's the way the system works. You come up—and she's just fourteen years old. If she was twenty and had proved herself year after year, then you'd really be upset and feel bad."

Ron knew his daughter's natural talent would impress the judges eventually. "She's such a good gymnast that she doesn't have to have the big-name notoriety coach to push her up above her ability. And we are very lucky to have Steve close enough and have his interest in producing an elite gymnast."[1]

Controversy surrounded the team selection since Sandy Woolsey, voted the 1991 Athlete of the Year by the gymnastics community, was bumped from the squad by Michelle Campi, a former Karolyi gymnast with no international experience. Michelle was the second alternate, placing eighth, while Sandy had clinched the last team spot by finishing sixth in the qualifying meet. Still, Bela and Steve thought the judges would like Michelle's elegant style, so they chose her to compete instead of Sandy.

Shannon had been in Indianapolis since the end of August, training twice a day with the team. Although she shared a chalk bin with the other American gymnasts, she did not get to know them very well. There was little talking; most of the time was spent in silent concentration on perfecting routines during workout.

Shannon did get to enjoy a parade and the opening ceremonies with her American teammates. The entire team wore dark blue shorts and white shirts with red sweaters draped around their shoulders. Everyone was dressed the same, down to the red ankle socks and white tennis shoes.

The 1991 World Championships, Shannon's biggest competition so far, began for her on Monday, September 9, 1991. Shannon had the honor of going last for the American team during the compulsories. Usually, the last session was filled with the world's top athletes. The U.S. team was desperately hoping to win a medal and redeem itself from a fourth-place finish in the 1989 Worlds.

Being the anchor did not bother Shannon; she thought it would help her scores. However, the prestigious final position was sometimes accompanied by the stress of living up to everyone's expectations. Fortunately, Shannon's teammates who had gone before had done really well, lessening her burden.

Shannon had an excellent compulsory meet. She was graceful on floor for a 9.875 and clean on bars for a 9.85. The highlight of the meet was her superb beam set that earned a 9.937 and a tie for first with the Soviet Svetlana Boginskaya. She stuck her vault cold for a 9.90, the top vault score of the meet.

Some American judges had once told Steve that Shannon was not doing the compulsory vault properly. Even after correcting the vault, her reputation for a certain error seemed to hinder her scores from American judges. Luckily, only foreign judges were scoring vault in Indianapolis, and their lack of a bias helped

Shannon win the event.

Shannon's mom remembered some competitions earlier in Shannon's career during which her compulsory scores had seemed a little too low. "We would always feel—of course we didn't really know and I'm sure we were biased in our thoughts— but we would think she was doing such wonderful compulsories," Claudia said, "and I'm a judge so I did have some idea of what the skills should look like and how they should be executed, and what to take execution for. And not that I thought she was grossly underscored ever, but I thought they were not quite as high as they should have been. So I felt maybe that was partly because she didn't have any reputation yet and neither did her coach."

After the compulsories, Shannon was in first place on the American team and in second place overall to Svetlana, the 1989 reigning World Champion. Shannon respected Svetlana and thought she was really good, although they did not know each other that well.

Shannon was up fourth on the first event, uneven bars, in the optional portion of the team competition. Placement strategy in the lineup was important. The first gymnast was typically very consistent but less known, and the order built up to the last gymnast, who was usually the strongest.

Dressed in white with a white scrunchy bound tightly around her hair, Shannon listened to Steve's last-minute pointers then bounced off the springboard and up to the high bar where she twisted, turned, and flipped her way to a 9.90. She did not pay attention to the score as she quickly put her hand grips back in her bag.

Meanwhile, the Soviet Union was already pulling ahead of the field on vault. Tatiana Gutsu, the little daredevil from the Ukraine, flew down the runway and spun a double-twisting Yurchenko into a blur. She stuck the landing for a 9.925. Surprisingly, after the first rotation, the U.S. was in second place with Romania in third.

The U.S. team marched in order of height to the balance beam. Shannon, at four feet six inches, was the shortest next to Kim Zmeskal.

Shannon practiced her beam routine on the sideline as she awaited her turn. She did not watch the other competitors. She just focused on the job at hand.

Shannon did an outstanding beam routine with an excellent dismount for a 9.95. One judge even gave her a 10, but the highest and lowest scores were dropped. Shannon seemed pleased with the routine and the score. Peggy Liddick, her beam coach, gave her a one-arm hug for a job well done. The U.S. maintained a slim lead over Romania with two rotations to go.

The American team had a few problems early on floor with a step out of bounds by Michelle Campi and a fall out of bounds by Hilary Grivich. Fortunately, the lowest score on each team was dropped, but the errors put extra pressure on the remaining gymnasts. They had to hit in order to remain in second place.

Shannon used a new music medley including *"When the Saints Go Marching In."* She did two full-twisting double backs, but she had a few unsteady landings. She scored a decent 9.887. Steve hugged Shannon and went over the improvements to be made.

As the team was moving to the next event, Betty Okino looked up at the scoreboard and realized that the U.S. was tied with Romania with one rotation to go. The excitement was building!

Shannon went fourth on the vault. Like all her teammates who had gone before, she stuck her landing cold. She punctuated the finish by lifting her arms and tossing her head back. She earned a 9.937.

"Good job!" Steve exclaimed as he gently shook Shannon's

shoulders.

Kim Zmeskal followed with a perfect 10. Bela and Steve hugged each other then the whole team piled together in a group embrace to celebrate their awesome performance.

The United States, for the first time in a World Championship, captured the silver medal, and the Romanians haplessly took the bronze. The last Romanian competitor on bars, Lavinia Milosovici, had fallen, and the disappointment she felt was evidenced by the tears streaming down her cheeks. This marked the first time the U.S. had beaten the Romanians in competition. The Soviets, as expected, had won the gold.

"It was good that it was in the U.S. because I think we all came together as a team a little bit more," Shannon said.

Shannon smiled proudly as she accepted her silver medal and flowers with a handshake and a thank you. She was happy to finish fourth in the world after the team competition. She had hoped to be in the top six and had done even better. Ironically, she had finished seventh against the best gymnasts in America at the 1991 U.S. Championships but had placed fourth against the whole world.

Shannon's quiet voice and low-key personality made interviews uncomfortable for her, although she was intensely motivated and aggressive in gymnastics. She was once described in an *International Gymnast* magazine article as "speaking softly and carrying big tricks." Kathy Johnson, the captain of the 1984 silver-medal-winning Olympic team, interviewed Shannon during the World Championships. She asked Shannon if she had dreamed of this moment.

Shannon responded in a tiny voice, "Yeah."

"Is this about how you dreamed it?"

"No." Shannon shook her head and paused. Then she added softly, "It's a lot different: it's more exciting."

Shannon did not easily open up to people that she did not

know or trust. "She's gotten a really bad rap [from the media] about being shy, but what they don't know is she's not dumb," Claudia said. "She has watched Steve put his foot in his mouth so many times. She's not going to do that. She is going to think before she speaks. She's not going to say any more than she has to, because if you really get on a roll you're going to say something you might be sorry for. You're going to give the media a chance to twist something you said. So just say as little as possible.

"When you take your time to answer or when you don't say a whole lot, they think you must be shy. If the interviewer did not understand gymnastics and he asked stupid questions, then that made it difficult, because she wondered, 'How do you respond to this question that doesn't make sense?' That was a problem for her."

At home, Shannon was not as reserved as the media portrayed her. "She's got an unbelievable sense of humor," her mother said. "She cracks us up. She and her brother have such sharp wit that they keep us in hysterics."

Shannon shared a bathroom with her brother. When he left a big mess, she was sure to tell him about it. She would also tell him when she thought his hair was too long or when his grades could have been better.

"She's quiet at school," Claudia said. "She doesn't volunteer with all the answers. But not at home—she's not shy at home. She tells everybody everything."

"She's not really shy, she's just quiet," Ron pointed out. "She's not going to run out and try to get in front of the spotlight."

After a competition, Shannon sometimes discussed the interviews with her parents. Occasionally she told her mother what she had really wanted to say in response to a ridiculous question from a reporter.

"Oh my gosh, why didn't you say that?" her mom would ask. "That's hysterical! That's great!"

"Oh Mom, no!" Shannon would exclaim. "I don't want to say something that's going to make Steve mad or Peggy mad. I don't want to say something you won't like or that's going to make some other coach mad or hurt some other gymnast's feelings."

Claudia knew her daughter was correct in her thinking. "Shannon's constantly filtering everything until you end up getting a plain answer," she said. "She would have these great comebacks that would just knock you down, but she's not going to say them because she's always thinking."

Steve, on the other hand, liked to talk freely to the media. He did not mind answering Shannon's questions for her, which reinforced the notion that Shannon was shy.

"I believe she is a modest girl," Steve said on national television. "But she really has her emotions she likes to show through her gymnastics. And so she really doesn't have a lot to *say*, but she has a lot to *do*."

The top thirty-three gymnasts from the preliminaries, limited to only three per country, qualified to the World Championship all-around final. Shannon, Betty, and Kim were the U.S. representatives.

Shannon began on the balance beam. She flowed smoothly and gracefully through her routine. On her second event, the floor, Shannon did not hold back. She threw all of her tough skills to her Dixieland music. She scored a 9.862, which drew boos from the spectators at the Hoosier Dome who thought it should have been higher.

"I had some little stumbles that I could have been better on," Shannon said, always thinking of ways to improve.

Hoping to better her seventh-place position, Shannon ran

hard down the vaulting runway, punched off the springboard, and soared through the air. The vault was good enough to move her up one place in the standings.

With one event to go, Shannon was not in the medal hunt, but she was performing admirably. On bars she had a lot of amplitude on her release moves and stuck the landing. She walked off the podium with a big smile on her face.

Steve greeted her with a hug, saying, "All right, that's a good one. That's the one we needed right there. Nice job." She placed sixth overall. Shannon's teammate, Kim, captured the all-around title, a first for American gymnastics.

In the event finals, Shannon qualified to compete on all four apparatuses due to her strong performance in the team competition. This marked the first time a U.S. woman had qualified for all four events in a World Championship.

"I'm not sure I expected it fully, but I was training really hard to make finals in all that I could," Shannon said.

Her vaults, a full-twisting Yurchenko and a handspring front tuck, were averaged for a 9.812. She placed fourth.

Shannon did a carbon copy of her bar routine from the all-around final for a 9.95. She tied with Soviet Tatiana Gutsu for the silver. Kim Gwang Suk of North Korea won with a 10.

"It was really exciting," Shannon declared about her medal-winning performance. "I did the best bar routine I've ever done. And I had just gotten it changed a few weeks ago, so I felt really good about it."

Steve frequently changed Shannon's bar routine, which drew some criticism, but it usually paid off in the end. "I was always changing her bar routines at the meet," Steve laughed. "I'd change something else, I'd put something else in to try to get her to place as high as she could. And she always placed very high, if not won."

Shannon's mother remembered one incident at a meet in

Arizona. Steve had changed Shannon's bar routine just before she was due to compete, but apparently he had not thought through everything properly. During her routine, it was apparent to her mother that she was in trouble.

" 'She's going the wrong way. How's she going to get to the low bar?' " Claudia remembered thinking during the meet. "So she just put in a few more moves until she got turned around and got to the low bar. I thought, 'Oh my gosh, it's going to be a horrible score.' She got like a 9.70 or 9.75. I couldn't believe the score. Steve said, 'She didn't have any execution [deductions]. She had too many moves on high bar because she had to get herself turned around, but that's only a tenth.' "

Shannon finished her first World Championships solidly, placing sixth on beam and fourth on floor.

"She sure matches up with the whole world here, you know, coming from the Romanians and the Soviet Union," Steve said at the conclusion of the 1991 Worlds. Shannon sat beside him, biting her lip. She seemed uncomfortable listening to his praise. "But we're real excited about being able to go through five days of strong competition and not missing one routine."

Shannon was awarded the Fédération Internationale de Gymnastique (FIG) insignia along with her teammates from the World Championships. A gymnast from any country who had averaged a 9.0 or higher in the World Championships or Olympic Games was bestowed this honor. She was also chosen from more than one hundred top young athletes as the recipient of the Women's Sports Foundation's 1991 Up & Coming Award.

After a successful World Championships, Shannon returned home and began ninth grade. She had missed the first four weeks of school because of Worlds, but she did not lighten her course load, and she still took several honors classes. She managed to catch up just in time to leave again.

In late November, Shannon headed across the Atlantic to gain some international recognition. Her first stop was the Swiss Cup Mixed Pairs on December 1 in St. Gallen, Switzerland. This meet was similar to the International Mixed Pairs competition in that each female athlete was paired with a male athlete from the same country. As the only American couple, Shannon and Scott Keswick took Europe by storm. Shannon scored a perfect 10 on balance beam, the first 10 of her career. Her lowest score was a not-too-shabby 9.875 on uneven bars. Scott was equally strong on his events, and the duo captured the gold.

Three days later at the Arthur Gander Memorial—named after a former FIG president—in nearby Montreux, Switzerland, Shannon outdid herself and the competition. She claimed the highest score on each event—including another 10 on beam—to win a second gold in the all-around over Romania's Mirela Pasca. Shannon admitted to having a good meet. In fact, she said it was one of the best meets of her life. She even set a new all-around record, scoring 39.875 total points.

"I believe it is the highest score that *any* gymnast in the United States has ever scored in *any* competition," Steve said.

With two recent victories, Shannon was confident going into the December 7 Deutscher Turner Bund (DTB) Cup in Stuttgart, Germany, and it showed. The competitive field was stronger than it had been at the two previous meets, consisting of the best upcoming gymnasts from the Soviet Union and Romania. Shannon scored highest on vault with a 9.95, but her score was only a 9.80 on bars, which Steve and 7,000 fans thought should have been higher. Even Shannon was a little disappointed in the score and said it could have been better.

Shannon finished strongly on beam and floor with a 9.875 on both. She ended up with the bronze, less than a tenth behind the winner, Romanian Lavinia Milosovici. Tatiana Gutsu was second.

Steve was not satisfied with the results. "She did just as well [as in the two previous meets] but yet she took third," he complained. "There was a lot of politics involved. . . . She should have won the competition. I felt that we got robbed."

A photographer told Steve after the meet, "This is the first time I've been to a gymnastics competition where a girl took two places in the all-around: third place in the all-around and first in the hearts of the people."

In the event finals, Shannon qualified to all four apparatuses. She did not leave empty-handed. She took the bronze on vault, the silver on bars, and the gold on floor.

"I didn't make a fuss," Steve stated, "but I knew—come Barcelona—our time has come."

A week after returning home, Shannon's parents received a nice letter from Tom Gibbs, the U.S. delegation leader to the meets Shannon had just attended. "She was not only a joy to travel with, but an absolute delight to watch compete," he wrote. "If ever there was a gymnast that was an ideal representative for her sport and ambassador for her country it is Shannon."

Shannon thought her trip to Western Europe had been fun. She now looked forward to the year for which she had long been preparing: 1992. She wanted to fulfill a dream by representing the United States at the Olympic Games.

Shannon had been in the shadow of Kim Zmeskal for years. She had gained the respect of the gymnastics community, but she had not gained the spotlight like Kim had done. Shannon had won some prestigious competitions in Europe, and now she needed to win some meets domestically.

Her hard work and persistence had kept her *near* the top but not *on* top. She needed an opportunity to become the number one U.S. gymnast and hoped that 1992 would be her year to shine.

A young Shannon competes on floor exercise at her first U.S. Championship. (© Steve Lange 1996)

Eyes glued to the floor, Shannon listens as Steve gives her some pointers. (© Steve Lange 1996)

Shannon executes her compulsory floor routine at the 1990 U.S.
Championships. (© Steve Lange 1996)

Shannon soars above the high bar on her full-twisting double back flyaway dismount. (© Steve Lange 1996)

Sure-footed Shannon steps into first place on balance beam at the
1991 U.S. Championships. (© Steve Lange 1996)

Peggy stretches Shannon's split more than 180 degrees. (© Barry Quiner 1996)

Peggy helps Shannon with some conditioning. (© Barry Quiner 1996)

Diving through the air in Denver. (© Steve Lange 1996)

Flying high in Indianapolis. (© Steve Lange 1996)

Shannon twirls around the bar on her Thomas release move. (© Steve Lange 1996)

A perfect leap. (© Barry Quiner 1996)

Shannon performs admirably at the 1991 World Championships.
(© Steve Lange 1996)

Chapter 3

Pins and Needles

With the start of the Olympic year, Shannon quickly nailed down her goals. Goals were an important part of her training; she had to be aiming for something to accomplish it. She wanted to win the 1992 U.S. Championships and the Olympic Trials. She really hoped to make the Olympic team and possibly win an Olympic medal.

To accomplish her goals, Shannon thought she needed to beef up her routines by adding more difficulty, especially on floor. She was training a double layout somersault, one of the most difficult tumbling passes ever attempted. In addition, she wanted to polish her existing routines. She worked with a ballet instructor twice a week for forty-five minutes to refine the dance in her floor and beam sets.

Shannon also hoped to improve her second vault for the

event finals, in which each athlete had to do two completely different vaults. Besides her full-twisting Yurchenko, she wanted to do a front handspring front flip with a barani-out (one-half twist) in either a tuck or pike position. She had been competing a front handspring front flip without a twist in the tuck position, which had a starting value of 9.90. This meant that if she did the vault perfectly, the best score she could receive was a 9.90. By learning the vault with a half twist she could increase her starting value to a 10.

Shannon trained twice a day for a total of six hours, three times a week. Sunday was her day off. The other three days she worked out for four to five hours.

On days when she had two practice sessions, Shannon usually woke up at the crack of dawn, around 6:00 A.M., hopped in the family car with her dad, and headed toward the Dynamo gym in Edmond. The morning workouts were at the Edmond gym, while all the others were at the main Dynamo gym in Oklahoma City. Sometimes Shannon caught extra sleep under a blanket in the back seat, and other times she worked on homework.

She liked spending the one-on-one time with her dad. They often talked about school or practice.

"Driving her to the gym and back is almost an hour a day," Ron said. "We're in the car doing homework, doing geometry, visiting. I may see her more than I see my other kids."[1]

Ron was happy that he and Claudia had not sent Shannon off somewhere, like Karolyi's, to train. He enjoyed being able to talk with her in person, unlike some other gymnasts' parents who were separated from their daughters by thousands of miles and only spoke to them on the phone.

Once at the gym, Shannon and her dedicated teammates started the morning with some conditioning. Shannon did oversplits—one leg on a mat and the other on the floor—to stretch more than 180 degrees. Her best split was with her left foot in front. Although right-handed, she was a left-sided gymnast: she performed splits, cartwheels, roundoffs, and turns better on the left side. She placed her left hand down first on her cartwheel and roundoff, and she was more flexible on the left side.

After splits and stretching, Shannon walked across the floor mat on her hands several times. This exercise built strong arm muscles and helped her learn to control her handstand, one of the most important maneuvers to master in gymnastics.

She continued with seemingly endless situps, pushups, V-ups, mountain climbers, and presses to handstand. In addition, she did pullups and leg lifts on the high bar with Steve right there counting and watching her every move. Conditioning lasted over an hour, with running, aerobics, and weightlifting included in her regimen. Dance and floor exercise work followed, then she changed her clothes, grabbed her books, and rushed to school.

Shannon did not lessen her school load even though it was the Olympic year. She attended the ninth grade with her classmates while other top gymnasts took the year off from school and did correspondence work while training for the Olympics. The Millers wanted to keep Shannon in public school, but Steve did not.

"We had to fight him tooth and nail to keep her in public school," Claudia said. "He wanted her out of school completely the year before [the Olympics]."

Shannon missed the first hour of class at Edmond North High School because of morning workout, but she attended the rest of her classes. She was excused from physical education class, for which she substituted study hall. She maintained a 4.0 grade point average and was a member of both the Oklahoma and National Honor Societies.

After school it was back to the gym for five more hours of

exhausting work. In the evening, Shannon began with a half hour warmup and stretching period, then she moved to the equipment for several vigorous hours of practice. She spent a little over an hour on each piece of equipment.

Steve could be heard yelling, "Speed it up," as Shannon ran toward the vault. She practiced her vaults over and over. There were always improvements to be made.

One time Steve suggested trying a certain move to improve her vaults. Shannon refused. She said she had tried the move and it had messed up her vaulting, and she did not want to risk that happening again. Steve immediately kicked her out of the gym. She sat on the couch in the lobby and waited for her mom to pick her up. It hurt Shannon's feelings to get kicked out, but it did not happen very often.

Steve yelled at her or kicked her out of the gym when he was not satisfied with her performance or when he thought she was not trying hard enough, but Shannon felt it was for the best.

"He knows how to motivate me," she said. "He usually knows what I'm thinking or how to help me if I'm doing something wrong. He knows how to get me to do it better. He knows a lot of the technical things as far as gymnastics goes. He's always been tough on me and it's always helped me. He's one of the best coaches."

"He knows when to stop short of going too far," Shannon's mom noticed. "Half the time when I'll be upset because he's really yelling at her or treating her unfairly, she'll come out and say, 'No, Mom, I wasn't giving a hundred percent today; I needed a kick,' and she'll take up for him. And then there are times when she thinks she's not being treated fairly, that he was too impatient. She was trying; couldn't he see it?"

"When I raise my voice just a little bit, she gets upset," Steve explained. "She doesn't want to be in that situation. She doesn't want me ever frustrated. She wants me proud of her. And I want to be proud of her."

Peggy Liddick usually got upset with Shannon for one of two reasons: "Loss of concentration and if she isn't performing up to expectation—her ability level. Everybody needs a kick in the butt once in a while. I'm not an easy coach by any means, but I respect Shannon and she respects me."

"I'm sure we haven't always agreed on everything," Shannon admitted, "but as far as I'm concerned I'm the gymnast and she's the coach. So far she's always known what's best for me, and so I'm always willing to try what she has to say."

Steve was normally firm but fair in his coaching approach, but he occasionally got out of hand. When his yelling turned personal or demeaning, Shannon's parents stepped into the situation and talked to him.

Claudia recalled one incident: "Once when Shannon was afraid he was getting close to [a personal attack] she came home and said, 'Mom, if he ever calls me a name I'm going to walk over to my locker, get everything out, and leave. I won't be called names.' We thought, 'Things are getting hot in the gym—we better pay him a visit.' We said [to Steve], 'She can be headstrong and she'll put up with an awful lot, but she does have her limits.' He noted that he had never called her a name, and we said, 'No, we know you haven't, but we're just letting you know you might want to get a little rein on your temper.' "

The Millers had their differences with Steve, but they knew he wanted what was best for Shannon. "We feel like he's a good coach and a good person," Claudia said. "We do have our disagreements with him. . . . The angrier he gets with her, usually the worse she gets. Then she gets angry with him and then *we* get angry. It becomes a vicious circle, and so pretty soon we're in his office saying, 'Wait a minute, what's going on here? Why are you kicking our child out of gym?' He's got his side. Usually by the time we leave his office, we're all okay again."

Practice ended around 9:00 P.M. Once at home, Shannon had a light snack and worked on her homework. She went to bed around 11:00 P.M., getting about seven hours of sleep each night. If she slept less than that she would be tired at workout the next day, so she was careful to get enough rest.

Shannon worked closely with both Steve and Peggy. Steve, the head coach, oversaw everything and primarily instructed vault, bars, and tumbling. Peggy, the assistant coach, concentrated on beam and the dance on floor.

Shannon respected her coaches and took practice seriously. She went to the gym even when she had a cold, rips on her hands, or minor aching injuries. She sometimes modified her workouts when she was not up to full strength, but she never missed one.

"She's never missed a practice in five years," Steve acknowledged. "Not for sickness, not for anything: illness, injury, nothing. And there isn't another girl, I don't think, in the country that can say that."

Dynamo Gymnastics was roomy and bright inside. A painted rainbow went all around the gym. Banners on the walls boasted of the club's state championships. In-ground pits filled with chunks of yellow foam allowed the athletes to learn new vaults, tumbling passes, and bar dismounts. There were rows of uneven bars and balance beams. A blue 40' x 40' floor exercise mat next to a wall of mirrors was used to perfect floor routines. Gymnasts watched themselves in the mirrors to correct hand positions and poses in their dance.

Hanging on the wall in Steve's office was a large framed picture of Shannon with a silver medal draped around her neck from the 1991 World Championships. Shannon's presence was definitely known in this gym.

Since she was one of the only top U.S. gymnasts not from Karolyi's, she was sometimes questioned about why she had not switched clubs. She replied with a smile, "I don't know how I'd do at Bela's, but I think I'm doing just fine here. I mean, I'm up with them and I'm doing as well as they are, and I don't have to be there."

Shannon's first competition of 1992 was used as a warmup meet for the American Cup. She traveled to St. Joseph, Missouri, for the Dragon Invitational held February 21-23. Shannon, now an inch taller than she had been at the 1991 World Championships, blew away the competition, finishing two points ahead of her teammate Soni Meduna, who placed second. Over five hundred gymnasts competed, and Shannon's team easily won.

After the meet, Shannon's face revealed that something was wrong. She seemed to be in anguish and close to tears. The reason was soon apparent: she had suffered a pulled hamstring. The pain was great, and she told her dad that she could "barely walk."

Shannon had endured a pulled hamstring in her right leg in 1989, and now she was suffering with one again, this time in her other leg. She tried to push the injury out of her mind and focus on her next meet.

With confidence from the World Championships, her triumphs in Europe during December, and her fresh Dragon Invitational victory, she entered the 1992 American Cup with assurance and the will to win. The American Cup was held March 6-7 in Orlando, Florida.

Shannon's optional exercises were sensational in the preliminaries. She won the all-around and had the highest score on every event except floor exercise. In so doing, she became the first to defeat the new World Champion, Kim Zmeskal.

"Obviously, she's the World Champion," Steve said about Kim, "but this is the American Cup. Kim is not the defending champion of the American Cup this year. It's anybody's ball game and we have two great champions, and I'm really excited to be in contention at all."

Unfortunately, Shannon's victory was only in the qualifying round. No scores would carry over to the finals the next day, and the finals were what counted and what people remembered. The competition was shaping up to be an interesting battle between the top two American gymnasts and the top two American coaches.

These coaches had enjoyed a friendly history together. Steve had met Bela in 1982 at a national meet, shortly after Bela had defected from Romania to the United States.

"[Bela] asked me if I was interested in coaching with him, and his girl, I think, took second place," Steve remembered. "I said to him, 'Well, my girl won, maybe you want to coach with me,' and he laughed like hell."

Steve was interested in coaching with Bela, so a year later he told Bela he wanted to take him up on his offer. Bela told Steve he needed someone right away. In the summer of 1983, Steve left the Gymnastics Junction in Massachusetts and moved to Houston.

Steve became Bela's right-hand man in training his top elites. Steve worked with Mary Lou Retton and Dianne Durham as well as the junior elites, Phoebe Mills and Kristie Phillips. Once a week he helped coach the "Hopes"—children who aspired to be elites—like Kim Zmeskal. When Bela traveled to do clinics, exhibitions, or camps, Steve became the head coach.

Steve realized right away what he needed to become a better coach. "Two weeks after I was there, I knew what I was lacking," he said. "I was lacking the motivation to coach the high-level kids. I knew the gymnastics part. Side by side with Bela for that time, and seeing some of the top athletes and what it really took to get those kids to that level, I knew right away that I didn't want to work for somebody. I needed to work for myself, and I was ready to get after it."

Steve learned the tricks of the trade from the legendary

54

Romanian couple for nine months. Then Bela told Steve the gym was suffering financially and Steve would have to take a serious pay cut if he wanted to stay. Steve felt that he had learned what he needed and decided it was time to move on.

He moved to Oklahoma and shortly afterwards opened Dynamo Gymnastics. He remembered and valued his experience from Bela's gym.

"What he did for me was taught me how to motivate a gymnast," Steve told a reporter interviewing him and Bela. "I believe that he is probably the best coach in the world. I think he could take a basketball team and coach a basketball team to a championship."

"He is crazy, though," Bela laughed as he jokingly pushed Steve. "He is flattering me too much. I believe that Bobby Knight guy would be really mad at me if he heard about this."

Bela's influence on Steve was evident from Steve's coaching style and from a picture of the two coaches on Steve's desk in his office. Steve also had a picture of Bela's scowling face plastered on a door in his gym.

He explained the reason for the photograph: "I said, 'I'm going to stare at this guy until I beat him' . . . and every time I saw his face, I knew how hard I had to work."[2]

Bela and Steve prepared to face off against each other on the first event of the American Cup all-around finals, the vault. Shannon was pleased about making the finals since she had narrowly missed qualifying in the two previous years. She sprinted down the runway and launched herself skyward for a beautiful vault. The judges flashed a 9.95.

Kim followed. She did the same vault, a full-twisting layout Yurchenko, but it was a little better for a 9.987 and the early lead.

Up first on bars, Shannon pulled out all the stops with a thrilling routine that scored a 9.937. Not wanting to relinquish her lead, Kim matched Shannon's score on what was possibly her weakest event.

Shannon's father watched in anticipation from the stands with his video camera in hand. Besides having a video collection of Shannon's competitions, Ron liked to use the tapes as teaching material for his physics classes. His most effective demonstration was of Shannon failing to catch a Tkatchev on bars. He would show the tape and have his students calculate the force with which she hit the ground. After viewing the tape, some students would wonder if Shannon was okay after the fall. Then Ron would pull out another tape that showed her catching the bar perfectly. The class would be relieved.

"Many of our lessons we teach in physics involve motion," Ron said, "and so it's nice to give a demonstration to the students rather than just dropping something on the floor to demonstrate."

At the halfway point of the meet, Kim emerged with a slim 0.037 lead over Shannon. It was shaping up to be quite a battle.

Shannon practiced her balance beam routine on the floor. She went over each skill, concentrating on making it perfect. She would be second to last up, with Kim following her once again.

"All right, ready to go. Be aggressive," Steve reminded her. He did not want Shannon to hold back or be conservative. It was easy to be cautious on the four-inch-wide apparatus when performing in front of judges and thousands of fans.

Shannon began confidently with an arched handstand in a split position followed by a back extension roll to an immediate back handspring whip (two-foot layout). Then she took an extra risk by adding a third layout to her tumbling sequence. The crowd recognized this tremendous difficulty and responded with loud cheers. She completed some nice leaps then turned to do her dismount. She had had problems in the touch warmups on her dismount, but she blocked them out of her mind and performed a magnificent full-twisting double back somersault with only a slight hop on the landing.

Steve raised his hands in triumph and let out a yell when she finished. He rushed over and hugged her tightly.

"What a good job! What a good job!" he exclaimed. "Go out there and wave to the people." And she did, which brought even more applause.

Shannon scored a 9.95. "Good job, perfect set, very nice," Steve continued. "Oh what a competitor you are," he said while playfully knocking on her head. Turning serious, he reminded her to stay focused. "Okay, one to go. Let's do it." Shannon nodded in agreement. She was psyched.

One of Shannon's greatest attributes was that she did not water down her routine if a skill was not going well in warmups. She was very strong mentally, and she was able to overcome her problems and force herself to do the skill correctly. That was the mark of a champion.

Shannon strode past Kim, who was preparing to begin her beam routine. Shannon had put the pressure on her. Kim responded with a solid set, and her only error was a hop on the dismount. Although she had less difficulty in her routine, she received the same score Shannon had received. Her status as the reigning World Champion was a definite factor in getting such high marks.

Shannon did not pay attention to the score, however. She knew her own routine had been more difficult, but she also knew there were politics involved in judging. Steve thought the scoring had been unfair. Even the NBC television commentators expressed concern that Shannon's score had been a little low. Shannon just pressed her lips firmly together, ignoring the politics as she prepared for the last event. She concentrated on hitting her routines, leaving the judges to handle the scores and Steve to deal with the politics.

Shannon began her three-minute touch warmup for floor

exercise. The pulled hamstring in her left leg visibly affected her performance for the first time during the warmup. She only executed her first tumbling pass and nearly landed on her face. Then the bells sounded, marking the conclusion of the warmup period.

Shannon was up first. Steve encouraged her to go for it.

"You're first up. Get ready. Be rested," Steve instructed. After seeing the doubt in her face he questioned, "Are you ready or do you want to wait?" She responded with an uneasy look but she started to step forward. Sensing her hesitation, Steve held his arm out to stop her and said, "Let's wait." Shannon practiced her landing for a few more seconds.

Steve squatted down next to her. "Powerful on the tumbling," he encouraged, "up on the take off, and stick it, okay? Keep your chin up. Let's go. Come on!"

As Steve finished, the announcer boomed, "She's spent nine years in gymnastics and trains at Dynamo Gymnastics in Edmond, Oklahoma. Please welcome back, from the United States, Shannon Miller!" The crowd roared as she stepped onto the mat. After seeing her worried facial expression, young gymnasts shouted words of encouragement as she struck her starting pose.

Shannon's body danced toward the corner but her face wore a blank stare. The audience was already clapping with the music. She raised herself up on her toes and dashed forward, doing a roundoff whip back through to a full-twisting double back. Although her tumbling was powerful, she overcorrected for her earlier problems and fell backwards, sliding out of bounds and off the floor. She had to rush to get back onto the floor and back in sync with her music.

Shannon could not believe she had fallen. She thought to herself, "How did this happen?" She had never fallen on this skill in a meet before. On her next tumbling pass, she also nearly touched her hands to the mat. The routine was falling apart. Her pulled hamstring was obviously bothering her; she grimaced in pain during her leaps and splits. When the routine was finished, she limped gingerly over to her coaches as the tears began to flow.

"Oh well, it's okay, that's all right," Steve consoled as Shannon sobbed. "You did a good job. Let's go get some ice on that thing, huh? You can rest over there." She put on her warm-up suit and walked toward the training table for some help.

Shannon scored a 9.212 and ended up third.

"It's tough, but you gotta be able to handle it," Steve said. "We have one more to go. We have the Mixed Pairs left." This would be her last meet before going home.

Shannon was upset with herself because she had wanted to hit her routine. "I underrotated it a little bit in warmups and I overdid it in the meet," she said with watery eyes about the mistake on her first tumbling pass. Showing true grit, she refused to let her pulled hamstring excuse her third-place finish.

Meanwhile, Kim turned in a stellar set to *"In the Mood"* for a 9.912 and first place. Although she had fallen at the end, Shannon had pressured Kim throughout the meet. Both young women had performed to the utmost of their ability.

Shannon earned $5,000 in prize money for her performance at the American Cup. Following the meet, the gymnasts and coaches attended a banquet that displeased Shannon's father.

"They had food that [gymnasts] don't eat," Ron said. "That's the first thing. And the second thing, they had a bar in there. I thought, 'There's a great education for my child to have a nice open bar where you watch all the coaches drink.' "

The next day, Shannon and the other gymnasts from the American Cup spent the afternoon at Disney World. Then they traveled north to Tallahassee for the 1992 McDonald's International Mixed Pairs held on March 10. Shannon was paired with Scott Keswick, who had been her partner in Europe when they had won the Swiss Cup. Both Shannon and Scott had been hoping to win the American Cup but had fallen short. Now they had a chance to beat the American Cup winners, Kim Zmeskal and Jarrod Hanks.

Steve was hoping his star pupil would win this competition. "This year we should be winning, and she wants to win," he commented. "We've been the person without the pressure. If you're going into the Olympic Games, you're not going to win unless you've won something. She's won a number of international competitions, and as I've said before, I think she's very well respected on the whole international scene. Unfortunately, she hasn't won a particular meet in America. [She's won] a lot of invitationals but not a big USGF-sanctioned competition, so it's our turn. She's got to earn it, she knows it, and we're ready for it."

Shannon chose to begin on uneven bars, one of her best events. She flew high above the bar on her two release moves, a Gienger and a Tkatchev, and only had a slight hop on her full-twisting double back flyaway. This solid routine got the ball rolling with a 9.925.

Scott did a beautiful still rings routine, and he nailed his double-twisting double back dismount. He scored a 9.85.

"Good job," Shannon told Scott as he walked toward her. After the first round they were in first place.

Kim and Jarrod both did floor. Kim performed a great routine for a 9.90, and Jarrod was solid for a 9.70. They qualified to the next round in third place. Also tied for third place was the strong Soviet pair of Svetlana Kozlova and Dimitri Karbonenko.

If the women wanted to vault, they had to do so in the second round. Kim did a great vault with only a slight hop on the landing for a 9.95, and Jarrod was good for a 9.60.

Shannon dashed down the vaulting runway, flew through the air, and stuck her vault for a 9.95. Steve gave her some pointers for her next try. Her second attempt was not as good—she almost touched her hands and knees to the mat—so her first score counted.

With only one American pair advancing to the final round, the pressure was on Scott. He swung an excellent parallel bar set for a 9.70, which earned him and Shannon a place in the final round and eliminated Jarrod and Kim.

Shannon, wanting to redeem herself from the American Cup, chose the floor as her last event. She landed her whip to a full-twisting double back somersault on her feet, although she took a few steps backward and went out of bounds. But she hit her remaining tumbling passes perfectly to rebuild her confidence and score a 9.775.

"I wanted to do floor for my last event," she said after her routine, "and it kind of made it easier to get through the first two [events] because I really wanted to redeem myself on the third."

All Scott had to do was get a 9.10 or better to clinch the title. He chose the daring high bar. He caught his two release moves early and then stuck the triple back dismount. Steve and Shannon rushed over to congratulate him. He scored a 9.90.

Shannon and Scott dominated the competition, easily defeating the couples from the Soviet Union and China to capture the International Mixed Pairs title. This was Shannon's first major international victory in the United States, and it helped to ease some of her frustration with the American Cup. This was also a great birthday present for Shannon, who turned fifteen on the day of the meet.

Shannon's fame in gymnastics was beginning to grow. In the March 1992 issue of *International Gymnast* magazine, she was featured in a large colorful poster accompanied by a lengthy interview. Shannon was pictured in a pretty red leotard on the balance beam during the 1991 World Championships.

Shannon said that kids treated her a little differently in school because of her celebrity status. Sometimes people would recognize her in local shopping malls and stop her for autographs. She also received about one or two pieces of fan mail each day, and more after she returned from a meet. She was diligent in answering them all, which was fun at first but began to occupy a good deal of time as her popularity increased.

As March came to a close, Shannon flew to Los Angeles for the 1992 Hilton's Superstars of Gymnastics. This event featured some of the best gymnasts of all time, including Olga Korbut, Nadia Comaneci, Mary Lou Retton, and three members of the 1984 gold-medal-winning men's team.

Shannon performed on uneven bars. She upgraded her difficulty by adding a third release move, a Thomas—named after the American gymnast Kurt Thomas—to her already-challenging routine. She accentuated this incredibly difficult set with a full-twisting double back flyaway dismount. With skills like these, she was certain to be a contender for medals in Barcelona, the site of the 1992 Olympics.

Unfortunately, tragedy struck two days after returning to Oklahoma following the exhibition. While practicing the compulsory uneven bar routine, Shannon caught her foot on the high bar while attempting a full-twisting flyaway dismount and fell. This would not have been a bad spill, but she stuck her left arm out the wrong way to catch herself. The weight and pressure on her arm were too great and she dislocated her elbow.

"It was one of those things: only *if*," Steve recalled. "I had just removed the crash mat out from underneath the bar so she could stick the last couple. She was tired. It was the last one. It was a great dismount, but she just happened to clip her feet [on the bar] and she reached out and dislocated her elbow.

"I looked down and Shannon looks at her arm, the first thing I didn't want her to do. She knew something got hurt. She looked at me and she said, 'What are *we* going to do?' And that's when I knew that *we* were not going to have a problem, because she [had] said, 'What are *we* going to do?' "

"I knew as soon as I looked at it that something wasn't right," Shannon said. "When I first did it I thought he would put it back in place and I'd ice it and then I'd go to beam."

The injury was extremely painful. Steve took off his warmup jacket and put it over Shannon's arm. He also packed ice around the protruding bone. He knew how to put a dislocated elbow back in place because he had done it before, but he did not want to risk anything with Shannon.

Steve ran to his car and rushed her to the hospital. He called the doctors from his car phone so they would be ready to set her elbow back in place once they got to the emergency room. Along the way, Steve assured her that everything would be okay. He told her the doctors would pop it back in place and she would be practicing a few days later.

"I think the worst part was looking at it, because that always makes it worse," Shannon said. "I'm not going to say it wasn't painful. It was, but I was so worried about what was going to happen in the next few weeks because I was supposed to go to Worlds."

Shortly after she and Steve reached the emergency room, her parents arrived.

"So in come the parents and they look at me," Steve said nervously as he recounted their initial meeting in the waiting room. "I'm thinking the first thing they're going to do is haul off and hit me or something; I hurt their kid. But they were really supportive."

After viewing the X-rays, the doctors discovered that Shannon had chipped a good-sized piece of bone off her elbow. Luckily, no ligaments had been torn. Dr. David Holden explained the options.

"We had a loose, unstable elbow, and some choices to make," Dr. Holden remembered. "I talked to her parents and coaches about it. We could treat the injury conservatively . . . that is, we could immobilize the arm in a cast for five or six weeks."[3]

The doctor knew that if Shannon had a cast for that long it would spell disaster. First, six weeks without any real practice would definitely take her out of the running for the Olympic team. Secondly, her arm would be very weak after being immobilized for that long. Finally, she would probably never be able to fully straighten her arm again.

Shannon's other choice was to have surgery to re-attach the bone chip. Steve knew this was the only realistic option and hoped that Shannon and her mom, who were Christian Scientists, would see it that way. Shannon and Claudia were not very enthusiastic about going to see doctors, but they did so when it was necessary.

Claudia explained: "Our religion says, 'Hey, if you don't feel comfortable with working it out through prayer, there's nothing wrong with going to a doctor.' "

Shannon was apprehensive. "Of course I didn't want to have it," she said about the surgery. "But I decided they knew best and that was the way to go."

"Shannon has relied heavily [on her religious beliefs]," her mom commented. "That's probably her psychological assistance."

"The main thing is that if I put my trust in God, he'll take care of me," Shannon stated confidently, "and I'll be able to do the best I can. He keeps me calm when everything's not going perfect."

Instead of going to a sports psychologist, Shannon depended on a Christian Science practitioner. "A lot of times if she's having a particular problem, whether it's physical or mental, she'll call and talk with her about it," Shannon's mom said. "She believes very strongly in God and that he takes care of her no matter what."

When Shannon arrived in the emergency room, the first thing she did was call her practitioner. She was hesitant about the surgery and explained her doubts to the practitioner, who helped to calm her down.

Steve tried to make the surgery option seem like no big deal. He told the Millers that it involved a small incision and a *micro-screw* the size of a hair to hold down the bone chip.

Ron, a Baptist, strongly believed that surgery was necessary. He ultimately made the decision to go ahead with it. Claudia, who knew that God would take care of her daughter, consented to it as well. There was no conflict surrounding the decision. Steve, however, breathed a sigh of relief when the Miller family agreed to have the surgery.

Shannon was nervous about the anesthetic and the procedure itself: "I remember going through the doors and laying there thinking, 'Oh gosh, is this going to hurt or not? What's going to happen?' "

Dr. Holden performed the operation. It went very well. After the surgery, Shannon slept through the night. A nurse came in periodically to tell her she needed pain medication, but each time Shannon said, "No, I don't want anything."

As she lay in her hospital bed, Shannon worried that she would not be fully recovered in time for the Olympics. Claudia, who spent the whole night at Shannon's side, tried to calm her, reassuring her that everything would be okay.

The next morning, in preparation for writing a prescription for pain medicine, Shannon's doctor inquired from the nurses what medicine Shannon had been taking. He was startled to learn that she had taken nothing. Shannon told him she did not want any medicine. Still, the doctor insisted that she have some. But he couldn't make her take it, and Shannon's mom admitted that years later she still carried around an unfilled prescription for Shannon's pain killers in her purse.

Ron and Claudia were thankful they did not have to pay the high medical bills related to Shannon's injury. The insurance company for the gym, Markel, paid for everything.

Eventually, Shannon had to return to the hospital. "About eight months later she had the screw removed," Steve explained with an impish grin. "It was about an inch-and-a-half-long screw. And Shannon goes, 'Some *micro*screw. What's that?' It was all in the papers how they had this microscrew in her arm. It was the biggest lie I ever made up and everybody took off on it. I just didn't want her to ever have to worry about it. The smaller I could make the problem, the less the problem she'd have with it."

Immediately after the surgery, Shannon's elbow was very stiff, but she had a good physical therapist, Mark Cranston, who began moving her arm and building back the muscle just one week after the operation. She performed daily exercises that strengthened her elbow and improved its range of motion. The rehabilitation was painful but necessary for her to make the Olympic team.

Shannon sat out only one day of workout because of the surgery. After that she was back in the gym—a splint on her arm—trying to do everything she could to prepare for the U.S. Championships in May. At first she could only do things that did not involve her elbow, but gradually she began to build up to her normal routines.

"I just worked around it," she said. "When everyone else was on bars, I would rub my hands on the bars so when I came back I wouldn't get a lot of rips. I would do swings on the bar or just hangs. I would do some one-arm tumbling like one-arm roundoffs. Once I could put weight on [the injured arm], it made it a lot easier."

Steve and Peggy were very careful with Shannon's elbow.

They did not want to push her too fast and risk re-injuring it.

"Every morning I had to stretch Shannon's arm out, and she didn't like it one bit," Steve said. "I did it every day until that thing was straight, and it took me two months. The doctor told me that it was just going to be scar tissue that was inhibiting it. I knew if that arm wasn't straight she wouldn't have a chance."

Steve could empathize with Shannon's discomfort. "I dislocated my own arm and had surgery," he said, a fact to which a scar on his left arm attests, "so I knew what would happen if we didn't start moving it right away."

Unfortunately, because of the injury, Shannon had to miss one major competition: the 1992 World Championships for Individual Apparatus held in Paris April 15-19. Steve thought the timing of the meet, with the Olympic Trials and the Olympics so close, was all wrong and would be too taxing on his athlete.

"It was the first time they ever had one," Steve commented. "I never wanted to go to that meet. And I got my wish."

With all the distress it caused, there were some positive consequences of the injury. Because of it, Shannon was able to give some other minor injuries a rest. Also, it created in her more of a hunger and determination to win.

The Olympics were only three months away. Shannon wondered if she would be at full strength by July. It was now a race against the clock; the lack of time posed the biggest threat to the fulfillment of her Olympic dream.

Chapter 4

Number One

On May 14, 1992, Shannon began her quest to become the best gymnast in America. The U.S. Championship was the first of two meets that would decide the top eight gymnasts in the country, six of whom would represent the United States at the 1992 Summer Olympics in Barcelona, Spain.

Shannon had to place in the top twelve at the Championships to advance to the Olympic Trials that would be held a month later. During the compulsories, Shannon, wearing a green and black tiger-striped leotard, dazzled the fans at the St. John Arena on the campus of Ohio State University with her near-perfect routines. She stuck her vault and did a marvelous floor routine. By the time the night was over, she had beaten Kim Zmeskal by 0.21 to earn the highest position going into the optional round.

"She got fired up," Steve said of Shannon's sparkling performance. "I thought it was a good mental thing for her to see that she was still in the hunt even though she had this injury. . . . It put all the rumors to rest that Shannon Miller wasn't going to be ready." But the question on everyone's mind was whether her body could handle the difficult optional routines.

When asked if she wanted to go for it the next day, Shannon responded without hesitation: "Yes, definitely."

She had not been able to train her full optional routines because of her elbow. However, after Shannon's victory in compulsories, Steve announced that she would go through her optional skills the next morning and then make a decision about competing.

Early the next day, Shannon and Steve arrived in the arena prepared for battle. Shannon began with her usual conditioning. She did leg lifts on the bar, with Steve there beside her, counting. Her left elbow bore the marks of recent surgery; the scar was red and puffy. As she worked out, the soreness and swelling increased. Still, she pressed on, ignoring the pain.

During practice, Shannon went through her complete bar routine for the first time since the surgery. Her elbow seemed to be faring well, but Steve was feeling a little apprehensive.

"If the Olympic Trials were today, we'd be in them and we would qualify for the team," he explained. "But I want to give Shannon every opportunity to not only be in the Trials, but to win the Trials. Why would you ever want to go into something that you're just not quite ready for?"

With the decision made, he and Shannon walked over to the scoring table. "This fine young lady right here is going to scratch the optional session of the meet," he told a woman at the table. "I just wanted to make that official to you. . . . I got an official acceptance into the Trials in writing, so we'll see you at Trials. We'll sit and watch, if you need us." The woman acknowledged Steve and congratulated Shannon on her first-place finish in compulsories. Then the two headed toward their seats to watch the competition.

Shannon wished she were competing. "It was hard to do," she admitted about watching the meet. "I would have definitely rather competed, but I knew that if I wasn't ready and I went ahead and competed, then you never know what's gonna happen."

Steve, explaining his position, said, "I didn't want to see her make mistakes that she would feel bad about [after] the competition. We could go out a winner—which she is—and go into [the next] meet feeling really great."

Shannon, along with an injured Betty Okino, petitioned directly into the Olympic Trials, where their scores would count 100%. Since neither finished the U.S. Championships, a score was not tallied. Normally, the U.S. Championships counted 40% and the Olympic Trials counted 60% toward selecting the Olympic team. Shannon and Betty were two prominent members of the 1991 World Championships team, and they deserved a fair chance to make the Olympic team.

"I hope that they'll be ready for the next competition because we'll really need them in Barcelona," Kim Zmeskal said about Shannon and Betty. With Shannon out of the competition, Kim easily won her third U.S. Championship.

Shannon returned to Oklahoma City and resumed training. Dynamo did not have air conditioning, so she had to endure the hot, humid weather. It was even hotter inside the gym than the ninety-plus degrees outside. This was among the most intense training of Shannon's career. She wanted to regain all her difficulty and consistency in time for the Olympic Trials.

"We work out, eat, rest up a bit, then come back and work out again, eat, shower, and go to bed," Steve said. "It is a very strict regimen, but you have to have it that way."[1]

Shannon and her coaches developed a new floor routine to the tune of Hungarian Gypsy violin music.

"It usually takes a day," Shannon said. "You actually get the whole floor routine done. It takes about five or six hours or more to get the routine and then you have to practice it for months."

The routine had a fresh, mature style that her coaches thought the European judges—particularly those in Barcelona, Spain— would enjoy. Shannon was working her hardest to prove to the United States gymnastics community that she was the number-one gymnast. Her elbow was almost fully healed. It had only taken her five weeks to completely rehabilitate; normally, such an injury took at least eight weeks.

"It's truly amazing she's where she's at," Steve remarked in an interview. "It was a miraculous recovery."[2]

Shannon's intense effort was paying off. She hoped to fulfill a dream that had begun in elementary school by making the United States Olympic team.

"My goals when I was little were just to have fun and do the best I could in competition," she remembered. "It wasn't until a couple years before the Olympics that I actually started believing that I might make the team. That was when it really started becoming a goal for me."

"We've been seeing it come for quite a while," Shannon's dad said. "First it was incredible, then it was unbelievable, and now it's gone far beyond that."[3]

Shannon flew to Baltimore for the 1992 Olympic Trials, which began Thursday, June 11. There she inched even closer to making her dream come true. The pressure was tremendous and the press constantly hounded the athletes, even during practice sessions. Shannon, who later admitted she was more nervous before the Trials than she was before the actual Olympics, tried to ignore the media hype surrounding her and Kim. The press was trying to pit the two gymnasts against each other.

Shannon worked out as she normally did, going through countless routines. She rarely made a mistake and looked superb.

She intended to win. Steve earnestly wanted her to prevail. He was hoping that his world-famous athlete would give Kim a good fight.

"Beating Kim Zmeskal, the World Champion, would be a tremendous feat for Shannon," he said. "I don't think that Shannon has ever lost to Kim, necessarily; Shannon has beaten herself every time we've been on the floor."

As she had done at the U.S. Championships a month prior, Shannon finished first after a strong showing in compulsories, edging out Kim on almost every event. Despite her brilliant performance, she admitted the compulsories had been nerve-wracking.

"I felt really good about what I did tonight," she said at the conclusion of the meet. "I hit all my routines, but there's still room for improvement before Barcelona."[4]

In the optionals, the gymnasts would all be competing together—one event at a time—in Olympic order: vault, bars, beam, and floor. The warmup period before the meet was usually about two hours. Each gymnast attempted all the skills in her routine, and sometimes—for example, on uneven bars—she did her entire routine.

At 2:30 P.M. the meet began. All the competitors marched in and listened to the national anthem, then they moved to the vault for a three-minute touch warmup. Each gymnast was allowed to "touch" the equipment one last time to make sure her springboard setting and her starting position were the proper distance from the vault.

Shannon's full-twisting Yurchenkos were excellent in the touch warmup. She looked confident and her elbow did not seem to be bothering her. Kim looked equally strong. She intended to remain the best U.S. gymnast and was not about to cede her title without a fight. Kim thrived on competition, while it was more of an acquired taste for Shannon.

It would be quite a coup for Shannon to upstage Kim and Bela Karolyi, considering Bela's experience. This was his third Olympic Trials in the United States. In 1984 his gymnast Mary Lou Retton had finished on top, and in 1988 another Karolyi student, Phoebe Mills, had won the competition. Bela expected the same outcome this time. On the other hand, this was Steve's first Olympic Trials. If Shannon made the team, this would be Steve's first trip to an Olympic Games.

Bela was no stranger to Olympic competition. Under his tutelage as Romanian head coach, Nadia Comaneci had won the 1976 Olympics and placed second in 1980. After his defection to the United States, he had coached two young women to the top of the 1984 U.S. team, Mary Lou Retton and Julianne McNamara, and the former had won the Olympic all-around gold. In 1988, his girls had taken three of the six spots on the team and both alternate positions. And in 1992, he hoped to place Kim, Kerri Strug, Hilary Grivich, and Betty Okino on the team. Steve and Shannon had their work cut out for them if they intended to unseat Kim and her legendary coach.

"I feel great coming into this meet," Shannon said confidently. "I'm really prepared and ready to hit my routines. And my elbow—it's fine. It feels as good as it did before the accident."

"We want to win the meet, there's no question in my mind," Steve said. "We are here to make the team—not only make the team, but to win the meet."

Shannon's diamond earrings sparkled under the bright lights of the arena as she stood at the end of the vaulting runway. At the head judge's signal, she began. She ran hard toward the vault but did not have enough power and landed low, taking a big lunge forward.

Steve was quick to suggest some improvements. "You were low on the board," he pointed out. "You have to get that run up faster so you get up off the horse faster." She scored a 9.70.

On her second attempt she was faster off the horse but had another unstable landing. However, the vault was better than the first one. The judges met for a conference to decide the score.

A conference was sometimes held because the range of scores was too wide. Normally, the scores were relatively close together, and if they were not, the judges needed to discuss the performance to make sure everyone had taken the proper deductions.

Shannon did not watch them. She prepared for the next event by putting on her hand grips. They flashed her score, a 9.787, but she did not pay attention.

Kim, meanwhile, was perfect on both of her vaults, scoring a 10 both times and taking the early lead.

Shannon nailed her uneven bar routine, catching all three release moves and sticking a full-twisting double back flyaway. In the stands, her dad breathed a sigh of relief. Some spectators at the Baltimore Arena waved a poster that said "It's Miller Time." They were thrilled with her performance.

Shannon scored a 9.937. She rushed back onto the mat to wave to the sold-out crowd of 11,832.

Kim rose to the occasion and hit her two release moves, although her arm awkwardly banged the low bar after her Gienger. She scored a 9.812.

Shannon kept warm on the sidelines by practicing her splits and other stretching. She tried to remain focused.

Kim was hesitant throughout her beam routine, with a series of wobbles and a hop on the landing. Bela was not pleased. She scored a 9.737, opening the door for Shannon to take the lead.

Shannon did not let the tension get to her. She hit all of her skills, including her three consecutive layouts, a back handspring whip, and a back handspring with a quarter twist. Her only mistake was a step on the landing. Shannon earned a 9.90 and big hugs from both of her coaches.

With one event to go, Shannon had a slim lead over Kim. She debuted her new floor routine. Unfortunately, on her first tumbling pass, she took a step back and crossed the white boundary line, an error which resulted in an automatic one-tenth deduction. However, she landed her second and third passes perfectly.

Steve was elated with her performance. He tossed her up into the air and caught her in a warm embrace. "Beautiful set, good job," he exclaimed approvingly, and added, "Only one step," about the slight mistake. The judges gave her a 9.762.

Kim had upgraded her tumbling to be competitive at the Olympics, and her fine performance scored a 9.95. But it was not enough to surpass Shannon.

"You're the champ," Steve reminded Shannon after Kim's floor set. They had both worked so hard to be recognized in the sport, and now their efforts were being rewarded. Shannon had earned the number-one ranking going into Barcelona. What a prestigious accomplishment!

"I've been training really hard and it just shows that all my work has paid off," Shannon said happily.

Her win, however, was a controversial subject. The complex calculations used to arrive at this conclusion were part of the problem. In both the U.S. Championships and the Olympic Trials, the scores were tallied using 60% of the compulsory score and 40% of the optional score. Of those totals, 70% of the Trials' score was combined with 30% of the U.S. Championships' score. Everything would have been fine except that Shannon had scratched from the U.S. Championships, so 100% of her score from the Trials counted against Kim's weighted score.

Kim had the highest score at the Trials and with the 60/40 factoring. But when Kim's U.S. Championship score was calculated into the equation, Shannon came out on top.

"My girl won," Steve said in defense of Shannon's victory.

"This is the procedure we've come up with, and Shannon won. . . . Two months ago, she's in a hospital facing surgery, and asking me if she'll be ready. It's unbelievable that she won."[5]

Bela felt that Kim had been penalized for competing in both meets and Shannon had benefitted from not finishing the U.S. Championships. Had Kim skipped the U.S. Championships, she would have had the number-one ranking. Bela thought it was a setup.

"Bela's admitted to being a bad loser," Steve said. "Tonight he has to raise his glass to me, and if he can't do it, then so be it. That's his problem. [Shannon] deserves every bit of credit for winning this meet."[6]

Bela and Steve's friendship was deteriorating. Bela would not acknowledge Shannon's victory, and Steve felt slighted.

"The Champion deserves to get some credit," Steve admitted about Kim's world title. "[But] Shannon's time was going to come. People knew it. And it's starting to come now. I realized Kim and Shannon, at some point, were going to be a controversial issue. They were two great competitors. Shannon wanted it. I wanted it. Kim wanted it. Bela wanted it."

"No doubt about it," Bela was quick to say. "It's a rivalry."[7]

"Absolutely," Steve seconded. "That's what drove us. It was a rivalry. . . . We both worked very, very hard for our athletes and for our programs. We're in competition with each other at every given time. I think he was tired of seeing my face at every competition because he hadn't seen someone be so determined." Steve thought Bela needed to learn to make room for someone else at the top, something he had never done before.

The final blow came when Shannon was supposed to appear with Kim on the NBC *Today* show after the Trials. Before her scheduled appearance, the show called and uninvited Shannon.

"I took the phone call myself," Claudia said. "I talked to the lady and she said, 'We're not going to be able to do it after all.

Instead, we're going to have Bela and Kim on. We just changed our minds.' She just said, 'We changed our minds.' She didn't give me any real reason or an excuse or anything. I think she said, 'We don't have time for Shannon. We're interviewing Bela and Kim.' "

The Millers did not buy that excuse. They felt that Bela had caused Shannon to be bumped from the show since he was not happy with the Trial results.

"We knew by then that it went deeper than just Bela," Ron revealed. "Bela had people behind him [like] IMG (International Management Group) and other names we could name. They're very powerful."

"Gymnastics is somewhat political," Claudia stated. "There is a certain amount of politics, especially when you get that close to the Olympics. We figured it might have been [political]. Bela and Kim were both with IMG, a very powerful agency, and we thought they could certainly have some influence in the media."

The incident offended Shannon, her family, and Steve. But Shannon tried not to involve herself in the controversy. She and Kim were friends, even if their coaches were not.

"I made the team," Shannon said proudly. "I won. But I didn't come here to beat any one person." She was clear about her goal: "I just want to go [to Barcelona] and do my best, and I would like to win a gold."[8]

"Really, the kids get along great; it's those forty-year-old kids that make things impossible," Ron joked. "I think if they let the kids run everything, we wouldn't have those types of problems."[9]

The Trials were supposed to pick a team, not a winner. But some questioned whether they even did that. An Olympic team is composed of six members. The Trials only narrowed the team down to eight. A final team still needed to be selected. The Trials team was made up of the seven athletes with the highest weighted total scores from the U.S. Championships and the Trials plus Betty Okino, who had petitioned onto the team. However, two gymnasts still had to be cut at a later date.

Shannon returned home and trained for a few weeks, then she packed her bags for the grueling month ahead. Just before she left, her town held a send-off Fourth of July parade to wish her well at the Olympics. She and Steve were the grand marshals of the parade. Her mother's bank also held a reception for her.

Shannon's first stop on the way to Barcelona was the Team USA summer gymnastics camp in Port Jervis, New York, where she worked out for a few days. She performed an exhibition for the campers then sat beside Steve to sign countless autographs for the young gymnasts.

On Tuesday, July 7, Shannon went to the Commodity Exchange in New York City and rang the bell to open trading in the gold ring. The purpose of her visit was to raise funds for her four family members to go to the Olympics. Her parents needed about $25,000. Shannon's expenses were already covered because she was on the Olympic team.

Steve Karvellas, who owned the Team USA camp, and Young Athletes of America made the arrangements at the Commodity Exchange. When Shannon appeared, the traders chanted, "USA! USA! USA!" Most left their posts to gather around Shannon, who received more than two hundred requests for her autograph.

Shannon's next stop was Florida for the third of a four-part team selection process. The first of two cuts took place at a private meet held July 9 at Brown's Gymnastics in Orlando. This competition was closed to the public. There were two sessions: first compulsories, then optionals, with no scores and no spectators, only coaches and athletes.

After the meet, all the coaches met in a tiny room. Their

objective was to select the 1992 Olympic team. They discussed around a table which gymnast would be the odd one out. Finally, they all voted.

"I thought it was a good idea that the coaches select the team," Steve remarked. "I think the coaches are intelligent and well trained enough that they understand that politics are not going to take precedence over winning. . . . In most other sports the coaches are the ones that select their team, not the judges. Can you imagine the basketball team being selected by the officials?"

The following morning, the seven team members were announced. Kim Kelly, who had finished sixth at Trials, was the unlucky person not chosen. Wendy Bruce, who had finished seventh, was placed ahead of her. Wendy had enjoyed, perhaps, a home field advantage since Brown's Gymnastics was where she trained.

"I think that it was good having two meets count . . . but I think they took it a little bit too far when they decided to have the training camp in Florida," Shannon stated. "A lot of people were confused about who was on the team and who wasn't."

Shannon, the top-ranked gymnast, was not threatened by this training camp because her position on the team was secure. She just concentrated on improving her routines.

"I'm planning to add a little bit of difficulty to my routines," she said, "and to polish them up and work real hard on them."

Although she had done so many routines she could have almost performed them in her sleep, Shannon pressed on, practicing them again and again. A key ingredient to her success was the large number of repetitions she did.

"What I respect most is her work ethic," Peggy once said. "If I say do something twenty times, she does thirty and asks what's next."[10]

To compensate for her delicate frame, Shannon had to put in

extra hours of work to develop the strength needed for the most difficult skills. She was not the stocky, Mary-Lou-like power-house gymnast. Shannon was quick, agile, and graceful. Her power was deceptive and her lean frame belied the fact that she could execute the most difficult tricks. Her secret was good old-fashioned training.

On Sunday, July 12, the U.S. team—Shannon Miller, Kim Zmeskal, Kerri Strug, Betty Okino, Dominique Dawes, Michelle Campi, and Wendy Bruce—left for yet another training camp, this time in France. The team went to France to get acclimated to the European equipment and the time change.

Once in France, Shannon shined. She looked stronger than she had ever looked before. Kim Zmeskal sustained a stress fracture in her leg and had trouble performing up to par, which made Shannon seem all the more the United States' best hope of winning an all-around medal.

"We trained six to eight hours a day," Steve recalled, describing Shannon's workouts during the two weeks before the Olympics. "I think the number of routines was anywhere from ten to fifteen optional beam routines, ten to fifteen compulsory beam routines, six to ten compulsory and optional bar routines, two to four [compulsory and optional] floor routines, and a dozen to twenty [of each] vault."

"It was a lot of hard training," Shannon remembered. "We did a lot of routines. It was stressful because we all wanted to do so well."

Once they arrived at the Olympics, practicing became more difficult. "We trained," Steve said, "depending on what you're allotted—at the Olympic Games you're allotted only a certain amount of time—and sometimes it's only four-and-a-half hours a day. And so it's a very intense time. You have to be ready to go."

The media began to follow the gymnasts and watch their every move when they arrived in Barcelona. Rumors circulated about how serious the U.S. women's gymnastics team was. The press suggested that these "children" were worked too hard. According to the other U.S. athletes, the gymnasts did not seem to be having any fun on the plane ride over, and they barely touched their meals in the dorms.

"The fun comes when you go to a competition, and you do well there, and you get excited," Shannon explained. "And you get to travel all over the place and meet new people." She did not feel that what she was doing was punishment. "I do gymnastics because it's fun, and if it wasn't I wouldn't do it. I would do something else."

Shannon roomed with Dominique Dawes at the Olympic Village. Shannon was closer to "Dom," as her friends called her, than to any of her other teammates. After the 1991 American Cup, Dominique had asked Shannon if she wanted to hang out, and together they had skipped a banquet. For "fun" the two had done conditioning and stretching in their hotel rooms. They had also played games, like seeing how many times they could jump from one bed to the other without stopping. Then they had settled down to watch television. From then on, the two had been close friends.

All the U.S. gymnasts stayed in dormitories built specifically for the Games. After the Olympics, the dorms were to be sold as apartments.

The girls were under very strict supervision before and during the competition. Shannon did not have time to go to the athletes' beach, bike ride, or play video games. She mostly stayed with Steve and concentrated on the job at hand. There would be time for fun sightseeing activities after the Games concluded.

The media criticized Steve's overprotection of Shannon,

saying that he controlled every move she made. But Steve did not see it in such a negative way. Gymnasts were typically the smallest and youngest Olympic athletes, and Steve wanted them to be safe.

"We've never left them alone," said Steve, who had a black belt in karate. "To go to the bathroom, they're escorted by a female coach; to go off the floor, they're with a teammate . . . so they won't get lost or distracted."[11]

A few practice sessions were held in Barcelona before the Olympics began so that the athletes could get used to the equipment. Shannon polished up all her routines, going through them in detail and sometimes picking them apart piece by piece to make sure each hand and foot position was correct.

The day before the team competition began, the U.S. decided to use Wendy Bruce as the sixth and final member of the squad instead of Michelle Campi, who had injured her hip. The group hardly seemed unified with a lawsuit initiated by Kim Kelly dangling over the U.S. Gymnastics Federation and some team members feeling that at any moment they could be yanked from the team for the smallest mistake during practice. E.M. Swift, a reporter for *Sports Illustrated*, wryly remarked that the women's gymnastics team "was as unified as a bagful of cats."

The controversial team selection process left the athletes feeling drained and unduly stressed. They should have been focused on the Olympics, not on trying to make the team. It was important to choose the best team, but not at the expense of team preparedness and confidence.

"We changed the process because the United States Olympic Committee has said to us, 'Your mandate is to pick the best team, to field a team that will best represent the United States,' " explained Mike Jacki, the executive director of the USGF. "And in doing so, we feel that we've got to allow every athlete to be evaluated up to the last moment. It may seem harsh, but that's

82

the reality of what this is."

Bela was named the head coach of the Olympic team. His wife, Martha, and Steve were the assistants.

Steve concentrated on the positive aspects of the team. He thought this was the strongest group ever assembled in American gymnastics, noting that every member had won national or international gold medals. In a sense, this was a little "dream team" with an unbelievable amount of experience. But would this near-perfect one-day-old team perform well enough to bring home a medal? The possibility of fulfilling a lifelong dream was only a few short days away.

Chapter 5

Barcelona

Shannon did not attend the opening ceremonies on Saturday night. The team compulsories started the next day, and she needed to be rested. Although the press was focusing on the battle between Kim Zmeskal and Svetlana Boginskaya, Shannon knew that she was also a contender. She was excited to begin competing. She had trained for so long, and now her dreams of representing the United States in the Olympic Games were only hours from becoming reality.

At age fifteen, Shannon was one of the youngest athletes in Barcelona. A gymnast had to have her fifteenth birthday some-time during the year of the Olympics to be eligible to compete. This rule was later changed so that, beginning with the 2000 Olympics, a gymnast had to turn sixteen in the Olympic year.

Her quest for gold began Sunday, July 26. It was the team

compulsories. Dominique Dawes and Wendy Bruce started the United States off well, and Kerri Strug and Betty Okino received decent scores in the next round, leaving the U.S. in third place with one round remaining. Kim and Shannon had a tall order to fill if they were going to take the lead. They each needed at least a 9.937 on every event to tie the Unified team (formerly of the Soviet Union).

A special video for the gymnastics team had been created to the song *"Wonderful Tonight"* by Eric Clapton. It featured Shannon preparing to compete, dressing in the locker room, and brushing her long blond hair. Her teammates were also shown in this tribute to the American team. NBC, the network covering the Games, played the video during the team competition.

Shannon and Kim, the top two gymnasts from the United States, prepared for the final round. Shannon was glad to go in this round because of the potential scoring advantage.

Wearing a white leotard with red and blue piping around the collar, Shannon mounted the uneven bar podium. She chalked her hands and stepped close to the low bar. She swung smoothly and cleanly, hit every handstand, and stuck the landing for a 9.912. Steve gave her a quick hug.

Preparing for her second event, Shannon walked to the balance beam and stood on the springboard with her hands hovering over the beam. Completely focused on her routine, she did not hear the music playing in the background. Her handstand mount was right on, and she moved through the routine gracefully. The only flaw was a hop on the dismount. She scored a 9.887 and seemed a little disappointed in her performance.

Next, on floor, she did not hold back at all. Each pose and gesture radiated all the exuberance she could muster.

"Way to go, Shannon!" her mom shouted from the stands. Shannon's parents and siblings had made the trip to Spain because of the generosity of the American people. The Millers were thankful to be able to watch their daughter's dream come true. They were also enjoying a certain celebrity status in Barcelona, as devoted followers of gymnastics recognized them from television and sometimes requested autographs.

"Beautiful," Steve commented as Shannon rushed toward him. "Excellent endurance. Super." After a quick hug, both turned and walked away. Steve flashed the audience the thumbs-up sign. Shannon scored a 9.887.

"Well, somebody liked you," Steve quipped after seeing the score. "Get ready for the vault now." Vault would be her last event of the evening.

Shannon had one try, because in compulsories the women get only one attempt. She sped down the runway and launched off the horse. She flew through the air, doing a Yamashita-half, and planted her feet firmly on the mat without budging. Steve was elated; she had nailed it. The judges gave her a 9.95.

As the first day of competition came to an end, Steve discovered that Shannon was in first place. She was leading the entire field.

"I'm real excited," she said shyly when asked by a reporter how she felt. "I had a little mistake on beam, but I'm going to get it cleaned up before optionals."

"Shannon has been better in practice than she was here tonight," Steve said. "She has been on fire in practice, throwing 10.0 routines."[1] He was very proud of his star pupil.

The Soviets also recognized Shannon's excellence. "You want to see ballet and beauty, Miller's got the classic style of the Soviet system," said the Unified coach, Alexander Alexandrov. "Her programs and aesthetics are the best on the U.S. team."[2]

The Unified coaches were amazed by Shannon's quick recovery from a dislocated elbow. A gymnast on their team had suffered a similar injury, and she had been out for almost a year.

In the team standings, the Unified team had a five-tenth lead over the United States, and the Romanians, in third, were less than a tenth behind the U.S. The American team was glad to be in second, especially after an uncharacteristic fall by Kim Zmeskal on balance beam.

Shannon did not know that Kim had fallen off beam until someone told her at the end of the evening. Shannon was so completely focused that she only concentrated on her own routines and did not watch anyone else's.

A day separated the compulsories from the optionals; the men competed on the alternate days. Shannon used this opportunity to go back to the practice gym and work hard on her optional skills. She looked forward to Tuesday's competition; she wanted to get as many points for the team as possible and qualify to all four event finals.

On Tuesday, Shannon and Steve traveled to the beautiful Palau Sant Jordi, the Olympic venue hosting the gymnastics competition. Water cascaded from fountains at the entrance and spotlights illuminated the arena.

The U. S. team began on uneven bars, and Shannon was last up. One by one her teammates went before her, all performing excellent routines but not sticking their dismounts.

Shannon walked up the stairs to the podium. Steve gave her some final instructions, and she nodded with an intense stare. When the judges signaled her to begin, she jumped off the board and grabbed the high bar, where she turned and executed her two consecutive release moves without a hitch. She swung over the low bar then back up to the high bar for another release move and a full-twisting giant swing. To cap it all off, she stuck her full-twisting double back flyaway. Shannon was the only American not to have a mistake on the landing. She was awarded a 9.95, the highest score of the U.S. team.

On the next event, Dominique Dawes and Wendy Bruce were a little shaky on beam, but Kerri Strug and Betty Okino turned in solid performances. Kim Zmeskal was superb for a 9.912.

True to form, Shannon did not watch the other competitors. She kept going through her routine in her mind and on the sideline, making sure everything was perfect.

Seventy-seven-pound Shannon seemed a little out of sync during her routine, with an assortment of wobbles after each major skill. Nonetheless, her set was more than adequate for a 9.90. The American section of the audience booed; they were not happy with many of the U.S. beam scores.

Kim gave Shannon a quick hug, saying, "Good job." Bela patted them both on the head to congratulate them.

At the midway point of the competition, the United States had dropped to third behind the Unified team and Romania.

Shannon was thrilling on floor. Her violin music fit her style beautifully. The judges liked it and gave her a 9.90. As she was performing, Tatiana Gutsu had a tragic fall on her beam mount. Touted as the new Soviet star, her coaches had been counting on her or Svetlana Boginskaya to bring home an all-around gold medal. Now she, like Kim Zmeskal, had to fight for third place on her team to qualify to the all-around final. This would be a difficult task given the depth of the Unified team.

On the final event, the Americans needed near-perfect vault scores to surpass Romania for second place. They were spectacular: the *lowest* score was Dominique Dawes' 9.90. Shannon hit both her vaults, and her best one earned a 9.925.

Kim squeaked by Kerri Strug to make it into the all-around final. She and her parents were relieved. On the other side of the arena, blond-haired, blue-eyed Tatiana burst into tears in Svetlana's arms. She had placed fourth on her team because of the fall on beam, so she would not be permitted to continue.

The Unified team, as expected, won the gold. The Romanians—narrowly edging out the Americans—captured the silver, leaving the United States with the bronze. The U.S. team was a little discouraged since they had wanted to challenge for the gold.

"Some people were disappointed that we didn't win the silver," Steve said. "And I was like, 'You don't understand. Winning an Olympic medal and the chances of even winning one are just so remote.' "

Shannon did not dwell on falling short of the team's aspirations. "We hit our routines the best we could," she said positively, "so we're happy with what we did."[3]

The last time the United States had won a gymnastics team medal in a non-boycotted Olympics had been forty-four years ago, and it had also been bronze. In the 1984 Olympics in Los Angeles, the U.S. women's team had finished second to Romania, but the Soviet Union had not attended.

The American women proudly accepted their medals. Shannon's name was announced, and she smiled and waved to the crowd. Then she bowed her head so the medal could be draped around her neck. She thanked the award presenter and shook his hand. Once the whole team had received medals, they all lifted their flowers and turned to face both sides of the arena. The Olympic banner and the flags of Romania and the United States were raised while the Olympic anthem played in place of the old Soviet anthem. In the next Olympics, the Soviets would compete as separate republics. This was the last time they would compete as a unified team before the dynasty was dismantled.

In the individual standings, Shannon was in first place, just as she had been the first night. Svetlana Boginskaya and Cristina Bontas were in second and third, respectively.

"She beat the whole world!" Steve exclaimed. "Everyone has to finally realize the greatness of Shannon Miller."[4] He did not think that even Shannon knew how great she was.

"She won the compulsory round, and she held onto the lead in the optionals," Steve pointed out. "Of course, this was a team meet . . . but Shannon—nobody can deny her. She's the best in the world. She proved it here at the Olympic Games, the biggest meet in the world. We're not finished. . . . That was just the second heat."[5]

With all the hoopla surrounding Shannon and her surprising first-place finish in the team competition, she tried to keep things in perspective.

"It was nice and all, but I still have the all-around finals and event finals to go," she reminded everyone. She did not have time to dwell on her successes because she was already focused on the next competition.

The top thirty-six competitors continued to the all-around final Thursday. However, only three per country advanced. The U.S. representatives were Shannon, Kim, and Betty—the same three as in the 1991 World Championship all-around final. Unfortunately, Shannon's lead was erased; all the contestants started equally in the all-around.

For the first time in the Olympic Games, the New Life rule was implemented. It stated that all the gymnasts would start over in the all-around final, and the scores from the previous team competition would be erased. This meant that only one day of competition would decide the champion. In the past, the gold medal had been awarded to the gymnast who performed the best throughout three grueling rounds: team compulsories, team optionals, and the all-around competition.

The new system benefitted those who had fallen in the team competition. Many were opposed to the idea, since the Olympic Champion would now have to hit only four routines instead of twelve to win the most coveted title.

Bela and Steve put aside their personal conflicts for the good of the U.S. team. Bela seemed to realize the potential both Shannon and Kim had to win medals. Kim had scored the most points in the optional round of the team competition, and Shannon had scored the most when both days were combined. Steve no longer saw it as a rivalry as he had at the Olympic Trials. He thought of it as a one-two punch.

In a shocking statement, Bela announced that he would be retiring when the competition ended. He had had enough of high-level competition. He wanted to take some time off and focus his energy in a different way for the advancement of American gymnastics.

Bela gave Steve a hug and said, "Handle it. I'm gone. Take the reins."[6] Steve thanked Bela for the inspiration.

There was again a day of rest before the next and toughest segment of the competition. Shannon, wearing a sparkling blue tank leotard and black tights, went through her routines with Steve watching every move. This was Shannon's final workout before the "big meet," the all-around final. Shannon looked superb and rarely even wobbled.

Surprisingly, Unified team member Tatiana Gutsu was also practicing. An alleged injury to Roza Galieva's knee allowed Tatiana to move up to third on the Unified team, so she was now eligible to compete. Roza had looked powerful and healthy in the team competition. Her knee had never been bandaged until after the Soviet coaches claimed she was too hurt to continue to the all-around final.

Tatiana knew she was stronger than Roza and tried not to feel guilty about her teammate's misfortune. In a kind gesture, she promised to give half of any prize money to Roza if she won.

Some were skeptical about the legitimacy of Roza's injury and suspected the Soviets had staged it so that Tatiana could advance to the all-around final. They had been known to pull stunts like this in the past. In the 1985 World Championships in Montreal, Canada, they had replaced two gymnasts who had qualified to the all-around final with Oksana Omelianchik and Elena Shushunova. Both had gone on to tie for the all-around title. The same situation had occurred in the 1990 Goodwill Games. Svetlana Boginskaya had fallen on bars in the team competition but still competed in the all-around final after the Soviets substituted her for Tatiana Lisenko, who had supposedly been injured.

The Soviets had high hopes for Tatiana Gutsu. Many speculated that the reason the Soviets made substitutions was to ensure their best gymnasts were in the all-around final regardless of how they had performed the day prior. These replacements were a controversial topic, and some people disagreed with the ethics of the Soviet Union. Still, the Soviets remained on top and produced some of the world's finest gymnasts.

Some in the gymnastics community believed the three-per-country rule should have been abolished so the top thirty-six athletes could qualify to the all-around final. This way no gymnast would be punished because of the depth of her team.

Steve thought the days of the Soviets' lying and cheating had passed. He admitted to seeing Roza with her knee bandaged. But he was quick to point out that if the same thing had occurred in the United States there would certainly be a lawsuit involved.

Shannon did not worry too much about Tatiana's controversial substitution into the final. "I wasn't really sure exactly what had happened," she said. "Of course, afterwards everyone knew. It bothered me a little bit. But really, if she was the better gymnast it wouldn't be fair not to have her in, because then even if you win you're never really sure."

Shannon concentrated on making herself ready. The ten years of long hours in the gym, the endless repetitions, the thousands of routines—all her preparation would now be put to the test. All her other victories paled in comparison to the importance of this evening's competition. To win the Olympic all-around gold medal would be the ultimate achievement in the sport of gymnastics.

Barcelona

The best from all over the world would be fighting for the gold. Shannon Miller, Tatiana Gutsu, Lavinia Milosovici, Kim Zmeskal, Svetlana Boginskaya, and Cristina Bontas all wanted to stand on that Olympic podium and hear the music playing for them.

Shannon and Kim remembered Mary Lou in 1984 with her gold medal and Olympic glory. Tatiana and Svetlana thought of the long list of champions from their country, and they hoped to carry on the tradition. Lavinia and Cristina thought of Nadia Comaneci, the hero of most of the women on the Romanian team.

Steve also reflected on his dream. He remembered all the sunny afternoons spent in a steamy gym with Shannon, all for this moment.

"I felt from the start that I was training Shannon to win the Olympic Games," he said. "I wanted to do it first for the country, second for Shannon, and third for me."

On Thursday, July 30, 1992, Shannon, who was normally not a morning person, awoke eager for the challenge ahead. Some athletes may have had trouble sleeping in Barcelona on an unfamiliar bed, but not Shannon.

"One thing about me—it's kind of a standing joke—I can sleep anytime, anywhere," she laughed.

She reminded herself as she prepared for the all-around competition that it was just like any other meet. "Just go out there and hit your routines," she thought. Of course, she wanted to win a medal, but first and foremost she wanted to execute her sets perfectly so that she could be satisfied with herself no matter what the outcome.

Shannon wore a white leotard with splashes of gold on it and a white scrunchy around her hair bun. She walked through the Olympic village with her teammates, wearing blue warmup pants and a white T-shirt over her leotard. It was a hot summer day in

93

Barcelona and the sun was shining brightly, so she carried her jacket. Steve walked beside her sporting a similar outfit—minus the leotard—and some sunglasses. He carried Shannon's gym bag. There was not much talking; everyone was thinking about the day ahead. The planning and preparation were complete, and all Shannon had to do was execute. She hoped she could hit her routines just as she had visualized them the night before.

Shannon, Kim, Betty, and their coaches caught an Olympic van to the Palau Sant Jordi. Upon arrival, Shannon hopped out first and carried her bags toward the entrance. The Olympic credentials dangling from her neck gave her access to restricted areas.

There was still a good deal of time before the competition. The warmup took over two hours.

"My warmup went pretty well," Shannon said. "My foot was hurting a lot. I had a minor problem on the tumbling and beam. This is the Olympics and my coaches kept reminding me of that. I knew that I wanted to go out there and do the best I could. I knew once I got out there, you get so involved and focused on your routine that you don't really pay attention to anything else, even pain."

Shannon made sure everything was in order for her first event. Her number, 303, was pinned to her back so the judges could see it. Her grips and wristbands were securely in place. She waited for the judges' signal to begin.

"That's good—that's enough," She told Steve, who was chalking the bars for her. He then placed the springboard in the proper position.

"Okay Shannon, be aggressive now!" Steve yelled to her. He crouched down beside the bars, waiting to pull the springboard away after her mount.

The music blaring on floor did not bother Shannon. In fact, she hardly heard it. The judges lit the green light and she raised both arms to acknowledge them. She ran, circled her arms as she bounced off the board, and reached for the high bar. She swung around the bar to build speed then let go on her first move, a Thomas, and regrasped the bar. Her second release was a pretty Gienger. So far, her routine was flawless and her form was exquisite. She completed her Tkatchev then let go of the high bar to do her dismount. She performed a single twist and flipped twice, landing perfectly, just like in the team competition.

Shannon jogged over to Steve. "Way to stick it!" he exclaimed. "Very good, aggressive routine. Good Gienger—tight form. Beautiful."

Shannon took off her grips and glanced at the 9.925 on the scoreboard. Kim, waiting at the floor exercise mat, also looked over at Shannon's score. After a long judges' conference, Kim began. Everything was going fine until her last tumbling pass, during which she came out of a high double back and bounced out of bounds. Her score was a disappointing 9.775.

Svetlana, one of the Soviets' best chances for victory, turned in an average set on floor. Her dance was exceptional, but her tumbling lacked difficulty. She scored a 9.912.

Tatiana Gutsu started on bars, the same event on which Shannon had begun. The contest between these two was becoming more interesting than the much-publicized feud between Svetlana and Kim.

Tatiana's set was similar to Shannon's except that she did not do a Thomas release move. Her dismount was an extremely difficult double layout flyaway, and she stuck it for a 9.95.

With the first event completed, Tatiana and Gina Gogean of Romania were tied for first, Shannon was in third, and Svetlana was fourth. Kim was twenty-third.

Tatiana was able to overcome her previous problems on beam from the team competition. She hit a tough roundoff layout mount and a standing full-twisting back somersault. She also did

95

two layouts in a row and a full-twisting back handspring swing down. To top it all off, she nailed her three back handsprings to a full-twisting double back dismount. She scored a 9.912.

Shannon had her work cut out for her. "Just like in the warmup gym," Steve reminded her. "Sharp, nice clean form. Really show it off. Show that dismount at the end. Take your time and let's stick it, all right?"

Shannon nodded. Steve pointed out some other things while nervously chewing his gum. Shannon tried to remain calm as the judges deliberated over the previous competitor's score.

"All right, the score's up. They're going to show it around once, then we're up," Steve thought aloud. "Sharp, clean, tight form. Let's get a good aggressive routine all the way through and a sharp dismount. Let's go." He sent her off with a wink.

Shannon was solid throughout her routine. She seemed to spend more time flipping above the beam than on it. She had two slight balance checks, but her difficulty was astounding and she stuck the dismount. She bettered Tatiana's score with a 9.925.

Svetlana, not wanting to be counted out, was almost flawless on her vault for a 9.962. Kim was also aggressive on vault for a 9.937.

Halfway through the meet, Svetlana was now leading, with Tatiana in second and Shannon in third. Betty Okino and Kim were tied for eighth.

Svetlana, with only one release move, scored a disappointing 9.887 on bars. Kim, never giving up, hit one of the best bar routines of her life for a 9.90.

Across the arena on floor exercise, Shannon kept warm by sitting in a split. Tatiana, just inches away, did standing back flips. They ignored each other. Shannon only watched her competitors at the end of the meet once all of her routines were completed.

"I don't focus on beating the competition, because that's not what I'm there for," she explained. "I'm not there to beat any person or team, because then I'd have to be looking over my shoulder and thinking about what they're doing. I'm just focused on what I'm going to do, on doing the best I can."[7]

Shannon later admitted that she was nervous during the Olympics, but one could have never guessed from her calm, cool exterior. She stepped up to the floor following a fantastic warm-up; all she had to do was repeat it to possibly take the lead. Her opening whip back to a full-twisting double back tuck was right on, and she mesmerized the audience with her classy dance to a classical violin piece. The landing on her second run was off slightly, but she covered nicely. This left only her final pass. She stood in the corner and took a deep breath, then she dashed across the floor and hit her full-twisting double back. Finished, she saluted the judges and waved to the crowd.

"A little wild on the last step on that double pike, but that was it," Steve said enthusiastically. "Nice and high. Good strong tumbling and good stuck landings. Beautiful." Shannon scored a 9.90.

Tatiana was also powerful on floor. Her only mistake was a big step forward on her first pass, a double layout. She scored a 9.925.

"One to go. Remember, we're in the first group on this one," Steve told Shannon, referring to the touch warmup on vault. Usually, the first four or five gymnasts took their touch warmup and competed before the second four or five gymnasts did their warmup. This way, the last person to perform did not have to wait so long after warming up.

With one event remaining, Tatiana and Lavinia Milosovici were tied for first, Svetlana was in third, and Shannon was in fourth. Kim was eighth and out of medal contention.

"We were going to the last event," Steve recalled, "and I just happened to look up [at the scoreboard]—I usually don't keep track too much of where they're placed; I just want them to get in there and do well and score well—and I see her in fourth place. I knew at the Olympic Games there's only three medals to be had. I said, 'Get in those medals, Miller! Get in those medals!' "

"I can remember Steve telling me before I went up, 'You need a big vault,' " Shannon said. "I knew what he meant. He meant that I needed to stick my landing and do a great vault to be in the medals."

With a beam routine that was not as good as usual, Svetlana scored a 9.912 and dropped to fifth place. Lavinia Milosovici finished on bars with a hop on the dismount, but the performance was good enough for the bronze medal.

The gold was up for grabs; all Shannon had to do was take it. She practiced her run on the sidelines and tried to stay focused.

The crowd in Barcelona and the billions of people around the world tuning in by television were anxiously awaiting the crowning of the Olympic Champion. In Shannon's hometown, people left work early and interrupted their daily routines to fit this event into their schedules. The locals crowded into restaurants with big-screen TVs to catch a glimpse of their miniature celebrity. Dynamo closed for the week so the students could watch their idol.

The past three Olympics had come down to the same final event, the vault: Mary Lou Retton versus Ecaterina Szabo in 1984, Elena Shushunova versus Daniela Silivas in 1988, and now Tatiana Gutsu versus Shannon Miller in 1992.

Shannon went first.

"Very important: a good strong run, pop it up there, open it, and stick it," Steve explained. "Fast on the run and straight arms."

Shannon practiced her landing by bending her knees and putting her hands out in front. It seemed like she was waiting up there for an eternity. Steve, who had left, came back up on the podium so she would not be alone.

"Steve gets right in her face, and I don't think she even knows what he's saying," Shannon's mom once said. "I don't think he even expects her to hear what he says, just his voice."[8]

"Pop it up there, open it up, and stick," Steve reminded Shannon again. "Nice high vault, open, and nail it, all right?"

Shannon went over the vault one more time in her mind. Then the green light came on and she raised her arms to the judges. She did not know what score she needed since she had not kept up with the running total. She just knew she needed the best vault of her life.

There was a hush in the arena. All eyes focused on Shannon. But she did not notice the cameras and the thousands of people staring at her. Nor did she think about the millions watching her on their television sets. There was only one thing on her mind: the vault.

Under enormous pressure, Shannon stepped forward. Her feet pounded against the padded mat as she rapidly approached the springboard. She performed a roundoff, hit the board squarely with her feet, and flew backwards to the horse. Her hands made contact and she pushed off, soaring through the air like Mary Lou Retton in 1984. She planted her feet firmly and without question on the mat.

It was one of the best vaults she had *ever* done.

Steve threw his arms over his head and cried, "That's the one!" He grabbed Shannon's arms and said, "One more time." The crowd was in a frenzy.

Shannon calmly headed back to her starting marker, eighty feet from the vault, for her second attempt.

"Straighter all the way, now, keep it open and nail it!" Steve yelled in a hoarse voice. Three of the judges posted a perfect 10, while the other three judges flashed a 9.95, resulting in a first score of 9.975.

Shannon dashed toward the vault and again flew through the air. Her landing was not quite as sharp, but she quickly turned to salute the judges.

"That was great!" Steve yelled as he swept her off the podium and spun her around. "Jump up there and wave to everybody," he suggested while setting her back on the podium. Shannon's whole face lit up as she smiled and waved to the screaming fans.

"Come on down," Steve said as he grabbed her. "Nice job little girl. You were unbelievable." Shannon hugged her assistant coach, Peggy Liddick. She scored a 9.95 on her second attempt, so the first score counted. All she could do now was wait and watch her opponent.

"They don't want to give that 10 out to us, squirt," Steve joked. "You'll have to get it tomorrow." Shannon nodded but did not speak. She wondered if the score would be enough.

Bart Conner and Nadia Comaneci came up to Steve and told him Shannon was in first place. Steve, who had not been watching Tatiana, turned to pay close attention to her vaults, as did Shannon and Peggy.

"After vault, when I was watching Gutsu, that's when I finally looked up [at the scoreboard] and knew where I was and knew what she needed and what I needed to be able to get the medal," Shannon recalled.

Tatiana mounted the podium needing a 9.939 to move ahead of Shannon. She performed a high vault, the same one as Shannon, but a tiny hop kept her at a 9.925. Still, she had one more chance.

On her second and final attempt, Tatiana had to do the best vault of her career. She sped down the runway, exploded off the board, twirled in the air, and looked for the landing.

She stuck the vault cold.

Shannon's hazel eyes registered concern. She knew. Even

before the score was flashed, she knew.

The judges slowly calculated the score. "It was a *long* wait," Steve recalled. "It was all maneuvered. I thought it felt like it was manufactured."

Once the score was tabulated, the head judge handed it to the score flasher. The flasher entered it on the scoreboard. The air was thick with anticipation.

Suddenly, the numbers that decided Shannon's fate glowed on the board. Shannon stared at the red digits. They read 9.95. Tatiana had scored just enough to win the gold.

Shannon chewed on her lip and blankly looked off in the distance. She and Peggy, who had been watching near the vault, stood up and walked away. Shannon could not conceal her disappointment, but she did not cry.

"No matter what, you did the best you could do," Steve said solemnly. "You did a great job, only small little wobbles on the beam. We'll fix them in the next few days."

Shannon did not think any of her performances had been bad. She was pleased with herself. She knew she had done her job. She also knew that she could not control the judges.

"When they raised the score, of course, I was a little disappointed at first," Shannon admitted, "but then you take a step back and think, 'There's like 0.012 between my score and hers; it could have easily been the other way. It could have easily been between third and fourth and I could have not gotten a medal.' So then you're thankful for being able to do that well."

Shannon smiled as she accepted her shining silver medal. She had fulfilled her dream.

"It's hard to put into words what you feel," she said about standing on the podium with her Olympic medal. "You just kind of want to thank everyone that made it possible. You are just happy at that moment. You almost want to cry, because you can't believe it's over. It's not the medal that I worked for, it's what it symbolizes: all the hard work and all the support that I've gotten. There's not really time to sit back and look at what you've achieved. You're always trying to achieve more. You're looking ahead all the time." Interestingly, the same three gymnasts standing together now had shared the podium about a half year earlier at the DTB Cup in Germany.

Shannon placed second in the closest battle in Olympic history. She had the highest American finish in a non-boycotted Olympics. She also had the highest point total when the scores from all three days were combined, proving she was one of the best in the world. Tatiana only outscored Shannon on the third day, and unfortunately for Shannon, that was the one day that counted.

A former East German Olympian, Steffi Kraeker, stated it best about the New Life rule: "[The female gymnasts] used to have to perform twelve perfect routines to become the World Champion, and now a gymnast can have mistakes and still become World Champion."[9]

Shannon would have won under the old system. Interestingly, under the New Life rule, Ecaterina Szabo would have beaten Mary Lou Retton in 1984, and Daniela Silivas would have defeated Elena Shushunova in 1988, not the other way around.

The more Steve thought about the situation, the angrier he became. "It ate me alive," he confessed. "Maybe the judges were waiting for a superhuman. It should have been a 10. We had the gold medal in our hands.[10]

"At the time I felt that Gutsu might have been the better gymnast in optionals, but she certainly wasn't that day, even though she was doing the bigger skills. She was doing a double layout on floor but I didn't see [her errors] until I watched the film, and I said, 'My athlete won that meet!' "

Saturday would be Shannon's last opportunity for gold. She had four chances, and she intended to give it her best shot.

Chapter 6

Awards and Autographs

August 1 marked the final day of competition for women's gymnastics in the 1992 Summer Olympic Games. Since Shannon was the only one on the U.S. team to qualify to all four event finals, she spent much of the day before training with Steve. The other American gymnasts had more time to relax. Half of them were finished, and the others had to compete in only one or two events.

Although the event finals were not as stressful as the other parts of the competition, Shannon was as serious as ever. She wanted to bring home a gold medal. She had already won a bronze and a silver; she just needed gold to complete her set. Her goal was to win as many medals as she could, possibly on each event.

The vault final was first. To qualify to an event final, a

gymnast had to place in the top eight on that particular event in the team competition.

"Strong run, pop it up there. Let's go!" Steve urged sternly.

Shannon ran fast and pushed off the padded vault. Her four-foot-seven-inch body was as straight as an arrow. As in the all-around competition, she landed without shuffling her feet for a 9.95. Steve was pleased.

"Straight up off the board," he reminded her before the next vault. "Heels up, front, and hands forward on the landing."

Shannon's second vault in the event finals had to be completely different from her first, and the scores from both were averaged. She chose to do a handspring front tuck somersault, a vault with a starting value of 9.90.

She launched herself high in the air on her second vault, and she grabbed her legs to form a tight tuck. However, she had to take a big step forward on the landing, scoring a low 9.725. Shannon was more inconsistent on this vault since she only competed it in the event finals and did not practice it frequently. Her average was a 9.837, which placed her sixth overall.

Tatiana Gutsu set the pace on the next event, bars, with an excellent performance that earned her a 9.975. To beat Tatiana, Shannon needed a perfect routine. She dazzled the fans with her three high-flying release moves and, like Tatiana, nailed her landing. She knew her routine had been outstanding, but she did not know if she would surpass her rival's mark.

Shannon had done three release moves and Tatiana had only done two. However, Tatiana's double layout dismount had been harder than Shannon's full-twisting double tuck. Both sets had contained roughly equal levels of difficulty. The deciding factor would be the judges' determination of which gymnast had executed her routine the best.

The judges posted a 9.962. The crowd immediately whistled and booed. Both Tatiana and Shannon, however, were later outdone by a Chinese athlete, Lu Li, who scored a 10. Shannon had to settle for the bronze.

Peggy and Steve had high hopes for Shannon's next event, balance beam. When asked by the NBC television announcers if there would be any changes to her beam routine, Shannon quipped, "Yes, I'm going to take out the wobbles."

She was up second on this event. Unfortunately, scores were usually lower for competitors early in the lineup. This did not seem to bother her, however, as she flawlessly performed her opening tumbling series. Her three layouts were magnificent, as was her back handspring with a quarter twist. She put an exclamation point on the routine with a stuck dismount.

Steve was elated. Shannon was happy, too. She waved to the crowd and elicited another round of cheering. The cheers turned to boos, however, when a score of 9.912 was flashed. Steve thought it was low. Shannon just stared in disbelief.

They tried to forget the scores and prepare for floor. Shannon sat in a split and Steve helped her with some stretching. They watched as many of the athletes wobbled and fell on beam, leaving Shannon in the lead. Soon only one competitor, Tatiana Lisenko, had not yet performed. She was the last one standing between Shannon and her long-awaited gold medal.

Tatiana mounted confidently and hit her one-arm handstand and her three layouts. She danced, spun, and leaped without error, and she capped off the routine with a stuck landing on her double tuck dismount. It was the best routine of her life.

Now it was up to the judges. Shannon's routine had been more difficult, but her three layouts had not been as crisp as Tatiana's. The scoreboard was turned, revealing a 9.975. Tatiana had snatched the gold away from Shannon, who was left with another silver.

Shannon's score on beam was later the subject of questions from the media about unjust scoring and politics. "Everyone asked me if I felt like I got gypped, but I really don't," she stated positively. "I went out there and I did the best I could, and that's the way the judges saw it. That's the way the sport goes."

Shannon pushed aside any thoughts of unfair treatment and headed to the floor exercise. She was up first on the event. Her chances of winning were slim, but she did not give up. Famous actors, like Jack Nicholson and Michael Douglas, were watching from the stands and pulling for her.

She performed very well. She enchanted the audience with her smile and elegant dance.

"The personality Shannon has on the floor can't be taught," her dance instructor Peggy Liddick observed. "She's a shy teenager in real life. But when she steps on the floor, she's an actress."[1]

"Awesome!" Steve shouted as she held her ending pose. "Flawless at the Olympics, baby. That was a great meet!" He enveloped her in his arms for a job well done. She scored a 9.912 on floor to win the bronze medal—quite a feat for the competitor who had to go first.

Shannon had accomplished something amazing. She had not missed a single routine throughout the Olympic Games. She had hit sixteen out of sixteen during a week of intense pressure and exhaustion. With thirteen of her sixteen routines she had scored at least a 9.90 or more—an incredible achievement. She had not received a score below 9.725.

Shannon looked for her parents in the stands. She found them and waved. Her dad, sporting a cowboy hat, and her mom waved back and yelled, "Way to go, Shannon!"

Her total medal count from the 1992 Summer Olympics was five: two silver (all-around and balance beam) and three bronze (team, uneven bars, and floor exercise). She had won the most medals of any U.S. athlete in Barcelona to become the most decorated American at the 1992 Olympics, both Summer and

Winter. She had also tied Mary Lou Retton's record for the most medals ever won by an American woman at an Olympics.

Steve was very proud of Shannon. "There's no question that the highlight of my coaching career was my athlete winning five Olympic medals in Barcelona," he said.

Before these Games, Shannon had not thought she would want to participate in the next Olympics four years down the road. But her experience in Barcelona changed all that.

"It was everything I dreamed of and more," she said. "It was fun getting there and fun being there. I hadn't planned to keep competing until '96, but after the Olympics were over I didn't want to stop. It's so much fun."[2]

She later put it more succinctly: "I'm definitely continuing. I still want gold."

Shannon seemed uncomfortable in post-meet interviews. Her voice was very soft and she often answered with only one word.

"It was really scary because I wasn't used to it and I didn't ever know what to say," she admitted about the interviews. Over time, giving interviews became easier for her, but even all the attention after the Olympics did not make her outgoing. She was very modest and did not talk freely around people that she did not know very well. Still, she and her family insisted she was not as timid as the press portrayed her.

"I'm not quite as shy as everyone thinks," Shannon said, "but I'm definitely not bouncing off the walls."

"Once you get to know her, she's just like a normal person and she's really friendly and talkative,"[3] Dominique Dawes said of Shannon. She enjoyed rooming with Shannon at the Olympic Village. Dominique thought Shannon was a good friend, and she was impressed by her performance at the Games.

Shannon's teammates were all very complimentary of her and proud of the job she had done for the United States. She was the only female American gymnast to win a medal outside the team competition. Trent Dimas won the only medal for the men's team, a gold on high bar.

Shannon was glad for Trent and his triumph, and she did not anguish over narrowly missing her own gold. She had hoped to win three or possibly four medals at the Olympics, and she had surpassed this goal.

"I would have loved to win the gold medal," she said. "It would have been great. But the silver is great, too. I'm real happy with that, and I don't want to look back and say, 'Oh, well, if I had only done this or only done that.' That's not really how it is. I did all I could. I hit all sixteen routines. I'm real happy with what I did."

Shannon was afraid to wear all five medals at the same time. She thought they would break. "I was scared whenever I had to take pictures, because they'd all clink together,"[4] she said.

When asked what she would do with the medals, Shannon responded, "I guess I'll take them home and hang them up on the wall. I'll have to find a place for them."[5] But the Millers worried that someone might steal Shannon's medals, so they locked them in a safety deposit box. Lavinia Milosovici lost four medals to thieves shortly after the Olympics, but fortunately, they were later recovered by police.

Once the gymnastics competition was over, Shannon had a free day to relax and enjoy herself.

"After all the hard work, I was relieved that it was finally over," she said. "But I was disappointed in a way because it was a lot of fun."

She toured the athletes' village and spent time sightseeing with her family. Given her popularity, Steve cautioned her not to venture outside the athletes' area by herself. Steve had to escort her when she traded pins outside the village.

"I think everyone recognized the gymnastics team because we were the shortest ones there," Shannon laughed.

"The village, it was all athletes . . . so it wasn't too bad as far as autographs," Steve said. "But boy, you couldn't step outside the village or we got hounded."

As Shannon shopped with her family in downtown Barcelona, many people recognized her, especially since gymnastics had just finished.

"Mostly, they were really nice," she said of her admirers. "They would come up and ask for an autograph or say, 'Congratulations, they saw me competing and how happy they were, how swell we did'—stuff like that."

The CBS *Evening News* caught up with Shannon for an interview later in the day. She and Steve talked to Mark Phillips. The media was a little critical of women's gymnastics, speculating that the sport stole the childhood from many of the top gymnasts competing at the Games. Shannon disagreed with the accusations. She did not think she had given up her youth. She pointed out that gymnastics had provided her the opportunity to travel a lot more than most kids her age. She loved gymnastics and was devoted to the sport. Otherwise, she would not have endured all the long hours of training and painful conditioning.

While in Barcelona, Shannon met several famous athletes, like Carl Lewis and Dan O'Brien. But she really wanted to meet the Dream Team. Bela's three gymnasts had met the famous basketball team at accreditation, but Shannon had missed the opportunity.

"The Karolyi's had gone and I was taking a nap at the time that they went, and they forgot to tell me, I guess," Shannon said resignedly.

Her coaches, upon sensing her disappointment in not meeting the Dream Team, decided to help. Over the years, Steve and Peggy had developed a friendship with NBC gymnastics commentator John Tesh. They asked him if there was any way for Shannon to meet the team. John came up with box-seat tickets and back-court passes for the USA versus Spain basketball game. These were among the hottest tickets in town.

After the game, they all went backstage for the press interviews. When they arrived, Magic Johnson said to Shannon, "I went to your gymnastics competition. Did you see me?" She smiled and said that she had. Someone had pointed him and Scottie Pippen out to her at one point during the competition.

"It was really neat that they would come watch gymnastics," she said later.

Larry Bird chimed in, "Five medals—is that all you won?"

Shannon even met the king of basketball, Michael Jordan.

"Michael Jordan was getting killed by the press at the time, and they were all around him," she remembered. "He just gave me an autograph while he was talking."

It was thrilling for Shannon to meet the team. She was excited to get their autographs and surprised that they knew who she was.

Shannon, being the lightest U.S. athlete at the Games, was also introduced to Mark Henry, the heaviest U.S. athlete. He was a weightlifter who weighed 367 pounds, almost 300 pounds more than her.

Shannon left Barcelona August 3. She flew into Dulles Airport in Washington, D.C., and was transported around the nation's capital in a limousine. She visited the White House, where she met President Bush and Arnold Schwarzenegger. She had her picture taken with both of them. She also stood next to the president when he spoke.

"They had a lot of Olympians there," Shannon said. "They were prepared for a lunch on the lawn and it ended up raining, so we were eating hot dogs in the hallways of the White House."

On the evening of August 4, a reception was held at the Capitol building during which Shannon was presented with a Senate resolution honoring her achievements at the Olympics.

The event was given by Oklahoma Senators Don Nickles and David Boren.

Shannon was reserved and soft-spoken at the reception. "I just want to thank everyone who supported me and my family in Barcelona," she said, "and I'm very proud to bring back medals for the United States."

During the evening, she drifted to a corner of the room where she noticed a television set replaying her vaults from the all-around competition. Intrigued, she stopped to watch.

Normally, she did not like to watch videotapes of her own performances. She liked to *do* gymnastics, not watch it. However, her mom sometimes videotaped meets and replayed them for Shannon while explaining what she had done wrong. Shannon also watched televised broadcasts on occasion just to hear what the commentators had to say about her.

Steve came over and reminisced with Shannon as they watched the tape. Soon the people at the reception began to notice Shannon watching herself on the television, and they crowded around to catch her reaction. They had seen her perform live in the all-around competition; this was the first time she had seen it.

After her second vault played, Senator Bob Dole congratulated her for a fine performance. The television audience and the Senate audience clapped, and Shannon smiled. The group agreed that she should have received a 10.

When the score was flashed on the screen, Shannon bit her lip and said nothing.

"Revoke their visas when they come over here,"[6] Senator Dole joked about the judges.

Soon after meeting some prestigious senators, Shannon appeared on morning talk shows like *Live with Regis and Kathie Lee* and *Today*. She was quite popular back in the States. The governor of Oklahoma even called to congratulate her for her fine performance at the Games.

Finally, after all her recent travels, competitions, and celebrations, Shannon got to go home. It had been a long time—over a month—since she had been able to relax in the comfort of her own home and her own bedroom.

The NBC television network affiliate in Oklahoma City, KFOR, flew Shannon home in a Learjet. Upon arriving at the Oklahoma City airport August 5, Shannon, wearing her U.S. team warmup suit, was greeted by over 5,000 fans chanting her name and holding signs with tens on them and posters saying "We love you, Shannon!"

She was escorted to downtown Edmond for a parade in her honor. She rode through town in the back of a convertible, down streets lined with 15,000 locals who cheered wildly. Her heart-shaped American flag earrings glistened in the sun as she smiled and waved to everyone. Shannon signed some autographs and eventually made her way to a stage set up for the occasion. After several people spoke to congratulate her, the Bob Moore car dealership of Edmond presented her with a 1993 red Saturn sports coupe brandishing a silver license plate with her name and "Olympic Champion" on it.

"I was so excited!" Shannon recalled. "But I didn't have my license yet, so that became my next goal."

Store windows displayed signs that read "Welcome Home Shannon" or "We're proud of you!" or "Good job Shannon!" or "Shannon Miller: Gymnast Extraordinaire." Her hometown even erected a road sign at the city line that said "City of Edmond, Home of Shannon Miller, Winner of 5 Olympic Medals, Barcelona 1992." Shannon appeared everywhere from billboards to the cover of the Edmond phone book. People stopped her on the street and said, "Are you who I think you are?"

Once when Shannon went out for dinner with her family, the waiter refused to bring the bill. He said he wanted her autograph, but not on a credit card receipt.

Shannon's home was flooded with over a thousand letters following the Games. Some were simply addressed "Shannon Miller, The Best Gymnast in the World, Edmond, OK." But home wasn't the only place she received fan mail. Dynamo, the U.S. Olympic Training Center, the U.S. Gymnastics Federation, the post office, the local chamber of commerce, the city of Edmond, her school, and the local television stations were all bombarded with letters for Shannon.

"It was coming from everywhere," her mom laughed.

Fans often questioned Shannon about her family or about how she had learned a particular trick. Claudia remembered one girl who asked Shannon for advice about her boyfriend: "Shannon said to me, 'Mom, how would I know?' So Shannon wrote her back and said that she didn't have any experience in that area, but when she does get a boyfriend, she will write *her* for advice."[7]

Apparently, lots of young men were willing to be Shannon's boyfriend, judging from all the pictures they sent her. She catalogued all the fan mail addresses on a computer and stored the letters and gifts in boxes. Shannon diligently tried to respond to them all. She autographed postcards designed to send to her fans that had her picture on them. She went through about 2,000 cards in a month so she ordered 5,000 more. They did not last very long.

"Most of the time all they wanted was a signed picture, and of course, you always have some that ask you a lot of questions," Shannon said. "I do as much as I can, but I'm still going to school."

Besides all the mail, the phone rang constantly, from early morning to late at night. Newspaper reporters, television stations, and radio announcers all wanted to talk to Shannon. Fans even called her home.

"If I actually answered the phone and they got to talk to me, mostly they asked questions," she said. "Just normal stuff: 'What was it like to be in the Olympics?' A lot of times they'd be little kids or people about my same age and they just wanted to know a little bit more about me, instead of what they read in the newspapers."

All the attention was tough on Shannon's family, especially her dad, who felt the need to protect his youngest daughter.

"After the Olympics I wasn't allowed to answer the phone, so my dad would," Shannon remarked. "He usually gave them the third degree before he let them talk to me. He wanted to know if they went to school with me. He would give them a quiz to see if they really knew me. I kept getting mad at him for it, but he thought it was for the best."

Eventually, it all became too overwhelming, so the Millers hired an agent to represent Shannon. Jerry Solomon with ProServ in Washington, D.C., began to handle her affairs outside the gym. He also represented other famous athletes like Gabriela Sabatini and Nancy Kerrigan, whom he later married.

Inside the gym, Shannon was still yearning to improve. "After the Olympics, I only had about a couple days off, so it was a little bit easier to get back into gymnastics," she explained. "I didn't really feel like I should stop or anything."

Her Olympic success proved beneficial to Steve. He claimed that over two hundred children signed up at his gym because of Shannon's performance in Barcelona.

Shannon did not stay at home very long because she had become a very popular commodity, especially at the World Trade Center in Manhattan. As promised, she went back to the Commodity Exchange to thank the traders for raising $5,000 for her family's trip to Spain. She and Steve held up her five medals and roused a barrage of cheers.

Through the generosity of many people, Shannon's parents had raised more than enough money to go to Barcelona. "Everyone in Oklahoma helped: ordinary people, businesses, all the radio and television stations, and my mother's bank," Shannon observed. "We ended up with $11,000 extra to donate to the Special Olympics."

Later in August, Shannon began her sophomore year at Edmond North High School. Although she was small and quiet, she could not blend into the crowd anymore.

"We drove her to school the first day," Erin Jones, a classmate of Shannon's, remembered. "My mom said she looked more nervous than she did at the Olympics. It was a huge deal. One guy tried to kiss her in the hall. She freaked out."[8]

"It was embarrassing," Shannon laughed. "I don't even know exactly why it happened or anything. It just kind of was a fast kiss and then I was embarrassed. I was afraid they were [all looking at me] but I guess no one really cared. I felt like everyone was staring at me. He didn't even say anything and I didn't know who it was. Erin knew more about it than I did."

Shannon felt a little uncomfortable at school with all the attention she was receiving after the Olympics. She rarely talked to her school friends about what it was like to compete in Barcelona.

"We don't really talk about gymnastics at school," she said.

Her longtime friends did not treat her any differently, but others did. "I think by some I am treated differently," she acknowledged. "They're afraid to talk to me, I guess."

Shannon did not get to know her classmates as well as her gym-mates. Her best friends were those with whom she trained.

"I don't think anyone knows me quite as well as the people in the gym do because I'm so quiet at school," she said. "I just mostly do homework all the time."

In the gym, other athletes looked up to her. "Shannon is a great role model," fellow teammate Marianna Webster said. "She works really hard and has a good attitude."

Shannon did not attend much school at the beginning of her sophomore year because she was invited to participate in two post-Olympic tours. First, she went to nine cities with the 1992 Gymnastics Spectacular tour. Then there was the 1992 Tour of Olympic and World Champion Gymnasts that visited twenty-five cities throughout the fall. Steve and Shannon used the tours to make her a more well rounded gymnast. She had to get used to the crowds and her overwhelming popularity.

"This is not a tour of just fooling around," Steve commented. "She's doing three release moves on the uneven bars. She's doing major elements on the balance beam, and we've been practicing our tumbling and vaulting on the side. I believe that she'll be a better gymnast because of it."

At one arena the gymnastics floor was placed over an ice rink. During practice, Shannon's feet kept going numb because the floor was so cold. She had to periodically go to the bathroom, put her feet in the sink, and run warm water over her toes to thaw them out so she could continue her workout.

Dubbed the Cinderella of gymnastics, Shannon was the most popular attraction on the tours. She received more applause than even Tatiana Gutsu and Svetlana Boginskaya. When advance ticket sales were slow, Shannon traveled to those cities to do radio and newspaper interviews. She did not brag about her medals; she would not even mention them unless specifically asked.

On tour, Shannon performed her uneven bar and balance beam routines. At one particular stop, she fell during her beam routine on her three consecutive layouts. In a gutsy move, she jumped back up, walked down the length of the beam, and did them again. This time they were perfect.

"There's not a lot of pressure," Shannon explained about the tour. "You're doing the same routines, but there aren't judges."[9]

Shannon occasionally took the microphone to tell the adoring fans about how her life had changed. "People ask for my autograph and I'm getting lots of mail," she would say to the crowd. "I also have different goals now, such as going for the 1996 Olympic Games."[10]

A highlight of the tour was the simultaneous performance of the compulsory floor routine by Shannon and Tatiana. They ended the routine side by side and held hands to wave to the crowd. Shannon and Tatiana, wearing matching black-and-white leotards, were the same size and looked like they could be sisters. These Barcelona rivals were becoming friends.

While Tatiana was the Olympic Champion, Shannon received more attention and better treatment—especially from her government. Tatiana would eventually move to the United States in August 1994 because of tense relations with the Ukrainian government, which gave her only $3,000 for winning the gold. In past years, Olympic Champions from the Soviet Union had earned at least four times that amount. In addition, the government allowed her to keep only a fraction of the money she had earned in post-Olympic tours in the United States and Europe.

Tatiana admitted that she had sometimes hated gymnastics and had been forced to continue training despite stress fractures in her back. She had been given shots of Novocain to numb the pain so she could continue competing during the two years prior to the Olympics. Like many gymnasts from the former Soviet Union, she fled her own country for the freedom of America.

Shannon, of course, was treated like a hero in the United States. When she finished her routines during the tour, little girls screamed out her name, thrusting papers and pictures in front of her to sign. Budding young gymnasts wanted to be like her, look like her, and do the moves that she did. Fans even tracked down which hotel she was at and called her room, so much so that her room could not be listed under her own name.

"It feels kind of weird to have them knowing your name and

stuff and asking for autographs," Shannon said with a laugh.

"She's actually never been a shy person," Steve observed. "She's been a modest person. She doesn't like to talk about what she's doing because she doesn't know how great she really is."

During the tour, Shannon found time to attend the USGF banquet and the annual Gymnastics Congress in Anaheim, California. She and Trent Dimas were given special awards that recognized their fine efforts at the Olympics. The two also appeared on ABC's *Good Morning America* together. Shannon did a balance beam routine that thrilled the hosts and audience.

Shannon thought traveling with the other athletes was enjoyable. Usually, they flew to each city then toured on a huge bus that contained a kitchen and two living rooms. It was like a big gymnastics family.

One time Shannon, who normally roomed with her tutor Terri Thomas on the trip, overslept and almost missed her flight. Terri had inadvertently set her alarm clock for 6:00 P.M. instead of A.M. Shannon had also set her alarm and requested a wake-up call, but the call never came and the two slept through Shannon's alarm. The coaches called at 7:30 A.M. saying it was time to go to the airport. In a panic, Shannon and Terri threw on some clothes, quickly packed their suitcases, and rushed out the door. From then on, they always set at least three alarms in the room.

Terri Thomas had begun traveling with Shannon after the Olympics. She was Shannon's tutor, and she also worked as an office manager at Dynamo. Shannon missed several weeks of tenth grade during the tour, and Terri helped her keep up with her courses, like algebra, biology, history, Spanish, world literature, and computer literacy. The two became close friends almost immediately.

Shannon could talk about her problems with Terri. She expressed how difficult it was to endure the demanding, pressure-filled workouts while the other Olympians, most of whom had retired after the Games, relaxed and enjoyed themselves.

"On the tour, everyone else was there having fun, and Shannon wasn't allowed to," Terri said. "She was still competing. She was in strict training. She was there for work."

Each day Shannon had to get up before dawn, do interviews, do conditioning, work out, do homework, then perform in the show until late in the evening. She even squeezed in school tests between performances.

"There wasn't that much time and she'd get tired," Terri observed. "Every once in a while something would happen. She'd have a bad workout or Steve would yell at her and she'd be a human for a few minutes. She'd cry for about ten minutes and we'd talk about it." Then Shannon would get back to work.

She drove herself to get good grades with the same fervor she displayed in gymnastics. "I push myself to get all my homework done, even if it's one or two in the morning," she admitted. "I guess I'm a perfectionist."[11] Consequently, she became stressed if she ever received a poor grade, which by her standards was a low B. But her grades were usually excellent, and she attributed her scholastic success to outstanding time management.

"I don't think I would do as well in school if I didn't have gymnastics," Shannon claimed. "I might not use my time as wisely; I would say I could do things later. Now I have to get them done."[12]

"When our family goes out to eat, Shannon spends time doing schoolwork in the car and at the table while waiting for her food," Shannon's mom said. "She sees to it that every spare moment is accounted for and used to its maximum."[13]

In addition to touring, Shannon filmed a television commercial for Trivial Pursuit. In the opening scene, a woman holding a Trivial Pursuit card asked, "What woman won the most medals in the 1992 Olympics?" The camera panned to Shannon sitting casually on the beam and wearing a silver medal. She smiled and said, "I don't wanna brag, but. . . ."

During the filming of the commercial, Shannon met basketball star Patrick Ewing. "[I] came up to about his kneecap,"[14] she joked.

Shannon saved the money she earned from the commercial and the tours to help pay for college. She would not be able to get a gymnastics scholarship because she had forfeited her eligibility to compete in college by accepting money for doing gymnastics.

Shannon was becoming quite a celebrity, but she did not let all the attention and fame go to her head. Winning recognition did not change her personality, nor did it change how her family treated her. Her mom still insisted that she clean her room, although Shannon found it hard to get rid of things she no longer needed. She liked to save everything.

"I still go to public school," Shannon said. "I still work out. My coach still yells at me in the gym. My brother and sister still pick on me, and I still pick on them. Many of my friends have known me since I was in the first grade, and they still treat me the same. I've never been accused of being big-headed."[15]

Once she was back home and things began to settle down, Shannon had to rearrange her skills on each event and learn new compulsory routines. It was not easy to master the new compulsories, which changed after each Olympics.

The Code of Points was also changed and updated after every Olympics. Some skills increased in value while others were devalued. This meant that more difficult tricks had to be added to a routine for it to be worth a 10. Naturally, scores were lower immediately after the Code was updated.

After two months of traveling the country, Shannon found herself behind in her training.

"I worked out during the tour but not quite as much as normal," she said, "so after the tour it's been a little bit harder to get back into full sets and top shape."

To improve her routines, Shannon had to learn new tricks. When she tried a new skill, like a double layout somersault on floor, she first attempted it on the trampoline to get a feel for it. At Dynamo the trampolines were in-ground, meaning they were level with the floor, which made them safer than normal trampolines. Next, she practiced the new move into an in-ground pit filled with square chunks of foam. When she was ready, she placed a mat over the foam so she could try landing on her feet but on a well-cushioned surface. Eventually, she attempted the move on the floor with Steve spotting, and then by herself. This safe progression aided Shannon in learning difficult skills without taking unnecessary risks.

By the time the autumn leaves were falling and the weather was becoming colder, she had reworked most of her routines to again be worth a 10. She did not pay much attention to the new rules; she liked the challenge of improving her routines and thought the spectators would enjoy the harder sets and more innovative skills. She left it up to Steve to worry about figuring the level of difficulty using the new Code of Points.

As the holiday season approached, Shannon got an early Christmas present. One dreary morning in November, her brother Troy heard some strange sounds coming from outside the house. Shannon's mom went to check on the noise and found a helpless newborn puppy squeaking in the mud. Shannon immediately fell in love with the tiny puppy and named him Dusty. She begged her parents to let her keep him. Troy had his own pets and so did Tessa, she reasoned. Reluctantly, Shannon's parents gave in and said she could keep Dusty.

At first Shannon had to use an eyedropper to feed little Dusty. No one knew where he had come from or who his mother was. Apparently, Tessa's dog Ebony had given birth to puppies, and no one in the family had even known she was pregnant. Shannon thought Dusty was half Golden Retriever, one-quarter Lab, and one-quarter German Shepherd, but she was not absolutely certain.

Since she did not compete during the holiday season, Shannon had some extra time to play with Dusty. She was not allowed to participate in the DTB Cup in December because she was just short of the new age minimum, sixteen. Unfortunately, this meant she would never again have the chance to face off against Tatiana Gutsu in amateur competition. Tatiana retired shortly after the DTB Cup, saying she felt like an old woman from all the years in gymnastics.

As 1992 came to an end, Shannon was voted the U.S. Olympic Committee's (USOC) Female Gymnast of the Year. She was also nominated for USOC SportsWoman of the Year, where she finished fifth in the ranking. She was a finalist for the Babe Zaharias Female Amateur Athlete Award and the Sudafed Amateur SportsWoman of the Year. Shannon won the 1992 Steve Reeves Fitness Award—she was the first woman to do so—and the 1992 Nuprin Comeback Award, honoring the tremendous comeback she had made after dislocating her elbow in the spring. In addition, she was named the 1992 March of Dimes Sports Headliner of the Year for Oklahoma.

The year had changed her life forever, but Shannon wasn't one to dwell on the past. "I don't look back at the Olympics too often," she said. "It was great—the experience and everything. It was great to be there. That's something I'll take with me the rest of my life, but I'm also looking forward to the competitions ahead."

Chapter 7

Winning Over the World

Shannon entered the 1993 gymnastics season with a new status. Now, *she* was the one to beat.

"I was used to being the underdog up until the Olympics, and now it's just a different role coming into a competition being on top," she said confidently.

Shannon still worked as hard as ever. As she had done for countless mornings over the last several years, she got up early almost every day and headed for Dynamo Gymnastics.

Steve, now thirty-five years old, also made the familiar morning trip to the gym. While driving in his red BMW, he sometimes recounted all the long hours spent fighting, scratching, and clawing his way to the top. Now he was the best coach in America. His life and the life of his star pupil had forever been changed by one competition in late July 1992 that had enthralled the entire world.

Though Shannon had danced on the world's stage at the Olympic Games, had been featured on morning television shows across the country, and had shaken the president's hand, one might have never known from looking at her. She was still a quiet sophomore in high school. She was humble and down to earth despite her impressive list of accomplishments that rivaled any professional athlete's.

As he had done for the last ten years, Ron Miller continued to drive his daughter to practice, only now they made the trip in Shannon's new red Saturn. She hopped out and entered the familiar gray building on which the words "Dynamo Gymnastics" were painted in white over a rainbow.

Shannon got right to work with 75 chinups, 100 V-ups, 75 pushups, and 25 presses, then she walked on her hands across the mat several times. She was not treated any differently than the other athletes.

Shannon's dad and other onlookers could peer through the small observation window on the second level to watch practice. The parents could not hear Steve's comments, but they could tell from his facial expressions if their daughters were performing up to par or not. Occasionally, Steve closed off the viewing area so that no outsiders could distract his gymnasts from their training.

These young women trained harder than most professional athletes. And even five Olympic medals did not keep Shannon from striving to improve her gymnastics.

"Motivation that she has gotten from me has been, in my opinion, given to her every time she does something, and I think that she feeds off that," Steve said. "I think that she feeds off the understanding that I want what's best for her and I'm willing to tell her right out what she's going to have to do to be the best."

Also pushing and motivating Shannon was 1992 Olympian Kerri Strug. After Bela Karolyi's retirement, Kerri had promptly left his gym and sought training elsewhere. She was a welcome addition to the Dynamo team, providing some healthy competition for Shannon that drove both of them to do their best. Kerri and Shannon learned from each other's strengths and weaknesses. Kerri was a powerful tumbler and vaulter, while Shannon's strengths were bars and beam.

"It is nice having someone else at an elite level that is on the national team and training for the same competitions that I am," Shannon said. Steve was developing other elites, but they were younger and less experienced. "She makes me do my best every day. If she learns a new skill, then it makes me want to learn a new one. If she's hitting her routines and I am missing some, then it motivates me to do better and better in the gym."

"I think it helps a lot because we push each other," Kerri agreed. "One day Shannon's on top and hopefully another day I will be. It's a good way of training because it pushes you to go harder. It's nice to have someone in the gym that can do that with you."

Shannon's first competition after her Olympic triumph was the 1993 Dynamo Classic in January. She did not do as well as she had hoped.

"I didn't win," Shannon admitted sheepishly; her teammate Kerri did. "I fell on beam. It's the curse of the Dynamo Classic. I've fallen on beam about three years in a row, but that's okay because they were new skills. It's hard because it's in front of a home crowd, but it's a great time to try new skills."

Next, Shannon entered the 1993 McDonald's American Cup in Orlando, Florida. Having lost the 1992 American Cup to Kim Zmeskal, she was determined not to let the title slip away this time.

"Even though Kim retired, I don't think that's any less motivation because that's not where I got my motivation all last year and the years before that," Shannon said. "It's from me wanting to do the best I can, and from my coaches and family supporting me all through gymnastics."

In the preliminaries, Shannon had a fall on beam on her three layouts and finished second to Kerri. However, she had the highest score on every other event.

In the finals, Shannon was the one to beat. She was determined not to fall off beam. She did a beautiful routine and scored a 9.875, the highest score awarded on any event at the American Cup. The young gymnasts in the audience loved her, waving posters of her and yelling out "We love you, Shannon!" whenever she took the floor. She easily defeated Kerri and took home $8,000 in prize money for her stellar performances.

1984 Olympic Champion Mary Lou Retton, whom Shannon greatly admired, could identify with the pressures a gymnast faced after a successful Olympic performance. "I think Shannon and my gymnastics careers are very similar," Mary Lou remarked. "We both went into the Olympics as kind of the underdog and came out as pretty successful and then competed the year after in the American Cup. I can remember in '85 feeling more pressure here at the McDonald's American Cup than at the Olympics. And I'm sure Shannon feels the same way. You're expected to win. The media, the press, and the public say, 'Hey, she's an Olympic Champion, she should win.' "

Four days later in Atlanta, Georgia, Shannon entered the Reebok International Mixed Pairs and was coupled with Lance Ringnald. She had won the meet in 1992 and wanted to repeat in 1993. This competition again fell on her birthday, and she hoped to treat herself to a first-place finish.

Reebok was a new sponsor for the U.S. gymnastics program and this event. Shannon received a colorful warmup suit, a leotard, and some shoes just her size: 5½.

Lance and Shannon started the competition well, advancing to the second round in first place. However, the pair was unstable on the next events and was knocked out of medal contention.

The following day on the flight home, Shannon tried to catch up on her homework. Her travels had caused her to fall behind; her classmates were already taking semester exams back in Edmond. She did not like to miss a lot of school, but that was part of the sacrifice she made for gymnastics.

On Saturday, March 13, after her five-hour morning practice, Shannon and over twenty of her friends gathered in the gym parking lot. They boarded a bus headed for Celebration Station, a local fun center, for Shannon's sweet sixteen birthday party.

Lots of hot pizza—one of Shannon's favorite foods—satisfied the hungry group. A magician thrilled the crowd with his amazing tricks. He even used Shannon as his assistant. He pulled a live rabbit out of a hat and offered to let her keep it, but she declined since the family already had so many animals. Besides, she thought her cat or dog might eat the helpless bunny!

Shannon's parents surprised her with a half-carat sweet sixteen diamond pendant draped around the neck of a furry, brown teddy bear. Her dad put it around her neck and gave her a gentle kiss on the cheek. The necklace and the party had been donated by Jim Clark of B.C. Clark Jewelers as a thank you to Shannon for putting her hometown on the map during the Olympics.

"Shannon hasn't had a birthday party since she was nine," her mom said. "That's when she started competing, and there hasn't been time since for parties and everyday kid things."[1]

Shannon's dad enjoyed the festivities but had mixed emotions about his daughter turning sixteen. He realized his little girl was becoming a woman.

As the television cameras, photographers, and her friends looked on, Shannon blew out—in one breath—the sixteen candles on her red, white, and blue cake that was shaped into a one and a six. After eating, it was time for some serious game playing.

Shannon even won a large stuffed flamingo. The finale of the evening was a slumber party at a nearby hotel, where she opened gifts and the entire crew watched the movie *A League of Their Own*.

The next morning, Shannon did not feel any older. However, she had received lots of neat presents from her friends, and Peggy had scheduled her for a sitting at a glamour photography studio.

Peggy had worked with Shannon since her elite career had begun to blossom, and the two of them enjoyed a special friendship. Peggy had thought up a new move on balance beam and was trying to teach it to Shannon. If Shannon were the first person to compete the skill internationally, it would be named after her, so she planned to try it at the upcoming World Championships.

With the 1993 Worlds only weeks away, Steve made practices tougher. Since Shannon was on spring break from school for part of the time, Steve increased the workout hours. But when her elbow bothered her on bars because of the scar tissue from her injury, Steve backed off and gave her a rest.

Shannon was also very busy outside the gym at this time. She filmed a public service announcement at her father's school, did interviews for a radio station and the ABC television network, and went to Pennsylvania to do a photo shoot for the Elite Gym-Kin catalog.

On Thursday, March 25, Shannon and her teammates left for the 1993 American Classic in Salt Lake City. Upon arriving, she did a television interview and went to a hospital to sign autographs.

The Classic was used as a trial for the World Championships squad. Since Shannon was guaranteed a spot on the team, she did not compete. Instead, she did an exhibition on every event. She hit her new vault, a double-twisting Yurchenko, but it was questionable whether she would use it at Worlds. She was lacking consistency and having trouble completing the second twist. The vault she had used in the Olympics, a full-twisting Yurchenko, had been downgraded to a starting value of 9.80.

Kerri Strug and Dominique Dawes qualified as the other two members of the team. At the 1993 World Championships there would not be a team competition, so only three gymnasts per country were allowed to participate.

Early the next morning, Shannon flew back to Oklahoma City. She had one week to touch up any problem areas before leaving again, this time for Birmingham, England, the site of the World Championships. Because Steve wanted to get in as much training as possible, he had Shannon and Kerri practice on Sunday—normally their day off. Shannon was going to the gym every day without a break. Steve even squeezed in a workout the morning before their plane left.

Shannon's lower back had been bothering her a little during practices, but she tried not to let it concern her. She saw a doctor and took it a little easier on some skills, but that was about all she could do for it.

"We've had a bunch of X-rays done," Steve said about her back problem, "and we're told it's nothing really serious. Only the pain is serious."[2]

Her mom helped by massaging it at night. Shannon told herself that after Worlds she would take some time to rest her aching back. For now, she had to press on to reach her goal, a World Championship victory.

It was a long flight to England. Shannon watched *Chaplin* and caught up on some homework on the plane. She had left Oklahoma City Wednesday morning. With the time change, layovers in different cities, and a flight in excess of nine hours, she did not arrive in England until Thursday morning. Steve let her rest in the hotel for a few hours, then it was off to the gym—despite the jet lag—for a workout.

Shannon had almost a week to get used to the new equipment and the time zone difference. She typically woke up early and went to the gym for a few hours. In the afternoon, she ate lunch and rested or did homework in the hotel. Then she headed back to the gym for several more grueling hours.

The press and television announcers were there watching practices, scoping out the top gymnasts, and adding additional pressures.

"The main goal I have is hitting my routines," Shannon said to the media before the meet, "because I know if I do my job, then whatever happens, I'll feel like a winner."

The competitive field was not as tough as usual. Generally, in the year after the Olympics, many athletes retired and were replaced by new, younger gymnasts who lacked experience. Tatiana Gutsu and Svetlana Boginskaya, the top two Soviets, were not there. The reigning World Champion, Kim Zmeskal, had decided not to go, as had Hungary's best, Henrietta Onodi. One of the leading Romanians, Cristina Bontas, was also absent. Still, there were serious contenders present, like Olympic gold medalists Lavinia Milosovici and Tatiana Lisenko.

Shannon cared little about who was competing or not. As always, she was there to hit her routines and win the meet, regardless of the roster.

Before the meet began, the international gymnastics committee had to evaluate Shannon's new beam move. Any skill that was not in the Code of Points had to be evaluated before a competition so the judges would know its value. Shannon showed them a perfect back handspring with a quarter twist to a handstand, to which she added another half twist. It had only taken her a few months to master the complex skill.

"Peggy dreamed it one night," Shannon said, "and she came in the gym the next day and said, 'Let's try this.' So I tried it and it worked out pretty well."

Her move would now be known as the Miller. The committee valued her skill as an E, the highest level of difficulty. All skills were rated from A to E. An A skill, like a single back flip, was the easiest.

Shannon was at the top of her game in Birmingham. Her dominance was evident when she won every event in the preliminaries and entered the finals holding the number-one position. She was the talk of the town and expected to sweep the meet.

Teammate Kerri Strug was strong in the preliminaries, but only two Americans could advance to the finals, and Shannon and Dominique Dawes had finished ahead of her. Steve was upset that Kerri, who placed fifth, could not advance. He joked that maybe the U.S. should compete as separate states, like the former Soviet Union now did with each republic represented, in order to get more gymnasts in the finals.

Everyone expected Shannon to win the all-around final. Kathy Johnson, the ABC television commentator, said she had not seen an athlete with a better chance of winning a competition since Nadia Comaneci in the 1976 Olympics. Bart Conner thought the only way the other competitors would have a chance was if Shannon made a big mistake.

"It's nice because it gives me a little bit more confidence going in," Shannon said, "but I still have to hit my routines and try hard for them."

She began the all-around final on uneven bars. She swung, twisted, and flipped around the bars with ease, taking only a small hop forward on the dismount. She had stuck her landing in the preliminaries, so she was a little disappointed with her routine in the finals. Still, she scored a 9.825.

Dominique started the competition on bars as well. She was dynamic and scored a 9.762. Gina Gogean was also nearly perfect on both of her vaults for 9.718 points out of a possible 9.80. Dominique and Gina claimed the two spots behind Shannon.

On the second event, Dominique proved she was a contender for gold by nailing her beam routine for a 9.775. Gina was a little weak on her bar routine, but her double layout dismount was spectacular. Both competitors pursued Shannon closely, hoping to take advantage of any mistake she might make.

That mistake came on balance beam. Shannon was sailing through her routine, with only a minor wobble on her two consecutive layouts, when she came to the dismount. She had plenty of height in the air, but she did not open up in time for a solid landing and overrotated, stumbling backwards. She did not fall, but the several steps were costly.

Shannon knew right away she was in trouble. After acknowledging the judges, she rushed toward Steve looking uneasy. Steve told her she would have to do better on floor to make up for it.

"You started out fine but became a little cautious in the middle," Peggy told her. Shannon had seemed uncharacteristically nervous throughout the routine. She scored a 9.625, which dropped her to fifth place.

Steve thought the error might cost Shannon the championship, but not wanting her to become discouraged, he kept that thought to himself. Shannon listened carefully to him as he encouraged her to put the mistake behind her and concentrate on doing the best routines of her life on floor and vault.

Shannon's mistake had opened the door for the other competitors, and they were fired up. Gina capitalized on the opportunity with a solid beam routine. She did not have any problems and earned a 9.725. Dominique, a crowd-pleaser on the floor, wowed the English with her complex tumbling and bright smile to capture the lead.

But only a fool would have imagined Shannon Miller out of contention. She fought back with grace and elegance on floor.

She showed why she was the favorite, nailing every landing and finishing all her difficult leaps and jumps for a 9.825. The routine propelled her from fifth to third place and less than a tenth out of first. With one event to go, the tension was high. Shannon needed to be perfect on her vaults. She knew it would come down to her landing.

Throughout the meet, Shannon had been feeling a bit queasy. She had taken Naprosyn, a potent pain killer, on an empty stomach to ease her back pain, and it had made her sick. She normally did not take medicine of any kind, so her body was not used to it. She had not been able to eat normally as a result and felt very weak. Steve was worried she might not have enough energy for her last event.

"I sat her down, gave her half a banana and Re-Vita, and she came to life," he said. "She was almost solely fueled on Re-Vita since she couldn't keep any other food down."

Steve debated whether to use the more difficult double-twisting Yurchenko that was worth a 10 or a single-twisting Yurchenko that could score only a 9.80. He decided that Shannon probably did not feel well enough to try the demanding double-twisting vault in this pressure-filled competition, so he told her to do the full-twisting Yurchenko.

Shannon concentrated on her vaults. "I needed to stick both vaults and hit them really well, because neither of them came from a 10," she remembered thinking.

With all eyes on Shannon, she dashed toward the vault and flipped high above it. She landed without error, just as she had done in the Olympics, scoring a 9.775 out of a possible 9.80. She still needed to hit one more vault, since for this competition the scores from the two would be averaged. Happily, her second attempt was even better than the first. She landed and triumphantly thrust her arms above her head like a referee signaling a touchdown. The vault was perfect, and the judges awarded her a

9.80.

Steve wrapped his arms about Shannon and twirled her around. "That was a beautiful vault!" he exclaimed. "That's the one!"

As in the Olympics, all Shannon could do now was sit back and watch everyone try to beat her. But she knew she had done her job and could be pleased with herself whatever the outcome.

Dominique stepped onto the podium eager to take the lead. On her first vault, a one-and-a-half-twisting Yurchenko, she took a large step forward. However, the vault was valued at a 10, and she scored a 9.712. Shannon leaned forward discreetly in her seat to catch a glimpse of the score. She was concerned. Dominique only needed one more good vault to surpass her.

Dominique spun through the air on her second and final attempt, but her hopes of winning were shattered in an instant. She ran out of power and sat down on her landing, knocking herself out of the running. Overwhelmed with disappointment, she immediately burst into tears. In an act of good sportsmanship, she walked over to Shannon and gave her a hug, even as she cried. Dominique was a favorite among the fans, who were touched by this show of emotion. Her costly mistake dropped her to fourth.

Everyone thought that Shannon had won, but there was one competitor left. Steve was worried.

Gina did a wonderful floor routine, hitting all of her skills cleanly. The decision would be left to the judges. Shannon waited in anticipation.

The score was flashed: 9.80. At first, Steve thought Gina had won. Then someone told him that Shannon had won by .007—"a James Bond" as Steve later put it.

At last, Shannon had won the long-awaited gold medal in the closest battle in World Championship history. In so doing, she had distinguished herself as one of only two Americans to ever win the all-around at a World Championship. Kim Zmeskal had won it in 1991 and now Shannon.

"It's a great feeling, especially after Barcelona, where I lost by such a little amount," she said. "It was great to be able to come back after having a little bit of trouble starting out."

The United States, Romania, and the Ukraine were all represented on the awards stand. Shannon placed her right hand over her heart and proudly watched the American flag raised as the *"Star-Spangled Banner"* played. Her eyes were watery. All of the hard training was worth it for this moment. She was on top of the world.

After a press interview, Shannon called home for just a minute to tell her family the good news. Her dad had heard the results on the radio and was bursting with pride.

The next day, April 17, Shannon awoke around 10:00 A.M. to a pleasant thought: it wasn't just a dream; she had really won the all-around. But there was little time to dwell on her victory from the previous night, for today the event finals on vault and bars would be held. She had qualified to all four event finals with the top score on each event, so she still had to get through two more days of competition.

"It's a great feeling that I was able to train hard and do so well," she said that afternoon. "But I know that I still have four more events to go."

Shannon could relax a little, since there was typically less pressure in the event finals. Steve decided to take her out of the vault competition because she was not feeling well. However, some of the other athletes did not think that was the real reason.

"We knew Shannon was out [because] she doesn't have a good second vault," Elena Piskun from Belarus stated bluntly. "They just wanted to keep her name in the winner's category."[3]

Steve admitted he and Shannon had not had much time to work on a second vault, but she was also ill. Nevertheless, on bars Shannon hit every skill. To put the icing on the cake, she stuck the landing cold.

"Unbelievable!" Steve shouted, clapping his hands. His star pupil was lighting up the arena. She scored a 9.887.

"It was one of my best sets that I've done since we've been here," she said with a smile. "I was really focused on the dismount, making sure that I stuck it, because I knew that I didn't in the previous competition."

Shannon faced no serious challenge for the gold. Dominique came the closest with a 9.80, but she had to settle for the silver. This became the first one-two sweep by Americans in a World or Olympic meet.

Following the awards ceremony, the gymnasts headed to a press room to answer questions from the media. Shannon rarely spoke up, so Steve sometimes answered her questions. This annoyed some members of the press who wanted to hear from the new World Champion.

"They asked her about why she didn't compete in vault," Shannon's mom said, "and she started to say something and [Steve] just jumped right in and totally contradicted what she was saying. She said, 'Mom, this is what he told me to say. Then he realized it wasn't sounding good so he jumped in and said something else.' "

Shannon was uncomfortable talking to the press with Steve around. She was a little intimidated by him and worried that he would censor her answers. She relaxed more when she was in the privacy of her home. Frequently, when she did phone interviews, she went up to her bedroom and closed the door so no one except the interviewer could hear her answers.

The beam and floor finals were the next day. A pale Shannon mounted the balance beam looking tired and frail. On her two back handsprings to a whip, she unfortunately was not straight over the beam and consequently fell off. The spill was frightening: both feet slid off the beam and her side banged against the edge. She stumbled backwards, then she took a deep breath before remounting the apparatus. Visibly shaken, Shannon fell again on her next skill, a back handspring with a quarter twist. She managed to hit her two layouts and the Miller before the bell sounded to let her know she had ten seconds to finish the dreadful routine. Her dismount was high, but she overrotated and rolled backward.

She walked away trying to fight back the tears. Peggy put her arm around Shannon. Although the routine had been a disaster, Shannon had to be commended for not watering it down. She had tried all of her difficult skills and had not substituted easier ones, even when things had begun to fall apart. With the three falls, she scored a dismal 7.85 to finish last. She had not received a score like that since she was nine years old. She later admitted that this was the most embarrassing moment of her career.

After all the balance beam participants had competed, the officials lined them up for awards. Steve had told Shannon to rest for floor, so she was nowhere to be seen. The officials thought she had left and thereby withdrawn from the final event, floor exercise, but Steve straightened everything out.

"I just didn't want her to go kiss somebody and throw up on them while receiving no award,"[4] Steve explained frankly.

Shannon was determined to redeem herself on floor, her last event of the 1993 Worlds. She put the troubles on beam behind her and did a beautiful routine. When she finished, the audience at the National Exhibition Centre clapped loudly.

Shannon looked exhausted as she walked off the floor and into the arms of her coaches.

"When's she's hot, she's hot, and when she's not, she's still pretty warm,"[5] Steve remarked.

Shannon scored a 9.787 to win her second event gold. Her overall total of three gold medals was the highest number ever won by any U.S. gymnast, male or female, in a World or Olympic competition. Shannon became only the third American woman to medal in both a World Championship and an Olympic Games. Kathy Johnson and Julianne McNamara were the other two.

Following the floor awards, Shannon was given a final drug test, then she was whisked away to interviews and a photo session. When all the business was taken care of, she attended a banquet with the other athletes. Shannon traded gifts and pins with the competitors from other countries. She enjoyed talking with them and getting to know them better. However, the language barrier was sometimes a problem.

Shannon had time for a little sightseeing before leaving. Usually on longer trips, Steve let his gymnasts do some touring. Shannon, Kerri, Steve, and Peggy took the train to London and visited Buckingham Palace, Big Ben, Windsor Castle, and the Hard Rock Cafe. Shannon also went to Harrod's, a department store where Queen Elizabeth shops, to pick up souvenirs. In the evening the gang caught a play, *Joseph and the Amazing Technicolor Dreamcoat*, at the Palladium.

Shannon had enjoyed England, but she was looking forward to going home. After layovers in New York and Dallas, she finally arrived in Oklahoma City. It was very late at night, but Shannon's family and the press gave her a warm welcome. She was glad to be back in the familiar surroundings of the "Sooner State," so nicknamed because early settlers had tried to enter the area and claim the land sooner than legally allowed by the U.S. government.

Shannon had a lot of catching up to do at school. She had missed many classes because of her numerous competitions. Her disciplined life helped in school, though. A test had been scheduled in biology class one day when neither the teacher nor the substitute showed up. While the other kids had thrown spit balls and squirted each other with water guns, Shannon had quietly found the test and taken it. She had known she would be missing school the next day and needed to take her test. Nobody had found the students until the class was over. Clearly, diligent Shannon was not a typical high school student!

In recognition of her recent string of impressive victories, Shannon won the United States Olympic Committee's Sports-Woman of the month designation for both March and April. Also in April, Shannon, her family, and Steve appeared on NBC's *I Witness Video*. They talked about the benefits of using videotape for training purposes. Steve filmed Shannon frequently so she could see her mistakes and correct any problems with her form. She could not always tell when she bent her legs, for example, but the tape showed it all.

"If she can see it, too, then all of a sudden, I'm on her side and not just a person criticizing her," Steve said during the show.

Shannon's popularity was high. In May 1993, she was featured on the cover of several prestigious gymnastics magazines: *World of Gymnastics*, *Gym Stars*, *USA Gymnastics*, and *International Gymnast*. Being modest, Shannon did not typically read any of her own press unless specifically asked to do so.

As the 1992-93 school year came to a close, Shannon looked forward to summer fun. But with school out, her workout schedule became even more intense. While most kids slept in, Shannon usually woke up at 6:50 A.M., tossed down a fat-free blueberry muffin and some orange juice, and left her house by 7:30 A.M. Having passed her driving test in early July, she could now drive her Saturn to practice. However, she was so small, even at age sixteen, she had to sit on a pillow to see the road.

When asked if she was a danger to other drivers, Shannon laughed and said, "Not too much. I haven't got to drive a lot."

Once, Shannon went to pick up a sandwich at an unfamiliar restaurant. As she pulled out of the parking lot, people started beeping and waving at her. She wondered what they were doing. Of course, she was well known in her community, but something did not seem quite right. A block later, she realized she was going the wrong way down a one-way street! Thinking the other drivers probably recognized her car, she was mortified.

"Oh my gosh, I can't believe I did that," she told her mom after the incident. "They probably think I'm a real dingbat."

Since Shannon was a new driver, her dad sometimes drove her to the gym to give her a break. The first of two demanding summer practices started at 8:00 A.M. and lasted until 1:00 P.M. Afterward, Shannon grabbed some lunch, like a sandwich or yogurt. In the afternoon she swam, played with her puppy, Dusty—who had developed a habit of chewing on her socks—or she visited her favorite store at the mall, The Limited Too. Then it was back to the gym from 6:00 P.M. until 8:30 P.M. She practiced six days a week and sometimes Sunday, too.

Shannon's lower back, particularly around the tailbone, was still bothering her during practice. The constant pounding and the stress of hard landings were taking their toll. Several important meets were scheduled near the end of the summer, so she wanted to be in top shape, but she also wanted to be healthy. Sometimes she took it easy in workout, but most of the time she had to block out the pain and continue. Doctors had told her that working out would not cause further deterioration of her back condition but would probably be painful.

Fortunately, Shannon did not have to do her full competitive routines every day. Her coaches broke up the monotony by having her work on isolated skills for a day, or sometimes she split her routines in half and worked on each part separately. On floor, she did only the dance parts or a routine with easy tumbling—a single back flip for every tumbling pass—when she was not doing her full set.

Like most people, Shannon liked to take a week's vacation in the summer. Her vacation, however, was spent at a gymnastics camp. She enjoyed a welcome change of pace and scenery at the Team USA gymnastics camp in Port Jervis, New York. There, she could train and have some fun at the same time. The 180 campers were thrilled to have their hero, gymnastics legend Shannon Miller, there with them. Her favorite activity was the zip-line into Root Beer Lake.

"It's really beautiful up there," Shannon said. "It's nice to get away from everything for a while and be able to train."

Shannon also attended a Republican Party function in Washington, D.C., where she met many members of Congress. She toured the White House and just missed catching a glimpse of the First Lady. Shannon was not registered with any political party because she was not old enough to vote. But when she turned eighteen she planned to vote for "whoever was the best person for the job."

Shannon had gone far with her gymnastics—quite literally: she had traveled all over the U.S., to the Commonwealth of Puerto Rico, and to ten foreign countries. By the time she was sixteen, Shannon had been to Canada, England, France, Germany, Holland, Italy, Japan, Russia, Spain, and Switzerland. She was known in many nations around the globe and was the hero of countless young athletes.

Shannon had defeated the best gymnasts in the world to claim her place at the top. But there were three more years ahead until the next Olympics. And that was a long time to stay on top, especially with upcoming gymnasts anxious for a chance to beat the World Champion.

Chapter 8

Unbeatable

Gymnastics insiders wondered if Shannon could stay on top until 1996. By the summer of 1993 she had already won five medals at the Olympics and three golds at the World Championships. Success was usually short-lived in gymnastics. Many thought her career could not last three more years.

As an athlete grows older and matures, her body naturally changes, making it more difficult to perform the high-level skills. Also, the constant pounding her body takes begins to wear it down. Shannon was susceptible to these problems, but as long as her body held up, she wanted to continue. She still enjoyed the sport.

"Most of all, I just keep telling myself to not put so much pressure on myself and that I will have good days and the rewards will come when I get to competition," she said. "I don't want to burn myself out in a couple of years and then have to stop before [1996]. I want to pace myself so that I'm at peak form in Atlanta."

In mid-July, Shannon flew to California for an exhibition at San Jose State University. She impressed the crowd with her spectacular uneven bar work. She also showed off a delightful new beam routine. Shannon had reworked the routine, changing around some of her dance and adding a front tuck somersault mount. Her new mount was worth more points than her old handstand mount.

A couple of days later, Shannon and the athletes from the exhibition traveled to Los Angeles for the Hilton Challenge, a tri-meet between the U.S. and two former Soviet republics, Belarus and the Ukraine. Despite a back injury, Shannon effortlessly won the meet. Dominique Dawes, after a break on bars, finished a distant second.

The United States easily won the team competition. With the breakup of the Soviet Union, the individual republics were not as strong as before and lacked depth. There were normally one or two excellent gymnasts on each republic's team, and the rest were good, but not great.

After a brief stop at home, Shannon was off to San Antonio, Texas, for the 1993 Olympic Sports Festival. Prior to the competition, Shannon, along with weightlifter Mark Henry, lit the Festival torch on top of Pike's Peak in Colorado Springs, Colorado, where it began its journey to San Antonio. She also visited San Antonio prior to the meet to promote the event.

This meet was special to Shannon because her grandparents from both sides of the family would be attending. She only saw her grandparents about twice a year, so this was a treat.

"We've got the Olympic flag flying on the pole in the yard like we always do," Shannon's grandfather Charles Miller said. "You know, it's sort of like they do in England when the queen is in residence."[1] His wife Mabel said they had to fight off the neighbors when Shannon was there.

Charles and Mabel Miller had lived in San Antonio for over forty years. Shannon's maternal grandparents also lived in the area.

Besides seeing her grandparents, Shannon wanted to use this trip as a tuneup for the U.S. Championships, which would be held in three weeks.

"I'm competing in the competition to mostly get my routines down before Championships," she explained. "And this is just kind of a fun meet that I get to do."

She pulled away from the field early with a near-perfect set on bars. Kerri tried to keep the distance to a minimum with a superb floor routine, but she lost ground on vault.

Shannon grabbed the lead and did not look back. Her beam routine exhibited her usual steadiness and class. She omitted one of her back layouts, but she had so much additional difficulty that she was not penalized. She landed her dismount adeptly and smiled briefly at the judges. But as she turned and walked toward her coaches, a vacant stare betrayed the fact that her back was hurting. Landing on the hard blue mats was not helping her injury any.

Kerri battled back after vault with a thrilling bar routine. Her release moves were well above the bar and she stuck her dismount. But Shannon refused to relinquish the lead to her Dynamo teammate. She was a little conservative in her tumbling to protect her irritated back but managed to stay ahead of everyone.

On her final event, floor, Kerri was at her best. She hit everything from start to finish. But her stellar performance was not enough to surpass Shannon, who hit her second vault perfectly for the title.

Shannon's excellent performance set a new all-around record at the Sports Festival, shattering the old one set in 1990 by

Brandy Johnson, whom Shannon considered one of her heroes.

Dynamo Gymnastics dominated the competition: Shannon captured first, Kerri took second, and Marianna Webster, an upcoming Dynamo student, came in third. Steve was pleased with the outcome. He thought his girls spurred each other on and fostered an atmosphere of healthy competition. The results spoke for themselves.

"This was a really fun meet to be in," Shannon said. "It was really a team thing, and that's different for me because a lot of the meets I go into are so high pressure."

Shannon got along well with her teammates and enjoyed traveling with them. The night before the competition, they usually went to a nice restaurant for dinner. It was a relaxed atmosphere with lots of laughter and joking, although the athletes were careful not to eat too much in front of their coaches. If the schedule permitted any free time, Steve took a quick vote to see what the evening activities of choice would be. The lure of the shopping mall usually steered the voting, because everyone, including Shannon, loved to shop for clothes.

"At nine o'clock we're going to meet right here," Steve told the girls once they arrived at the mall. "That means you have forty-five minutes. Any strange looking characters, avoid them, okay? Ready . . . break." The huddle disbursed in groups of two or three that rushed to their favorite stores. The younger ones stuck together, as did the veterans. Sometimes Shannon could slip in and out of stores without being recognized. Other times, people would spot her and say, "Hey, there's Shannon Miller" and ask for her autograph. After buying a few things, like jeans or T-shirts, the girls returned to the hotel.

Steve and Peggy closely monitored their athletes' whereabouts. The gymnasts were not allowed to leave their rooms, even to go down the hall for ice or soft drinks. But the athletes did not seem to mind this rule too much.

"Steve protects us," Marianna Webster observed. "He makes sure people don't bother us on trips. He makes sure we're in bed at a decent hour."

"It's pretty strict," Shannon's tutor Terri Thomas said. "He knows where they are all the time, but that's good for safety reasons."

The coaches had to be even more careful with Shannon because of her celebrity status. "Shannon is who she is," Terri commented. "She goes downstairs and people see her. She's the best-hearted person I know, but she's still a little bit naïve. She's getting better. She believes the best in people and she tries to see the best. She believes the best of all strangers, which sometimes isn't always good."

On the morning of the meet, Shannon and her teammates woke up early, piled into a rented van, and went to the gym for some conditioning and a light workout. Steve liked to "play a little more music to pump them up and get them motivated" on the day of the competition.

Shannon qualified to all four apparatuses at the Festival and hoped to take home a medal from each event. When the chalk settled, she walked away with three golds (vault, beam, floor) and one silver (bars).

It was not an easy victory for Shannon. She was in pain many times throughout the competition. She tried to hide it, but once in a while a wince or a grimace betrayed the pain. While sitting in a split after her floor routine, her face showed the anguish she felt. But when a score of 9.90 was announced, she quickly stood, smiled, and waved to the 13,500 screaming fans at the HemisFair Arena. The approval of her grandparents, the admiration of the crowd, and the standing ovation seemed to diminish the pain for a moment.

After a few draining weeks of travel and competition, Shannon went home to unwind and train for the big meet of the summer: the U.S. Championships in Salt Lake City, Utah.

"I still know I have a lot of work to do on compulsories, so I have a lot more cleaning up to do," she said. "I'm going to start working back my tumbling again for Championships."

Shannon returned to the U.S. Championships on August 25 as the most successful American gymnast in history. A year earlier at the 1992 U.S. Championships she had only competed in compulsories because of her elbow injury. Then, she had wondered if she would be able to make the Olympic team. Now, everything had changed. She had gone from underdog to favorite. She had won almost every U.S. title imaginable over the last year. The only one missing from her sparkling résumé was that of U.S. Champion, which Kim Zmeskal had held for the past three years.

Steve suggested that Shannon was winning competitions in reverse order. Normally, a gymnast won nationally in a U.S. Championships, then internationally in a World Championships, and finally the Olympics. Shannon was doing it backwards.

In the compulsories, which counted 30% toward the overall total, Shannon had the highest score on every event. It seemed like no one would be able to surpass her unless she made a mistake. She could only beat herself in this competition.

One worry was her injured back. She had begun having problems with it in January, and by August it had worsened. The doctors could not find the cause of her pain, so they labeled it a lower back sprain. Shannon's trainer, Mark Cranston, worked with her daily to improve her condition. He massaged her back to mobilize the soft tissue.

Shannon had to spend a lot of time treating her injury. On the day of the optional portion of the Championships, she began therapy at 7:30 A.M. then went back for more at 1:30 P.M. and again just prior to the warmup at 4:30. Following the competition, she would again work with the trainer.

Kerri was up first of the major players. She nailed her bar set for a 9.85. Dominique also hit her bar routine for a 9.825.

Shannon, also starting on bars, had a perfect routine in the touch warmup and duplicated it in the competition. The only mistake was a hop on the dismount. She scored a 9.90 and, as expected, took the early lead.

Kerri, unfortunately, fell during her two layouts on beam, scoring a disappointing 8.85 which knocked her out of the running. Dominique, however, was exquisite, sticking her three consecutive layouts, a front flip, and a full-twisting double back dismount. She scored a 9.675.

When asked if other athletes' falls affected her, Shannon replied, "I really didn't see many of them. . . . I just knew that I had to hit my routines and do well."

Shannon showed why she was the best in the world on beam, scoring a 9.875 to further her lead. She hit her three layouts and made her patented Miller move look easy. A truly talented gymnast can make extremely difficult maneuvers seem simple. Many gymnasts performed a back handspring with a quarter twist, but no one could do the Miller as well as Shannon, who felt more pressure performing the skill because she did not want to botch a move named after her.

As always, Dominique was powerful on floor with her new dramatic routine to *"Malaguena"* from *Carmen.* She scored a 9.80 to keep pace with Shannon.

"Be sharp out there, bright eyes. Let's go!" Steve barked to Shannon before her floor routine.

Shannon put the difficult tumbling back into her routine that she had taken out at the Sports Festival. She hit all of her passes, but she had an awkward wobble on her three-leap series. She equaled Dominique's floor score of 9.80.

On her final event, Shannon performed a decent first vault, but Steve wanted more. He knew she could do better. As she walked back to her starting marker, Steve encouraged her to go harder on the second try and to stick it. She was higher on the second one but still hopped on the landing. She scored a 9.75.

"Excellent meet. You're the president," Steve joked while massaging Shannon's shoulders. She barely smiled; her back had been hurting throughout the competition. Still, when asked about her back pain by a reporter, she downplayed her discomfort: "With the adrenaline flow you don't notice it much. Your mind's on other things."

Dominique's vault was solid for a 9.825. She had worked hard to improve it after the disaster at the World Championships. She finished second, almost a full point behind Shannon. Kerri placed third.

Shannon had clinched her first national title. "It's really exciting because last year I wasn't able to finish the meet because of my elbow, and this year I've been able to compete all eight events and do great on them," she said with a grin.

In the event finals the next day, she and Dominique split up the medals, each winning two golds, a silver, and a bronze. Shannon did not have to look very far to find her new rival; Dominique was quickly improving and building a name for herself.

After the U.S. Championships, Shannon and her family traveled to the country music haven of Branson, Missouri, for a short vacation. Shannon usually tried to take two small vacations with her family each year. She was happy to have a much needed mental and physical break from gymnastics.

When the Millers returned, Shannon began her junior year of high school. She and Steve decided to cut back her practice schedule. Instead of going twice a day, she just went after school. She arrived at the gym at 4:00 P.M., and finished around 9:00 P.M., Monday through Friday. She also went to the gym Saturday mornings for five hours.

Shannon missed the first couple of weeks of school to attend a training camp for the national team in Atlanta, Georgia. After the camp, she attended the National Congress Ceremony of Honors and banquet on September 11. Peggy and Steve were voted Coaches of the Year, and Shannon received the Master of Sport Award, one of the highest honors bestowed in gymnastics. She was the nineteenth person to receive the award in its twenty-one-year history. The last person to receive it had been Glenn Sundby, the founder of the Gymnastics Hall of Fame, in 1982.

Shannon met Billy Payne, the President and CEO of the Atlanta Committee for the Olympic Games. He gave an inspiring speech about the upcoming Games in which Shannon hoped to participate.

In October, Shannon, along with Mary Lou Retton, Wendy Bruce, Svetlana Boginskaya, and Dominique Dawes, traveled to eight Midwestern cities for the Montgomery Ward 1993 Tour of Champions. The first stop was the Myriad Arena, which was virtually in Shannon's back yard. She was the favorite, of course, and received deafening applause for everything she did. Two of her teammates, Jennie Thompson and Soni Meduna, also joined the group.

Shannon had a blast. She enjoyed catching up with Svetlana and Wendy, with whom she had toured following the Olympics. She really let loose during the shows, performing a 1950s dance routine with some of the other athletes. The tour finished in early November.

After the exhibitions, Shannon and her mom traveled across the Oklahoma border to Beaumont, Texas, for the Babe Zaharias reception. Shannon was again one of the four finalists for the Female Amateur Athlete Award, an annual presentation for women who pursue athletic excellence.

Mildred "Babe" Didrikson Zaharias had been one of the

greatest female athletes of all time. In the first half of the twentieth century, she had excelled at a plethora of sports, including basketball, football, track and field, figure skating, swimming, diving, and professional golf.

Shannon liked the people of Beaumont and felt honored to be a finalist. The winner was a Texas Tech basketball player, Sheryl Swoopes. The other finalists were a UCLA softball player, Lisa Fernandez, and an Olympic swimmer from Stanford University, Jenny Thompson.

Shannon was also picked as the U.S. Olympic Committee's Female Gymnast of the Year, and from there she was chosen as one of the top ten SportsWomen of the Year. Members of the media, the USOC Board of Directors, and the USOC Athletes' Advisory Council ranked Shannon second of the ten finalists. Gail Devers, a sprinter, edged out Shannon for the top spot.

Shannon's achievements afforded her the opportunity to meet several famous people. At the USOC banquet she met Phoenix Suns basketball sensation Charles Barkley. He even autographed a basketball for her. The Suns and the Chicago Bulls were Shannon's two favorite basketball teams. She also met Gail Devers and speedskater Bonnie Blair.

With the help of the American Floral Society, Shannon and her family met radio personality Paul Harvey when he passed through Oklahoma City. Shannon liked to listen to him on the way to practice. She also met TV mogul Ted Turner and his wife, Jane Fonda, while attending a promotion for the 1994 Goodwill Games that were to be held in St. Petersburg, Russia.

Among her many fall activities, Shannon managed to fly to Boston with Steve to promote the John Hancock Insurance Company, an Olympic sponsor. She endorsed several products or companies, including Elite Gym-Kin, Evian, John Hancock Insurance, Ray-Ban, Re-Vita, Xerox, and York International.

Shannon tried not to take much time off from practice.

Usually she traveled on her day off, but some trips lasted longer than a day. Between the tours and appearances, she stayed very busy. She had been traveling all over the world competing—and winning—since her eye-opening performance at the Olympics.

Shannon's parents and Steve decided she needed a rest, so she took the fall of 1993 off. Although they did not know it at the time, their decision to have Shannon take a break from competition almost caused a premature end to her career.

Steve focused on preparing his other elite gymnasts for several upcoming international meets. Since Shannon was the only one not going, Steve did not give her as much attention. With her next competition several months away, she began to feel that she did not have any immediate goals. She began to feel lost.

"[Steve] didn't realize that he had always set her goals for her," Claudia explained. "I mean, yeah, she had her own goals, too, but their goals were intertwined. He was always laying it out for her: 'This is what we have to do this year, I *want* you on that World Championship team.' And then it was, 'We're going to *win* Worlds!' He was always pumping her up . . . and then we didn't have anything that they were going to do."

Thoughts of quitting began to seep into Shannon's mind. She had made the Olympic team and won five medals. She had won the World Championships and the U.S. Championships. She had also captured many domestic and international titles. With medals from almost every possible gymnastics event, what more was there to win?

"I didn't know where to go from there," she said. "I looked around and I was like, 'What else was there?' "

Besides, her body was tired and beat up, and the next Olympics seemed light years away. She had sacrificed herself to be the best in gymnastics. How much more could she take of the endless pounding?

"Between the physical pain and being kind of lost, she got

really down on herself," Claudia observed. "I think her workouts weren't as good as they should have been in the gym because she didn't have anything that she had to go out and get. . . . It was hard to really drive herself, and consequently Steve got very frustrated with her. He's always had a kid that came to gym every day and gave 110%, and now she wasn't doing that."

Shannon was considering walking away from the sport she loved. She did not make any hasty decisions, but she dreamed of what it would be like to be a normal teenager—to come home from school, lounge, watch television, and have some free time. How different that seemed from the pressures and hectic schedules she faced as a world-class gymnast.

Shannon and Steve seemed caught in a vicious circle. Shannon was lacking her spark during practice, and that angered Steve. Then he yelled at her and made her more miserable.

Most elite-level coaches were quite critical of their athletes. There were always corrections to be made to routines. Although this attitude sometimes made practices unpleasant, the coaches' exacting standards helped motivate the gymnasts to work hard and make the improvements necessary to be competitive in the world arena.

"I don't watch their workout; I don't have the same philosophy that he does," Terri Thomas admitted about Steve. "I respect him as a coach, but I just can't watch him because I believe in positive reinforcement. It upsets me to hear the kids being yelled at. I see how hard they're trying."

But Steve knew the kids needed balance. He realized his athletes needed encouraging words and someone with whom to share their frustrations. He admitted to Terri that he liked having her on trips for that reason. If the girls were bothered by a comment he had made, Terri could console them when they thought Steve was not looking.

Although Terri's friendship helped, Shannon's discouragement persisted, so the Millers tried to improve the situation by meeting with Steve. But after a few weeks the problems emerged again. This time, Shannon's trainer, Mark Cranston, talked to Steve and suggested he needed to make a heroic effort or he would lose Shannon. Steve agreed.

Steve talked to Shannon and tried to convince her she had not physically or mentally peaked yet. He knew she needed a reason to keep going.

"I like gymnastics because it challenges me," Shannon remarked. "When I ran out of challenges it kind of just left me there. I didn't know, really, what I was supposed to do next. I had to ask myself, 'What else is there left for me to do?' But I sat down with Steve and worked out some new goals, and that helped me a lot because then I knew where I'd go from there. I'm always having to set new goals for myself.

"My new goals were to continue until '96, and that was my number-one goal, as well as getting new skills on each of the events. I think the smaller goals are just as important as the bigger ones because I can do those in gym and I can look forward to those in gym every day."

Steve was relieved that Shannon wanted to stay with gymnastics. He suggested that he and Shannon work one-on-one to get through this crisis. Shannon's parents were a little skeptical at first. They knew their daughter preferred to work in a group and enjoyed being with the other gymnasts. In addition, she would have to miss school to get the private time with Steve, which she also did not like to do.

"We thought, 'She's never going to go for this,' " Claudia remembered. "And just the opposite [happened]. She said, 'Mom, I think that's exactly what I need.' She was smart enough to know we had to take some drastic action here."

For the next three weeks, Shannon was tutored from home while she worked only with Steve. The results were fantastic.

"It made all the difference in the world," Claudia exclaimed. Soon, Shannon was back on track, improving in the gym and aiming for her next goal.

Shannon and Steve had spent a lot of time together, and because of that they enjoyed a special bond.

"It's a coach-athlete relationship," Steve pointed out. "It's not a deep relationship at all. It's one of mutual respect. . . . We've been through so many things together that I think she knows number one, if there's anyone she could go to with anything, she could come to me. There's just a real special kind of a tie there. There's still that magical feeling when she looks me in the eye and I look at her. I know I can get the most out of her, and she wants to get the most out of what I'm teaching."

With things going better in the gym, Shannon was in good spirits for the holiday season. She enjoyed a nice Thanksgiving dinner with her family.

"I mainly just like the turkey," she said. "I'm a pretty picky eater."[2]

Shannon was sad that her sister, Tessa, would not be coming home from Cal Tech University for Thanksgiving. Like many siblings, Shannon and Tessa had experienced their share of fights when they were younger, but just as they were becoming close friends, it was time for Tessa to go to college.

"I never really saw her a whole bunch because I was always at gym," Shannon lamented, "so I wish I would have gotten to see her a little more."

Since California was far from Oklahoma, Tessa did not get home very often. Tessa ran cross country for the university; she had performed and coached gymnastics when she was younger, but only for a short time.

"I'm going to ask Santa to bring my sister home from college for Christmas,"[3] Shannon said wistfully. Although they spoke on the phone frequently, Shannon missed Tessa.

Christmas was Shannon's favorite holiday. She loved to wake up Christmas morning and open gifts with her family. Then they all feasted on a big dinner later that afternoon. The next day, everyone piled in the family car and headed to Grandma's house in San Antonio, Texas. Shannon thought it was fun to see her relatives. They stayed through New Year's Day.

"Usually, my parents go out to dinner and a movie," Shannon said of her family's New Year's Eve traditions. "Me, my sister, and my brother stay at the house, rent movies, and do fireworks."

As 1993 ended, Shannon was voted the top newsmaker of the year for the second time in a row by her hometown newspaper, the *Edmond Evening Sun*. She also found herself all over a popularity poll in *International Gymnast* magazine. The readers voted her their favorite female gymnast of the year, with the best floor music, choreography, new trick (the Miller), and hair. She was also credited with the most exciting moment for winning Worlds, and she was predicted to win the meet again in 1994.

Kathy Johnson asked Shannon what the key to her resounding success was. "Mostly just a lot of workout and just hard training on the routines over and over," she responded.

That hard work, in addition to her natural talent, had paid handsome dividends. Shannon was now the most popular and well-known gymnast on the planet, not to mention the most decorated gymnast in the United States. She had not lost a competition since the Olympics and was expected to ride this tide of success into 1994.

Shannon springs off the floor at the 1994 U.S. Championships.
(© Steve Lange 1996)

Shannon works on each pose in her floor routine. (© Barry Quiner 1996)

A warm embrace from Peggy in Nashville. (© Steve Lange 1996)

Shannon is straight as an arrow on her Yurchenko Arabian vault.
(© Steve Lange 1996)

Steve tells her some corrections to be made before her second attempt.
(© Steve Lange 1996)

Shannon practices her bar set at the Team USA summer camp in
Port Jervis, New York. (© Barry Quiner 1996)

Shannon, with the ability to make complex moves look simple, floats above the beam. (© Steve Lange 1996)

Shannon's ballet-like hand positions . . .

. . . contribute to her unique style. (© Steve Lange 1996)

Grace has always been a Shannon Miller trademark on the floor.
(© Steve Lange 1996)

Shannon holds the ending pose of her new floor routine, which she debuted at the 1995 U.S. Championships. (© Steve Lange 1996)

Shannon and Dusty relax in front of a trophy cabinet in her home in Edmond. (James Coburn/*Edmond Evening Sun*)

Shannon flows through the compulsory beam routine in New Orleans.
(© Steve Lange 1996)

Despite falling on beam, Shannon came back to win the 1996 U.S. Championships. (© Steve Lange 1996)

Though Shannon cannot compete in the 1996 Olympic Trials, Peggy stretches her shoulders while the others warm up. (© Steve Lange 1996)

Shannon looks to catch the high bar on her Gienger during the 1996 Olympic Games. (© Steve Lange 1996)

The Magnificent Seven: Amanda Borden, Dominique Dawes, Amy Chow, Jaycie Phelps, Dominique Moceanu, Kerri Strug, and Shannon Miller. (© Steve Lange 1996)

Shannon executes a high fish jump in the Olympic event finals.
(© Steve Lange 1996)

After performing the beam routine of her life, Shannon waves to the fans in Atlanta. (© Steve Lange 1996)

Moments after being crowned Olympic Champion on balance beam, Shannon poses for pictures with bronze medalist Gina Gogean and silver medalist Lilia Podkopayeva. (© Steve Lange 1996)

Shannon performs with her gold-medal-winning teammates during the
post-Olympic tour. (© Barry Quiner 1996)

Shannon Miller, the first American to win back-to-back World Championships and member of the first U.S. women's gymnastics team to win an Olympic gold medal. (© Steve Lange 1996)

Chapter 9

A Repeat Down Under

With a new focus and the start of a new year, Shannon was anxious to compete.

"My main goals as far as competitions for this year are Goodwill Games and World Championships," she said.

Because of her stature in the gymnastics community, she enjoyed the luxury of choosing the meets she would attend. She decided to scale back her competitive schedule to avoid another burnout.

Teammate Kerri Strug, on the other hand, had already been pushed too far. She had attended a few meets in Europe in December 1993 and had experienced many problems, never finishing in medal position. Deeply discouraged with her performances and with her torn calf and stomach muscles, she left Dynamo Gymnastics and returned home in search of a new coach.

157

She said she really missed Bela and was sad he had retired.

Shannon was left without her training partner, who had pushed and competed with her daily in the gym. Without Kerri, Shannon had to look to her younger teammates for a challenge.

"I'm at an awkward age right now, because everyone at school is sixteen, seventeen, or eighteen years old, while everyone at the gym is much younger," Shannon commented. "I'm right in the middle."[1] She was the oldest in the gym and was beginning to face the trials of doing gymnastics as a maturing woman instead of a little girl.

Shannon's first meet of 1994 was the Reese's World Gymnastics Cup in Baltimore, Maryland, a professional meet with $50,000 in prize money to award. This competition was unique in that it consisted of only three events (bars, beam, and floor) and a perfect score was 100, not 10. In addition, costumes were allowed and music was used on all events, not just floor.

All the participants had won World or Olympic medals. Shannon and Dominique Dawes were the U.S. women's representatives.

This was a more casual competition for Shannon. While in town, she and the other athletes were even treated to a Washington Bullets professional basketball game with VIP seats. Dominique boldly stood near the court checking out the players, while Shannon sat inconspicuously in the stands talking to her friends and laughing.

The meet began January 23. Shannon, wearing a sparkling blue leotard, performed exceptionally well on bars to the tune *"Get on Your Feet"* by Gloria Estefan. She added a new trick after her Gienger: a one-and-a-half pirouette on the high bar. She removed her Tkatchev release move, but her double layout dismount was in the rafters.

Steve embraced her and said, "That was a great one. Good job."

Shannon scored a 96 to tie Dominique for second and claim a $1,000 prize. Dominique refused to accept her money since she did not want to forfeit her college eligibility. She had signed a letter of intent to attend Stanford University in the fall of 1996.

Dominique and Shannon were the only competitors lacking elaborate costumes and creative routines. Both just performed their normal sets in their usual gymnastics attire. Kelli Hill, Dominique's coach, and Steve claimed they had not been told about the special rules. Costumes were optional, however, and not required.

On beam, 1992 Olympic Champion Tatiana Gutsu was radiant in a red outfit complete with a hat. She did her routine to *"Lady in Red"* and was awarded a 98. Dominique was personable during her beam set, encouraging her hometown audience to clap at one point. The judges liked her effort and gave her a 97.

Shannon needed a good set to keep up with Dominique and Tatiana. She changed into an all-black leotard and nonchalantly executed her routine. She had a big step on the dismount, and she smiled sheepishly at the judges and fans. The routine was good for a 97, again tying Dominique's score and earning another $1,000 in prize money.

Shannon did not compete on the last event. "I'm in the process of working on new skills on the floor, and I'm not ready to compete," she explained. "Also, my back is sore."[2] Steve and Shannon did not stay to watch the final event or the award presentations.

After returning to Oklahoma, Shannon showcased her routines at the Lazy E Arena during the Dynamo Classic. She was a bit nervous performing in front of her friends, but she did very well. Although Shannon's routines were for exhibition only, her friends were impressed and Dynamo Gymnastics walked away with the victory.

In February, Shannon was busy with another photo shoot for

her Elite Gym-Kin personal workout line. She flew to Williamsport, Pennsylvania, and was escorted to a large renovated barn in a secluded mountain setting. She found the location peaceful and breathtakingly beautiful. It was an enjoyable trip for Shannon, and the pictures turned out well.

"They're fun," Shannon said of the sessions. "They're mostly a lot of trying on of different leotards and taking pictures in different poses."

Elite Gym-Kin also offered a solution to Shannon's over-abundance of fan mail: The Shannon Miller Fan Club. Keeping up with her mail had become quite a chore. Even years after the Olympics, she was still working on the same pile of fan mail.

"Let me put it this way: I still have a box of letters to answer from '92," Shannon admitted. "I'm a little behind. I used to answer them all by hand because I just thought that it was right. If they took the time to write me, I should take the time to write back. It just got so out of hand that I had to have some help with it."

Her mom sorted through her mail every day—about fifteen letters when she was not competing and more after a meet. Besides regular fan mail, there were notes from critically ill children that needed to be answered right away, letters from schools that were having special programs and wanted signed pictures to encourage their classes, and appeals from all sorts of charitable auctions that wanted Shannon's used leotards, not to mention the requests for Shannon to attend events and other offers that were handled by her manager.

To minimize the amount of time Shannon spent with her mail, Claudia laid out all the pictures to be signed in a row. She put sticky notes on certain items with special instructions. Then, like a worker on an assembly line, Shannon went down the table and signed each item. It took the Millers additional time to address the envelopes, weigh packages, and mail them out.

Postage was expensive and a cost Shannon usually incurred.

Elite Gym-Kin's suggestion for The Shannon Miller Fan Club was a welcome relief. For $19.95 a year, fans received a poster, a signed picture, and a quarterly newsletter called *Shannon's News*. Shannon answered certain letters in the quarterly, which helped alleviate some of the need to answer fan mail. Through the newsletter, Shannon could update everyone at once on what she was doing.

Interestingly, the fan club did not answer letters from men. As Shannon matured, she began receiving a lot of love notes and marriage proposals from young gentlemen.

"She's becoming quite a good-looking girl and attracting a different category of fans,"[3] Steve observed. He was more careful to monitor the letters she received at the gym. A large portion of her mail went to Dynamo because gymnastics magazines published the gym's address.

Being famous brought other dilemmas. Shannon had a stalker who frequently sent her lengthy love notes. After the Olympics, another man had sat in his car outside the Miller's home every day for a week trying to catch a glimpse of Shannon until the neighbors chased him away. She had once even received a death threat, but the FBI had tracked down those responsible.

"That's what you have to deal with being a champion," Steve said matter-of-factly.

Shannon flew to Atlanta for the 1994 Peachtree Classic held February 11-13. Despite an injury and not enough training, she easily won the meet. Originally, she had planned to do only three events but decided to do floor—her final event—at the last minute. As soon as she completed her routine, half the arena cleared out; they had come just to see her.

Back at home, Shannon was again honored at the annual March of Dimes Headliner banquet. She met Super Bowl champ

Troy Aikman, the quarterback for her favorite football team, the Dallas Cowboys. He signed a football for her, which she added to her growing collection of autographed memorabilia. Troy was named Headliner of the Year.

Shannon was training hard for the American Cup and the upcoming World Championships in Australia. She was hoping to change her vault to a Yurchenko Arabian (properly called a Hristakieva), a Yurchenko with a half twist to a front flip.

Her preparation came to a screeching halt Monday, February 28. While practicing a set of kips on uneven bars, she pulled a stomach muscle.

"It [happened] during training," Shannon said. "I think with me getting prepared for [the American Cup] and working out really hard, I just kind of overdid it."

Shannon wanted to compete despite the injury, but Steve said no. "I had to make the decision," he said, "because Shannon had her heart set on defending her title, but I didn't want to risk any further damage if there was a serious problem. We didn't know the extent of it, and she had the World Championships coming up."

So Shannon scratched from the 1994 McDonald's American Cup, which was later that week, and the International Mixed Pairs competition. She flew to Orlando anyway on Thursday to support her teammates and compete on one event. To qualify for the World Championships, she had to place in the top six on one event at the American Cup.

Shannon chose vault as her one event. Given her injury, she thought it would be the least risky and would provide the best chance to finish in the top six.

On Friday, March 4 in the preliminaries, Shannon and Steve unveiled Shannon's new Yurchenko Arabian vault. Beginning at the foot of the runway—dressed in purple, her favorite color—Shannon dashed toward the horse, blasted off the board, and soared through the air. She landed and took only a bunny hop forward, then she turned to smile and salute the judges. Unfortunately, the wrong number had been posted for her vault, so her score was reduced to a 9.625—remarkably still good enough for fifth place and a spot on the World squad. If this error had not been made, Shannon would have won the event.

According to the rules, Shannon had to be presented on each of the remaining three events for the vault score to count. To satisfy this requirement, she simply raised her arms, touched the equipment, and raised her arms again. Of course, she scored a zero on the other events.

Shannon thought her injured stomach muscle was improving. "It feels like it's getting better," she said. "I think just rest is going to help it."

During the finals the next day, Shannon had to watch from the stands. She found it quite frustrating sitting on the sidelines while Dominique Dawes electrified the crowd. Shannon was very competitive and yearned for the chance to defend her title.

"I would much rather be competing right now," she admitted. "It's hard to sit here and watch."

As Shannon relaxed in the stands and autographed T-shirts, Dominique performed superbly on each event. She stole the title and established herself as a new darling in American gymnastics and Shannon's primary opponent.

Shannon returned home to celebrate her seventeenth birthday March 10, then she was off again, this time to Indianapolis, Indiana, for the Amateur Athletic Union's (AAU) Sullivan Award. At a March 14 banquet, she was honored as one of ten finalists for this "Oscar" of sports awards. Established in 1930 in honor of James E. Sullivan, the founder and former president of the AAU, the Sullivan Award was the highest honor in U.S. amateur athletics.

Shannon again saw Bonnie Blair, Brian Boitano, Gail

Devers, and Sheryl Swoopes at the banquet. She also met other finalists like Bruce Baumgartner, Bobby Hurley, Dan Jansen, Jenny Thompson, and Charlie Ward, who won the award.

Shannon headed home to prepare for her biggest meet of 1994, the World Championships in Brisbane, Australia. Since she had already made the team, she did not have to compete in the World Championship Trials held March 26 in Orlando. The top three Americans plus one alternate were chosen for the team: Shannon, Dominique, Larissa Fontaine, and Amanda Borden.

On Monday, April 11, Shannon began her journey to Brisbane, located on the eastern seaboard of Australia. The flight was very long. She did not arrive until April 13 since she passed over the international date line and lost a day.

Shannon had never been to Australia before and was looking forward to experiencing the land "down under." Unfortunately, she would miss over two weeks of school and would have a lot of catching up to do when she returned.

Once she arrived, Shannon trained for about a week, getting used to the time change and the equipment. But her frustrating stomach muscle injury prevented her from completing her usual rigorous workout on each event. The major barrier between Shannon and a second World Championship title was the uneven bars. She had trouble doing a simple kip, and Steve had to spot her on even the most basic skills, like a cast to handstand. To make matters worse, she also had shin splints with which to contend. These difficulties made it seem unlikely she would repeat as World Champion. Still, neither she nor her coaches were willing to throw in the towel.

"I had a couple of injuries earlier this year that I had to come back from, so I was really hoping that I was going to be able to train hard for this competition," Shannon commented. "This is really important to me."

Even with Shannon in less-than-top form, the Americans—for the first time—found themselves the dominant team. A local newspaper referred to the U.S. as the superpower of gymnastics. But the Romanians were also very strong and anxious to prove their program was flourishing despite political upheaval in their homeland.

The first day of competition was April 19. No compulsories were performed, only optionals. The first round qualified the top eight finishers on each event to the event finals to be held later in the week.

Shannon hit her vault, but she had problems on bars. Her new one-and-a-half twirl to a straddle back was a little off, as was her dismount. But she remained strong on beam and floor to qualify for three event finals. She finished the preliminaries in fourth place on vault, ninth on bars, second on beam, and third on floor. This was the first time she did not qualify to all four apparatus finals in a World or Olympic meet. She had just missed qualifying to bar finals and was the alternate.

To the extent her injury allowed, Shannon spent the next two days working on her routines. She was worried about her upcoming performance, and her coaches were beginning to have their doubts. A repeat seemed *very* unlikely.

Friday, April 22 was the big day, the all-around final. Last year, Shannon had been the overwhelming favorite; this year she was far from it. Her recent string of injuries had left her broken and lacking adequate preparation. Also, her competitors had grown stronger. Lavinia Milosovici was in top form and expected to win, while Dominique Dawes still hungered for the title and hoped to redeem herself from the previous year's vaulting disaster.

The all-around final took place in three sessions, with one gymnast per country in each session. Larissa Fontaine went first for the Americans. She had some problems on balance beam and wound up finishing seventeenth.

Dominique was in the middle round. This was a disadvantage for her and other strong competitors, like Gina Gogean, who were vying for the gold, because scores were typically lower and fewer fans came to cheer. Kelli Hill, Dominique's coach, wished that all the all-around competitors could compete in one round. She knew performing in the middle was a handicap for Dominique, but she respected Shannon's right to defend her title in the final round.

Dominique began on bars. She swung cleanly for a 9.85. She was remarkable on balance beam, nailing everything for a 9.812. Nicknamed "Awesome Dawesome," Dominique was powerful and theatrical on floor to maintain first place with one event to go.

Dominique stepped up to the vault, brushing aside thoughts of last year's tragedy. But to her dismay she overrotated on her first attempt, which forced her to take a big leap forward into a somersault to keep from landing on her face. Once again, she had blown her chances of winning because of a bad vault. She tried to fight back the tears and concentrate on her second attempt. Young girls in the audience screamed out "Come on, Dominique!" to encourage her, and she performed the next one much better. She averaged a 9.506, but that would not be good enough to compete with Lavinia Milosovici and Shannon, who were still to come.

In the third round, Lavinia put the pressure on Shannon early with a powerful floor routine that included a double layout somersault and a triple twist. She earned a 9.812.

Shannon began the night on bars, her hardest event to stomach. Since the Olympics, she had begun all major competitions on bars. She and Steve liked this rotation schedule; it had always brought good results in the past.

Shannon blocked out the pain and pulled together the best

performance she could muster, complete with a stuck landing. She was elated, and so were the fans.

Steve enveloped Shannon in his arms and exclaimed, "That's how you do it!" She bettered Lavinia's first mark with a 9.85.

Lavinia moved to the vault, an event that had brought her World and Olympic gold. She hit both her Yurchenko Arabians and smiled confidently at the judges. She averaged another 9.812.

Shannon went to the beam. She stood on the springboard and gave the beam an intense stare as if to let the apparatus know she was its master. She was focused. Her face turned very serious, which some people mistook for unhappiness. She did not often smile during a competition because she was always concentrating.

Although her body was hurting and not in top form, Shannon forced herself to do the moves with exceptional quality and accuracy. She omitted her front flip mount, opting for a safer press to a handstand, but her back handspring with a quarter twist was right on. She danced to the end of the beam, posed, and executed two layouts down the length of the four-inch wide apparatus. Her Miller move was exquisite, ending in a split handstand held with perfect control. Shannon concluded with two leaps and turned to dismount. She needed to stick it. She twisted and flipped through the air and looked for the mat. Her feet slid back a tiny bit upon landing, but the set was beautiful and good for a 9.862. Her coaches were delighted.

Lavinia, trying to wrest the lead from Shannon's grasp, was solid on uneven bars. The routine was good, but not extraordinary, and earned her a 9.775.

Shannon's lack of preparation became evident for the first time during her third event. Her tumbling was not as sharp as usual, and she almost fell on her final pass. She watered down her difficulty, using front tumbling for the last two passes. While front tumbling was worth a lot in the Code of Points, it was less appealing to the crowd and less demanding to perform. Shannon solemnly jogged over to Steve. She knew there had been mistakes.

"A little slip up on that one," Steve told her. "That's all right. You pulled it out in the end. You had a good cover; everything else was great."

Shannon looked away despondently. She was worried. The judges were not too harsh, though, giving her a 9.75. She was still in the lead with one event to go, but Lavinia was closing in.

Lavinia began her final event. She wobbled as if surfing on the beam after her side somersault, and she seemed uncertain of herself throughout the routine. Given her errors, her score of 9.837 seemed high. But the door was open for Shannon.

Shannon had been in this position before—many times, in fact. All she had to do was keep her cool and hit her vaults.

Her first attempt was good, but she took a big hop forward and earned a 9.80. She needed at least a 9.775 on her second try to win. Lavinia looked on nervously, and Dominique, who was pulling for Shannon in the stands, also paid close attention.

Shannon stood on the vaulting runway waiting for the judges. The brace on her right wrist seemed a fitting tribute to her many battle wounds. When given the green light, she dashed forward—head bobbing, arms chopping the air—and rocketed skyward off the horse. She landed solidly, taking only a small step forward, but she quickly brought her foot back and turned to smile broadly at the judges.

Everyone waited for the score. The board lit up: 9.812. Shannon had done it! To the amazement of many, she had captured a second all-around World Championship. Steve raised his arms in triumph, then he hugged Shannon warmly. She looked up at him and smiled.

"I didn't even know what place I was in," Shannon remembered thinking before her last event, "so I was really happy when I finished."

Lavinia was devastated. A tear streaked down her cheek. This was a tough blow. She was in better shape than Shannon, but her mental game was not as sharp, and she had cracked under the pressure.

Steve lifted Shannon up and the crowd continued to cheer. She waved happily. After several minutes, Steve became concerned about the noise everyone was making.

"We still have some vaulters left," he reminded the fans. He wanted to be considerate of the other competitors.

Shannon became the first American to win back-to-back World Championships. The last gymnast to win Worlds twice in a row had been the Soviet Ludmilla Tourischeva, and she had done it twenty years ago in 1974.

Peggy quickly rushed to a phone in the arena to call Shannon's parents at their home in Edmond. She did not have much time before the awards ceremony, but she wanted to personally tell the Millers about the victory instead of having them hear about it on the radio like they had the previous year.

"The phone rang a little after 6:30 this morning and it was Peggy," Shannon's mom told reporters. "She yelled, 'We won! We won! We made history!' "

"We were both asleep this morning when the phone rang," Shannon's dad added. "We knew it had to be them calling from Australia. My first thought was 'Oh my gosh, it's them.' We were wide awake after they told us. We're just so excited."[4]

As the gold medal was draped around her neck and the national anthem played, Shannon reveled in the knowledge that her competitive spirit was back. Lately, she had not been as nervous competing, and she had worried she might be losing her excitement for the sport. But she had been very nervous competing at Worlds. As the last notes of the anthem faded away, she lifted her flowers and turned to acknowledge both sides of the arena with a smile. She was greeted by more cheers. What a proud day for American gymnastics!

"It's hard to put into words what I was feeling," she said. "I was just really proud to bring home the medal to the United States. It was definitely better the second time around."

"That was a sweet win," Steve admitted with a grin. "All the critics—all the people that said 'No, Shannon's just out of it'—they just could not believe [in] her on the night that it counted. It was really a feather in my cap, too, because coaches just came up and thought it was a tremendous job of coaching and pacing an athlete, and keeping an athlete confident in herself."

Once a tiny, unknown girl from Oklahoma, Shannon now stood as the most dominant figure in the sport of gymnastics. When comparing individual gold medals earned in Olympic or World competition, Shannon, with five gold, ranked eighth in the history of the sport. She was the only American on the list and was tied, ironically, with Lavinia Milosovici. Other past gold medal winners included famous names like Larissa Latynina (12 gold), Daniela Silivas (9), Ludmilla Tourischeva (6), and Nadia Comaneci (6).

Shannon thought this victory was more special than the one in 1993. "I think it's even better this year," she explained, "just because I wasn't the favorite coming in and I've had a rough year with injuries and everything. And just being able to come back from that, for me that was something to look forward to."

Shannon's parents had not been in Australia to see their daughter win her second title, so Shannon said hi to them on national television and thanked them for their support. She and her family were very close, and she wished that they could have been there to share this special moment.

The next morning during practice, Kathy Johnson asked Shannon if her repeat victory had sunk in yet and what it felt like.

"It feels great," Shannon responded. "I don't think it's quite sunk in all the way because I still have two more competitions to go, but I'm sure it will when I get home."

Later that day, Shannon participated in the vault event finals. She was strong on her Yurchenko Arabian, but she landed sitting down on her new second vault, a Phelps—a Tsukahara Arabian which was named after American Jaycie Phelps. She averaged a 9.543 for seventh place.

The next day Shannon was determined to win more gold. Her quest began on beam. She had not won a World title on this event, although she was considered by many to be the best. She had fallen three times in the 1993 World Championships, so she had something to prove this year.

There was an extra difficulty requirement in the finals, so Shannon put her front flip mount back into her routine, and it went perfectly. All of her skills were clean and graceful. She did not even wobble. Shannon displayed an uncanny sense of balance on the beam. Her dismount was stuck cold—one of the most steady landings she had ever done. She smiled as she walked off the podium, knowing she had performed a glorious routine. The score was a 9.875, and Shannon glowed with excitement. She had gone first and put the pressure on everyone else with an almost unreachable score.

Shannon's coaches thought this had been her best performance in Australia. She watched as the other athletes wobbled their way through mediocre routines or hopped on their landings. Her near-perfect effort was more than adequate to win the gold and dismiss the stigma of the three falls from 1993.

"I was really happy to be able to redeem myself from last year and what happened," she said. "I worked really hard for it."

Shannon did not win any medals in the last event, floor, but she was thrilled to be taking home two golds from these World Championships. It had been a very successful meet.

"I felt good about the competition," she said after the meet concluded. "I tried a lot of new skills and I made most of them, except for the vault."

Shannon, Steve, and Peggy got the chance to squeeze in a little sightseeing before leaving Australia. Shannon went to a koala sanctuary and held one of the bears, which was heavier than it looked. She even had her picture taken with it. She also petted some kangaroos and saw an emu bird. Shannon liked the Australian people and this interesting part of the world. As in England, the people drove on the left side of the road, which at times was scary for an American passenger.

Following her Worlds victory, Shannon's popularity soared. In the summer she found herself on the cover of *USA Gymnastics* magazine and the English publication *Gym Stars* along with Ivan Ivankov, the men's World Champion. There was also a poster of her ending pose on floor in the Swiss magazine *World of Gymnastics*.

When asked by Bart Conner if she ever just sat around and thought about how great she was with five Olympic medals and five World gold medals, Shannon laughed modestly and said, "I haven't had a lot of chances to sit around and think about it yet. Um . . . I probably won't. I'll probably just look forward to the next competition."

Arriving back in Oklahoma, Shannon unpacked, did some laundry, and repacked for a trip to New York. There, she made a commercial for the Goodwill Games that were to be held in July.

When Shannon returned home, she tried to catch up on all her school work. She was in eleventh grade and most interested in math and science classes. Chemistry was her favorite subject; English was her least favorite.

"There's always an exception," Shannon said, explaining

why English was harder to take. "Math is set in stone: two plus two is always four."[5]

Shannon considered grammar her weakest area. "She's better than average," her tutor Terri said, "but to her she doesn't do as well as she would like to."

Shannon did not have time to do many social activities. But sometimes she liked to play miniature golf, go to a water park, or watch hockey games—very popular in Oklahoma City—when her schedule allowed. She also went to a few high school football games, but she did not attend any dances.

Shannon enjoyed the music of Tom Petty, Boyz II Men, and Sheryl Crow. She really liked to watch television, particularly her favorite shows *Friends*, *Mad About You*, *Seinfeld*, and *Roseanne*. She also enjoyed movies, especially comedies.

"I haven't seen a lot of movies lately," she noted. "Probably my favorite was *Jurassic Park*."

Remarkably, Shannon also found time for community service. An important issue for her was drug and alcohol abuse by young people.

"That's something I feel real strongly about—keeping kids off drugs," she said solemnly. "I'm trying to help kids because I think they can identify with me more than some adult."

Shannon volunteered for The Red Ribbon Campaign, making public service announcements and speeches on MTV, ESPN, and Nickelodeon on behalf of Drug Free Youth. She also did a "Say No to Drugs" poster sponsored by the Oklahoma Foundation of Parents and a "Stay in School" poster distributed by the U.S. Army. In addition, she worked for Montgomery Ward's Kid Care program, helping inform parents about ways to prevent their children from getting kidnaped or becoming lost.

Shannon was the Chairman of the Miracle Balloon Campaign, a part of The Children's Miracle Network. She helped with telethons, donated money, and participated in several autograph sessions to raise funds for the Oklahoma Children's Hospital. She also supported anti-hunger campaigns and spent time helping organizations fighting muscular dystrophy, Alzheimer's disease, and lung disease. In addition, she performed special exhibitions and clinics at Sports and Swimfest in Oklahoma City to raise money for the American Red Cross.

In May, Shannon traveled to sunny Phoenix, Arizona, for the Hilton Challenge. She had won this meet in 1993 but had decided not to compete this time. She needed a break from the intense competition and wanted to give her body a rest, so she sat on the sidelines and watched. However, she did demonstrate the compulsory beam and floor routines during the meet. Dominique gladly stepped into the leadership role on the American team and narrowly edged Belorussian Elena Piskun for the title. The U.S. beat Belarus and China in the team competition.

Shannon's hectic schedule included performing an exhibition in Greensboro, North Carolina, and a clinic at Tops Gymnastics in Dayton, Ohio. She was also honored at the OKPEX stamp collectors show in Oklahoma City. Being a living legend, Shannon was featured on a cachet, a stamp used to seal an envelope.

Shannon flew to Worcester, Massachusetts, for the 1994 Budget Rent-A-Car Invitational: USA versus Romania, held on June 11. She was given the Budget Service Award by the meet sponsor because of her leadership abilities and community service work.

Once again, Shannon competed head to head with Romania's Lavinia Milosovici and Gina Gogean. She was solid throughout the meet but had a mishap on bars when her one-and-a-half twist did not go as planned, and she had to quickly change her routine. She stuck her double layout dismount, though, for a 9.75.

"How to improvise," Steve laughed when he greeted her. "Make up a bar routine as you go along."

Although Romania easily won the team competition, the top

Romanians had problems on beam. Lavinia had a fall and Gina was not as sharp as usual. Needless to say, Shannon walked away with another major international title, and her two-year winning streak continued.

Shannon realized she needed to improve some things. She was struggling on her tumbling in practice, and she wanted to upgrade her difficulty. She had temporarily put in some front tumbling before the 1994 World Championships because of her stomach muscle injury. Now that the injury had mostly healed, she wanted to go home and put back some of her old tumbling.

"I tried to get ready really quick for this competition, and hopefully I'll be able to put in some more difficulty for the next one," she said. "I'm really happy with what I did."

On Monday, June 20, in Tulsa, Oklahoma, Shannon became the first female recipient of the new Henry P. Iba Citizen Athlete Award. The award was given in honor of two-time Olympic basketball coach and former Oklahoma State basketball coach Henry Iba. Along with the award, a $5,000 donation was made to Shannon's charity of choice.

"I felt very honored to have been given this prestigious award,"[6] she said.

Professional football quarterback Mark Rypien became the first male winner. Shannon enjoyed meeting him and other distinguished individuals, like sportscaster Curt Gowdy and Duke basketball coach Mike Krzyzewski.

With so many engagements, Shannon was not able to finish the school year with her classmates. While everyone else at Edmond High got out at the end of May, she did not finish until the end of June.

On Wednesday, June 22, Shannon's 1994 summer vacation had finally begun. She still had to wake up at 6:45 A.M., but occasionally she rebelled and shut her alarm off for a few minutes, sleeping until it went off again or her mom peeked in to tell her it was time to get up. Shannon put on a leotard, some tights, and a T-shirt and went downstairs. A bowl of Frosted Flakes often sufficed for breakfast, and she concluded her forty-five-minute morning ritual by brushing her teeth. Then it was time for practice.

Shannon was at the gym for almost eight hours a day during the summer break. The Goodwill Games and U.S. Championships were quickly approaching, and she needed to be ready. The five-hour morning session was usually devoted to conditioning and full routines, and sometimes new skills were practiced.

In the afternoon, Shannon and her brother Troy, who was involved with karate and on the Dynamo boys team, liked to go for a swim. She also used the free time to call friends, watch television, answer fan mail, or just relax. Troy adopted a new gray kitten that he named Carmen. Both he and Shannon liked to hold and pet the frisky kitty.

Soon it was time to go back to Dynamo. At the two-and-a-half-hour evening practice, Shannon perfected the compulsory routines. In addition to practice, she spent extra time with the athletic trainer doing ultrasound and physical therapy for any injuries. After a brief team meeting during which Steve talked about the next day's activities, Shannon was free to leave.

At home, her mom had dinner waiting and was eager to hear about her day. "Shannon rarely talks about gym at home," Claudia observed. Shannon unwound from the exhausting day by reading or watching television. After a hot shower to relieve her aching body, it was time for some shut-eye, because in eight hours she had to wake up and begin all over again.

The summer included some fun activities as well. Among other things, Shannon enjoyed the State Fair. She also posed with her dog Dusty for a photo session featured in the *Sports Illustrated for Kids* July 1994 issue.

Shannon and Dusty were pals. It was good to know that no

matter how bad a meet or a practice went, Dusty would be happy to see her. Sometimes, Shannon's parents even brought him to the airport to greet her after a trip. Shannon tried to teach her dog a few tricks, and she liked to run with him on the track at the University of Central Oklahoma.

"It's a treat for him," she said. "When we get halfway there, he starts whining because he knows where we're going."[7]

Shannon met the crew from *Lifestyles*, a television show hosted by Robin Leech, when she was interviewed for an upcoming episode. The program was scheduled to air during the 1995-96 season.

Shannon traveled for the third time to the Team USA gymnastics camp for a week. She enjoyed the change of pace and fun activities like the adventure rope course, the schmatterhorn climbing wall, and "the blob," a water trampoline.

At the halfway point between Olympics, Shannon was still the best in the world. Everyone was chasing her. Her motivation was high, and she had a compelling reason to continue: an American team had never won an Olympic gold medal. Shannon did not just want to be on the team; she wanted to be a contributing factor in Atlanta on the squad that had a chance to win gold.

"There's only two years left until the Olympics, and I thought it would be long hard training—which it is—but not quite as bad as I thought," Shannon said with a grin. "It's a lot of fun still. Mostly what keeps me hanging in there is that it's going to be in the U.S., and I think that's going to be really great."

Chapter 10

Hanging On

In late July, Shannon left for the biggest competition of the summer, the 1994 Goodwill Games. She and three Dynamo teammates were the U.S. representatives for the gymnastics competition. Shannon had received a personal invitation from Ted Turner, the man responsible for creating the Goodwill Games and founder of the WTBS and CNN cable networks.

First held in Moscow in 1986, the Goodwill Games took place every four years to promote good relations between the United States and the former Soviet Union. The location alternated between the two countries. The next Goodwill Games were to be held in New York City in 1998.

The Dynamo clan flew to St. Petersburg, Russia, which a few years prior had been called Leningrad in the Soviet Union. Shannon liked being in Russia again. She had last been there eight years ago at the beginning of her gymnastics career. Now she was the best-known gymnast in the competition.

Shannon and her teammates had a few days to get used to the equipment and the time zone change before the meet, which would begin July 30. The Dynamo team was scheduled for its first workout Thursday, July 28. When Steve walked into the practice arena, he noticed the gym was very tiny and the equipment was close to the walls. He worried that one of his gymnasts might accidentally hit the wall and injure herself, so he refused to hold practice there. The officials let Steve and his team train later that afternoon at the competition site. The United States was playing Russia in basketball only a few feet away, but Steve decided his athletes needed to practice despite the distractions.

Over the next two days, Shannon missed two workouts because her ride to the arena never showed up. When she did get the opportunity to work out, she had problems with her timing, and many of her skills were just shy of completion. She seemed a little off her game.

Day eight of the Goodwill Games marked the start of one of its most popular attractions, women's gymnastics—the team competition. It was a warm Saturday evening at the Lenin Sport and Concert Complex.

"Shannon never ceases to amaze me," Kathy Johnson said at the start of the event. "I gain more and more respect for her even when she is struggling, which she has been a little bit here. She pulls together amazing routines. She has incredible will."

Shannon, with the weight of the team on her shoulders, was a little shaky on bars and beam but came through on floor and vault. She was not happy with her sub-par performance and felt like she had disappointed her younger teammates.

The American squad had been hoping to win a bronze, but fell just short, placing fourth. The Russians won the gold.

Shannon was not one to make excuses for her performances,

but she found competing in Russia a challenge. The competitive arena was uncomfortably warm and technical problems prevented the gymnasts from starting on time. The Russians also had difficulty with their computer scoring system. It had not been programmed properly, so many calculations had to be done by hand, causing further delays.

"The workout gym had a vault runway that was not regulation length," Steve complained. "[After the team competition] we waited for a bus until 12:30 A.M. When you can't get a ride home after the meet, it makes you feel like you're not welcome."[1] Once the athletes arrived back at the hotel, all the restaurants were closed. The group ate tuna and dry cereal that they had brought from home.

There were other minor adjustments to get used to as well. For example, drinking the water was a definite no-no, and eating unfamiliar meats was discouraged. They used bottled water at all times, even when brushing their teeth or washing their faces. Showering without drinking any water was more difficult than it seemed.

"I think if you're prepared for this competition, you can be prepared for anything," Shannon laughed.

Shannon returned to the sports complex Sunday ready to fight and regain her confidence in the all-around competition. She started on vault. Her first attempt was very high in the air, with only a step on the landing. Her second try was not as good, and she had to take several steps backward.

Shannon's main opponent was Dina Kochetkova, a Russian who had placed first overall in the team competition. She had also placed third in the all-around at the 1994 World Championships. Dina stuck her vault to take the early lead.

Shannon tried to improve on her fourth-place position with an excellent bar routine. It was much better than it had been the previous day. Dina, meanwhile, was strong and quick on her bar set to hold the rest of the competitors at bay.

Shannon brought the house down with a sparkling beam routine and punctuated the set with a stuck dismount. She smiled, a rare sight during the meet, and ran toward her coaches.

"I was happy that I got my beam routine together for tonight, and hopefully it will be even better tomorrow night for event finals," she remarked.

Dina was phenomenal on beam, throwing every trick imaginable, including a full-twisting back handspring step out. She held on to her lead with Shannon nipping closely at her heels. There was one event to go.

"Now the one, the best one left," Steve said soberly to Shannon about her floor routine. "It's got to be a strong first pass. Be focused." Shannon nodded but did not say a word. She rarely did. She just listened then tried her hardest to do what Steve or Peggy said. They had gotten her this far, and she knew she could trust them to bring out her best.

Peggy pushed Shannon's hair behind her ear, making sure every detail was in place before Shannon stepped onto the mat. She was very elegant on floor; the only error was an awkward step after her first pass, but that was barely noticeable. She finished solidly and remained close to the floor podium to watch Dina's routine.

Dina was dynamic on floor, ending with a high full-twisting double back somersault. She had not missed a beat. She hopped off the podium and waited for the judges' decision. Shannon cast a concerned glance in Dina's direction.

The score was posted. Dina finished slightly ahead, dealing Shannon her first defeat since the Olympics.

"I knew if she hit she'd win, and she did," Shannon said matter-of-factly. "She had a great floor routine. She had a lot of difficulty and she stuck."

At a press conference after the meet, Shannon said, "I won't say that it's not disappointing at all, but I know I did well. I just need to clean up my landings and learn from my mistakes."

Steve did not think Shannon should have placed second. "I feel that I got hometowned," he complained. "I've felt a little out of place since I got here. Second place just doesn't feel right."[2]

But one loss was not the end of the world. There were still the event finals and the mixed team competition. Besides, there were many other meets ahead, and Shannon needed to keep pressing on toward 1996 and the next Olympics.

"I'm definitely taking it one meet at a time," she said, "but I also have that in the back of my head for definitely competing there. I really want to make the team."

Shannon had to pace herself to remain competitive and not burn out before 1996. Having grown five inches in two years, she also had to get used to a new center of gravity.

"Everybody thinks she's very large," Steve said jokingly. "She actually weighs about ninety-five pounds and she wants to say she's five feet tall, but I think that may be a high heel."

"Getting older is, you know, growing up, gaining a little weight, getting taller," Shannon chatted pleasantly. "And it's harder to keep doing the tough skills and staying up with the juniors that are coming along and learning everything in a couple of weeks which takes you a few months to learn."

As Shannon was beginning to mature physically, she now took weight control more seriously. She ran on the treadmill at her house to burn off excess calories and to build endurance. Also, if a practice was canceled, she ran a couple of miles on the treadmill to make up for it.

Once in a while, the fact that Shannon was maturing and naturally gaining a little weight seemed to bother Steve.

"Sometimes he starts getting onto the weight thing," Claudia said, "and we pay him a little visit. He'd like to have that twelve-year-old body back, and we have to periodically remind him that

that's not going to happen."

But Steve was not always willing to tolerate the meddling of Shannon's parents in the gym. When he felt like he had had enough of their comments, he did not let them watch Shannon's workouts.

"He's got warped ideas that all parents are problems," Claudia said, "and if you let them in the gym to watch then it's only going to mean trouble for you."

But some inside the Dynamo gym felt that Shannon's parents had a tendency to get too involved with Shannon's gymnastics. "I think that they would be better off if they would just be her parents and stop trying to do everything else," Terri Thomas disclosed. "I think that's where the conflict starts in. Her mom feels like it's important for her to be in control of everything, which includes the gym, what her floor music is, what appearances she goes to, what she doesn't. She gets so stressed over all of that, sometimes she forgets just to be Shannon's mom, just to be supportive. But she means well. She just lets it get to her."

The frequent friction between Steve and her parents bothered Shannon somewhat. "It's hard," she quietly admitted, "when I get stuck in the middle."

"She has basically three things in her life," Terri noted. "She has her family, she has the gym, and then she has school. So when two of them pull back and forth—she's trying to please them both at the same time, and it's hard when they see things differently. I think that's the hardest part for her."

Shannon tried to keep everyone happy, which was next to impossible at times. She rarely voiced her opinions because she did not want either party to feel like she was choosing sides. At least she knew that both sides wanted what was best for her.

"In some cases Steve's right," Terri explained. "In some cases her parents are right. In some cases I think they're both full of baloney."

Eventually, the issues got resolved and everything returned to normal. The tension between parent and coach, in proper balance, was a healthy system of checks and balances that benefitted the athlete in the long run. Both sides agreed there needed to be a happy medium. Steve needed space to coach without the distraction of constant comments, but the Millers had the right to be a part of their daughter's gymnastics and watch her work out whenever they wanted.

"Basically, we get along fine," Shannon's mom stated. "We couldn't have lasted in his gym this long if we didn't."

The day after the all-around competition marked the beginning of the event finals.

"You have another chance," Steve told Shannon in a discussion after the all-around meet. "You can prove it by showing you are better in every event. You have the opportunity to redeem yourself."[3]

Shannon looked forward to the challenge. She knew she had made mistakes in the all-around, and she vowed to do better in the event finals.

She was phenomenal. Each day of competition, she seemed to get better and better. Although she was not one to complain about the equipment, as time went on she felt more comfortable with the Russian apparatuses.

Shannon hit both her vaults to capture the silver medal. This was the highest she had ever placed during a vault final in major international competition. Shannon's bar set was almost flawless—the best one she had done all week, even in practice—and good for a second silver.

Shannon was calm and precise on beam to win her first gold medal of the Games. On floor she again outdid the other contestants for a second gold.

Steve joked for the television camera after her floor routine, saying, "Number one girl right here, proved it again today one more time." Shannon shook her head as her cheeks flushed with embarrassment. "We love Russia," Steve said with a wink. "Really, we do." While Steve hammed it up for the camera, Shannon shied away from it.

In an interview after the meet, Shannon said, "I like to rise to the challenge, and I did in this competition, so I feel really good about that. I just wish I would have done this well in the team competition."

Later in the week, Shannon paired up with teammate Jennie Thompson and two American men, Chainey Umphrey and Scott Keswick, for the mixed team competition. It was tiring to compete again, especially for Shannon, who had already put in three tough days of competition. The U.S. pairs team wound up fourth.

The people of Russia were very fond of Shannon. They gave her an award for being the most popular gymnast at the Games.

"This is my first time competing in Russia, and it's also my first time competing in any Goodwill Games," Shannon said. "Last time, I was the alternate and I didn't get to compete, so this has been a good experience for me."

Before leaving, Shannon and the Dynamo entourage found some spare time to enjoy the city of St. Petersburg, nicknamed "Venice of the North" because of its intricate canals, waterways, and beautiful buildings. The group saw St. Isaac's Cathedral with its elaborate walls and ceilings and the ballet *Swan Lake*, where they ran into some gymnasts from other countries. In addition, they went on a boat ride of the city, with an interpreter pointing out all the important sites along the way.

Upon returning to Oklahoma, Shannon had only about two weeks to regroup and prepare for the U.S. Championships. She returned to the meet as the defending National Champion. She was still a bit tired and jet lagged from her trip to Russia, but she pressed on anyway.

This year's competitive field was much stronger and more experienced than last year's. Dominique Dawes and Amanda Borden were in top shape and well prepared. Shannon had her work cut out for her.

After the compulsories, Shannon had a slim lead over Dominique. Shannon was pleased, especially since she had not trained her compulsories like she would have liked.

On Friday, August 26, throngs of people poured into the Municipal Auditorium in the Music City, Nashville, Tennessee. They were anticipating an exciting showdown to decide who would become the next U.S. Champion. They wondered if Shannon would repeat or be outdone by Dominique. Dominique had been close to Shannon at the 1993 and 1994 World Championships, but each time the vault had stood in her way.

Wearing a pretty white leotard with stars and colors splashed across the front in a V-shape, Shannon began on bars. Her routine flowed smoothly, and she managed to pull around her double layout flyaway, thrusting her arms in the air to accentuate the finish.

"All right! That's how you do it!" Steve yelled as he rushed to congratulate her. He asked how she felt, and she weakly mumbled she was fine. But she looked exhausted and not as enthusiastic as usual.

Meanwhile on the vaulting runway, Dominique drew a chalk line across the blue carpet to mark her starting position. She powdered her hands and stepped up to the mark. She ran hard and attacked her nemesis, the vault, finishing her difficult one-and-a-half twisting Yurchenko without a quiver. Her second vault was also very strong. Coach Kelli Hill lifted her off the floor and gave her a hug. They were both thrilled to have that event behind them. With her outstanding effort, Dominique gained valuable ground, inching even closer to Shannon in the standings.

A few athletes competed ahead of Shannon on her next event, so she had time to go to the rest room. When she came out, her eyes met the stare of a strange man dressed in black standing inches from the door. He had been waiting for her.

Shannon recognized this mysterious character. He was the man who had ridden an elevator alone with her in Las Vegas at a stop on the 1992 Olympic tour, the one who had stared at her the entire time then handed her a stuffed fox and a note as she stepped off and fled to her room. He was the gentleman who had attended a private autograph session at her mother's bank the week prior to the Championships. Shannon had thought he looked familiar but had not been able to place his face, though his black trench coat in the middle of summer had seemed odd. He was the same man who had parked his black Cadillac with the license plate "FOX"—which Steve likened to a hearse—outside the Dynamo gym the week before she left for Nashville.

This was the obsessed fan who constantly sent her long love letters and packages, each containing a fox, the one who had made her special trophies and had once even mailed her a compact disc player.

Shannon knew who he was all right. This man was her stalker, the one whom Steve had nicknamed "The Fox."

Shannon was startled and froze for a moment. She wondered how he had gotten into the restricted area. When he tried to talk to her she quickly darted back into the arena and rushed toward her coaches. Her heart was pounding. She was frightened, and her eyes were filled with tears by the time she reached Steve.

Steve assured her he would handle the situation. He told Shannon to think about her beam routine. She was up next, but her mind was still racing. The stalker, now seated, was located in the front row close to the balance beam.

"Let's do it," Peggy encouraged Shannon before her beam

routine. "Right down the middle, keep your eyes on the beam."

Shannon, trying to keep her emotions under control, solidly flipped onto the wooden plank. She leaped, spun, and somersaulted confidently through the routine. Everything was going as planned.

Until the dismount.

Shannon's feet punched off the beam and she seemed fine in the air. But as she landed, her hands brushed across the mat. She quickly pulled them away as if the mat were hot to the touch. Shannon could not believe this had happened. She saluted the judges and turned to walk away, her fists stiffly clinched.

Peggy talked through the routine and the mistakes with her. Shannon looked uneasy.

"I can't believe I did that," she said numbly.

"Don't worry about it," Peggy suggested. She told Shannon to think about her next event, floor exercise, and to be aggressive.

The error counted as a fall, and Shannon scored a 9.40. She said the accident was a freak thing, something that normally did not happen. Steve knew the stalker had thrown her off mentally.

Dominique seized the opportunity and took the lead after a stellar bar set.

"I just went through the obituaries and you're not dead yet, okay?" Steve said to a very serious-looking Shannon. "There was no Shannon Miller in the paper so you gotta get going. You gotta pick it up. You gotta really be intense from this point forward. No careless landings. I want strong, stuck in there, tight body landings. All right, you ready?" She stared into his eyes and nodded. "Let's get to it," he growled.

Shannon stepped onto the floor. The violin music began and she did a nice full-twisting straddle jump. Her dance and tumbling were delightful. Having performed the same routine for over two years, every movement, down to the tiniest hand position, was perfect. She scored a 9.90.

Steve and Peggy seemed satisfied. They told Shannon to get ready for her last event, the vault.

Dominique, on her third event, nailed her three layouts and her full-twisting double back dismount off beam. On her last event, not succumbing to the front-tumbling fad, Dominique was powerful and vibrant on floor. She scored a 9.925 to clinch her first national title.

Even a perfect 10 on vault would not be enough for Shannon to overtake Dominique. It didn't matter. Shannon was going to do her best anyway, and she stuck her vault cold.

"That's how you do it," Steve laughed as he put his arm around her. Shannon smiled genuinely. Then she went back and duplicated the vault on her second attempt.

"That was great; just that one mistake, but you came back," Steve said about her unfortunate beam mishap. She finished second.

"Dominique deserved to win," Shannon said good-naturedly. "She hit all of her routines and did really well." Shannon was competitive, though. When asked what her plans were for next year's Championships, she responded firmly: "Come back and win."

Some began to wonder if her second defeat in only a couple weeks was a sign that Shannon was declining as the top female gymnast in the world. Dominique had beaten her on every event except vault in the all-around meet.

"I definitely don't think I'm on my way down," Shannon declared confidently after the meet. "I think it shows that I'm a real person. I can make mistakes and hopefully I'll learn from it and go back to the gym and train this much harder for the next competition."

True to form, Shannon did not use her busy schedule, her fatigue, or the stalker run-in as excuses for the outcome of the meet. Steve, though, was not as reserved and voiced his opinion that Shannon's exhaustion and leg injuries from her recent trip to Russia had been factors.

"The floors over in Russia were a little bit harder when you tumbled on them," Steve explained. "[Shannon] developed some shin splints that turned into some slight stress fractures. So when she competed she was in quite a bit of pain."

Steve did not tell the media about Shannon's stalker. But back at the hotel, he got a phone call. It was the man who had been following Shannon.

The call was brief. "He said he knew he was the cause of her demise on the beam and said he wouldn't come see her anymore,"[4] Steve later recalled.

The man kept his promise. He continued to send Shannon letters and packages, but she felt less threatened by them.

"I think he was just lonely," Shannon told reporters a year after the episode. "I think he's probably a nice guy who wanted to write me. He never did anything wrong. He just kind of got me freaked out."

"All he does is send her these [stuffed] foxes and he writes her these *long* books," Claudia acknowledged. "But they're not nasty or bad or anything. They just talk about how much he cares about her. He tells her about his whole life."

The Millers were reluctant to talk about the stalker affair because they did not want to encourage this sort of behavior. The story was not leaked to the media until a year after it happened.

In the event finals on Saturday, Shannon again placed second, this time on every event. She was noticeably tired and had been seen limping during the practice sessions. Still, she offered no excuse for her second-place finishes.

Skeptics continued to hint that she was losing her edge. "I may not go out and win every event," she responded. "I may not win every competition I'm in, but at least I've been throwing difficulty and doing the best I can on making all-around finals and all four events."

Critics pointed to her maturing physique as the cause of her decline, but Shannon disagreed. "I think it's helped me in my gymnastics," she countered. "It's given me a little bit more strength and a little bit more power on my tumbling and vaulting." Some things were harder, of course, but she was dealing with the adjustment.

Shannon's dad, being a physics professor, helped her to understand why some skills were harder now that she had grown.

"When you get taller, it slows you down in terms of your rotation," Ron said to her. "It has nothing to do with your weight."

He explained: "I could show her the equation, and the mass isn't in there, it's just the length. And so once she understood that spinning around the bars would take a little longer, not because of her weight but because she was taller, then that was just fine because she liked to get a little taller."

Shannon, who was usually polite during interviews, did not enjoy the constant questioning about her age and maturing body. She did not think it was that important and was quick to point out that she was still upgrading the difficulty in her routines.

Shannon had been under fire during the U.S. Championships about everything from her height to her floor music. Some were wondering when Shannon would change her floor routine. They charged that it was becoming old and stale since she had used the same piece of music since 1992. Shannon was working on a new routine to new music, but it had not been finished in time. She hoped to unveil the new routine at the next meet.

On Sunday, August 28, Shannon attended the Ceremony of Honors banquet at the Opryland Hotel. She was awarded Women's Athlete of the Year and the Presidential Medallion.

After Championships, Shannon took a much needed break from gymnastics. She and her family drove to Colorado Springs, Colorado, for a brief vacation.

"We always made sure Shannon got a real week of vacation in the summer and at Christmas," Claudia noted. "I think she was the only gymnast at Dynamo who did."

Shannon enjoyed horseback riding through the beautiful Garden of the Gods and mountain biking on a trail that had been used in the gold mining days. She and her family also hiked thirteen miles up Pike's Peak. Walking at the high altitude became quite difficult and strenuous near the top for everyone except Shannon.

"She left us in her dust," her mom remembered.

Once back in Oklahoma, Shannon started her senior year of high school. She had already missed the first two weeks, but she jumped into the school year with her usual zeal.

Shannon awoke at 6:30 A.M. three times a week for an hour of conditioning at the Dynamo gym in Edmond. She then ate breakfast and went to school. Her first class was sociology, followed by nutrition, then English, and finally physics. Each class was almost an hour. Shannon also took a calculus class at home. She ate a quick lunch and dashed to the main Dynamo gym to practice from 2:30 P.M. until 7:30. After a light dinner, she worked on her homework for about two hours and went to bed around 11:30 P.M.

Shannon had more motivation to do well in the gym because of her two second-place finishes during the summer. She practiced new skills—at least two—on each event to freshen up her routines for the new season. She was still plagued with injuries, like a stress fracture in her leg, so she tumbled into the pit and on a Tumbl-Trak. The Tumbl-Trak was a long trampoline that helped a gymnast learn the air sense and timing of difficult maneuvers without the pounding of the floor. Shannon was working on a difficult double layout somersault which she hoped to add to her floor routine by the 1996 Olympics.

In addition to her training, Shannon gave clinics and made appearances, like at a local mall to sign autographs as part of a promotion. She also filmed a commercial for Bemco Bedding.

There was one meet left for the year that Steve was debating whether to attend: the 1994 Team World Championships. He did not like the idea of having a second World Championship in the same year and in the off-season. Shannon had been competing nonstop since January, and she needed a rest. She also wanted to learn some new skills.

"She's been competing so many times this year," Steve said. "She's been in five international competitions. At some point you have to have an off-season."

As if there were not already enough World Championship competitions, a trial meet was held in Richmond, Virginia, October 15-16 for gymnasts wanting to qualify to Worlds. That was another meet requiring preparation, and besides, Steve thought it was unfair that Shannon, the 1994 World Champion, would have to requalify for a World Championship in the same year. He decided to have Shannon skip the trials and petition directly into Worlds, citing overuse as her reason. Overuse and injury were both valid grounds to miss meets and, depending on the accomplishments of the athlete, make the team without competing. Shannon's score from the U.S. Championships was used to place her second behind Dominique at the trials.

Steve finally decided that Shannon would not compete at the Team World Championships, and he told USA Gymnastics, formerly the United States Gymnastics Federation. He did not want to hurt the U.S. team's chances for a medal, but he wanted to do what was best for Shannon.

"I think it's probably in her best interest not to go," Steve said during the trials. "One of the things that we were trying to find out with this trials was to make sure the USA was going to send a very healthy, strong team. It looks like they've got a great team, so I think we're going to hold out on this one."

The other coaches at the trials pressured Steve to reconsider his decision. They wanted the best U.S. team possible at Worlds, and Shannon was an important member. This World Championship would be the first team competition since the 1992 Olympics to use six members, and the American delegation wanted a strong showing.

"[What] meant the most to me was that the coaches of the athletes that made the team really wanted me to go and wanted me to be there for my leadership," Steve said.

Two weeks before the World Championships, Shannon was formally asked by USA Gymnastics to join the team, and Steve finally gave in to the pressure. Also, he decided he wanted to show the other countries that Shannon was not out of the sport and was still a vital part of the American team. However, since the meet was imminent, Steve decided it would be best to only do compulsories. Shannon had not been vaulting or tumbling because of lingering leg injuries.

In mid-November, Shannon flew to Dortmund, Germany, to compete. She thought she would quietly go through her compulsory routines then go home to resume training. But that was not to be the case.

The U.S. team began the compulsory round on beam. There were a few problems early on, but Shannon was smooth as silk to log the highest score of the day, a 9.887. Her floor and vault went without a hitch for a 9.787 and 9.712, respectively. The American team was performing with style and class after three events.

Things started to fall apart, though, on the last event, uneven bars. Amy Chow fell and so did Larissa Fontaine—twice. Kerri Strug was not up to par, either. Shannon was up last and needed to regain some lost ground for the team.

Everything went fine until the end. Shannon waited a bit too long to put her feet on the bar for the dismount, a toe-on front flip with a half twist. Her toes slipped off the bar and she ended up in a dead hang, from which she kipped back up to the high bar and did the maneuver again. This second attempt at the dismount was right on, and she finished with a stuck landing.

Shannon bit her lip in anticipation of the score. To everyone's disbelief, a 9.525 was flashed on the scoreboard. The crowd immediately started to whistle and boo. The audience knew a fall was an automatic deduction of five tenths, and they thought the judges had failed to take the full amount.

"Basically an impossible score," observed NBC commentator Tim Daggett. "She's embarrassed by it. Nobody likes to see that."

Shannon had not actually fallen off the equipment, the judges claimed, so they had only taken three tenths for an extra swing.

The Russian head coach, Leonid Arkayev, dashed toward the scoring table to protest. He thought that Shannon, with her world-class status, had been given preferential treatment.

Steve disagreed. "I felt that it was almost appropriate," he said of the infamous bar score. "She didn't fall; she had an extra swing. It wasn't a score that we wanted. It was still a bad punishment to score a 9.50.

"It was really funny to see the Russians booing us for once. Someone yelled out of the crowd when I was walking away, 'Shoe's on the other foot' to the Russians; 'How do you like it?' "

It was not Shannon's fault; she had not done anything wrong. The officials had made the call. Regardless, the U.S. team marched out of the arena under a barrage of jeers. Shannon ended up placing fourth overall in the compulsories.

The next morning, Shannon and Steve immediately left Germany and headed home. They did not stay for the optional part of the preliminaries or for the finals. In fact, they were already on American soil before the team preliminaries finished. Their departure brought much criticism from the media and surprised the other American coaches because they had not been in on the decision. They first realized Steve and Shannon had left when the two did not show up to take the bus to the arena.

"I personally would still be here, so would my athlete," Kelli Hill admitted to the press. "I think that's what the United States expects of all their coaches and athletes."

But in its aggressive pursuit of this story, the media tried to exaggerate the impact of Shannon's unexpected exit.

"I sat in an interview probably forty-five minutes, with them trying to get me to be negative against Steve," Kelli Hill remembered. "And I wasn't. Nobody was mad at him; nobody was against him. It was totally media portrayal.

"I had said over and over again, 'Steve has to do what's right for his athlete.' I do feel that way. He had to do what was best for Shannon. Shannon needed to go home and heal a stress fracture. . . . They needed to get it taken care."

Mary Lee Tracy, the coach of Amanda Borden, had this to say about the episode: "I'm always disappointed when you're on a USA team and Shannon Miller can't be on the team, because she's such an asset—not just on the floor as a competitor, but her hardworking ethic and her training motivate other people to work that hard. She's one of the hardest workers I've ever seen in my life. She's a role model. She's taught Amanda a lot about training. So when Steve announced [that Shannon wasn't competing in optionals] I was disappointed, but I wasn't angry."

Steve had told the U.S. delegation that Shannon was just doing compulsories, but the other team members had thought she would at least be there for the rest of the meet. With Shannon gone, the U.S. team lost its alternate.

"I think what people are so upset about is the way they

decided to leave," Tim Daggett stated. "It's really important to note, however, that this is not Shannon Miller. Steve Nunno, he's the boss, he makes the call."

As soon as Shannon and Steve arrived at the Chicago-O'Hare International Airport, reporters approached them and asked about their untimely departure. Shannon, her straight hair flowing to the shoulders of her bright blue warmup suit, looked tiredly at the camera.

"I don't think we left midway through," Steve told reporters. "We did exactly what we were supposed to do and that was help the USA team."

As the pair approached the security checkpoint before boarding their final flight home, they wished the U.S. team well.

"I'd like to send a message to the USA girls who stayed back behind," Steve said, with Shannon chiming in, "Good luck. Bring home a medal to the USA."

The remaining team members pushed the incident out of their minds and prepared for the rest of the meet.

"There's a lot of other talented kids, and we can't just all revolve around Shannon," one-time training partner Kerri Strug stated. "It's hard that she's not here with us, but I think we can do it without her."

The U.S. team had a rough time in the preliminaries but came back to hit all their routines in the finals and take home the silver. Romania won the gold.

Shannon got home shortly before Thanksgiving. Within the shelter of her close-knit family, she felt safe from the nagging press.

"I'm thankful that I have such understanding parents," Shannon said. "I'm also thankful to have coaches that have stood by me in all situations."[5]

Shannon really looked forward to the holidays, especially

Christmas. She was glad to spend time with her sister Tessa, who was home from college. Among her holiday activities, Shannon took Dusty to meet Santa and have his picture taken, and she served as grand marshal of the Christmas parade in Tulsa.

The Dynamo elites drew names for "secret Santa" gifts to be given at the team's Christmas party. But many of them had trouble keeping secrets and blabbed who they had drawn to the others. After the intersquad Christmas meet at the gym, everyone exchanged presents.

Shannon was happy to get a couple of days off from practice. On Christmas Eve, each member of the Miller household picked one present to open. Then they all gathered around for the reading of the Christmas story about the birth of Jesus.

Christmas morning was also special. "My parents hide one gift and we have to find it in the morning," Shannon said. "They write a poem that hints where it is in the house. It gives us something to do while they sleep a little longer."

Together, Shannon, her mom, and her sister prepared a yuletide feast that took much of the day to make. The meal was similar to that of Thanksgiving, with turkey, mashed potatoes, cranberries, peas, sweet potatoes, corn bread, and raw vegetables. Shannon, a finicky eater, normally ate only the turkey, mashed potatoes—without gravy—and vegetables. The neighbors, Steve, and Steve's father were also invited to dinner.

Although Steve had been a bachelor for many years, all that was about to change. He planned to ask his girlfriend Laurie to marry him. He popped the question in January, she said yes, and the couple set their wedding for November 10, 1995.

The year 1994 had been an interesting one for Shannon. It had brought more honors and titles, and a few defeats. Her inspiring performances during the World Championships, the Goodwill Games, and the U.S. Championships garnered impres-

sive award nominations, including ones for the AAU Sullivan
Award, the Sudafed Women's Sports Foundation SportsWoman
of the Year, and the Babe Zaharias Female Amateur Athlete
Award. In addition, Shannon was named a Team Xerox Olympian and voted the USOC Athlete of the Year in women's gymnastics. She was also presented with the most prestigious award
for high school seniors, the Dial Award.

With the start of 1995, Shannon began the year on a good
note by winning the Peachtree Classic the first week in February.
She debuted a new routine on floor to *"Bei Mir Bist Du Schoen."*
Soviet choreographer Irena Mulagradova and Peggy Liddick had
composed the routine. It had taken many long hours to create and
a lot of hard work to perfect. The results were fantastic, and
Shannon shined by winning the event.

"It's different from my last routine," she remarked. "There's
not really any ballet. All the dance has changed."[6]

Two weeks later in Oakland, California, she regained her
confidence and national number-one status by winning the
American Classic. The Classic also served as the trials for the
Pan American Games, to which she qualified.

Shannon looked great at the Classic. Her jazzy new floor
routine with four tumbling passes—the last a full-twisting double
back—was a hit, and she played to the crowd. On beam she put
back her three layouts, and she executed three release moves at
the beginning of her bar set. Also, her one-and-a-half twisting
Yurchenko on vault was more challenging than her old Yurchenko Arabian.

In March, Shannon went to Seattle, Washington, for the
McDonald's American Cup. She hoped to recapture the title she
had been unable to defend in 1994 because of injuries.

In the preliminaries, Shannon hit her vault and bars solidly.
She had changed her beam set during the fall, adding new dance
and rearranging her skills, and the mature style worked well for

her. She executed a high switch leap into a back handspring with a quarter twist, finishing in a split handstand. She began to arch—too much—and suddenly she was off the beam. The crowd gasped in surprise.

The mistake caused her to drop in the standings. She finished in fourth place and did not qualify for the finals since two Americans, Kristy Powell and Amanda Borden, had placed ahead of her.

Immediately, the press came running after Shannon, bombarding her with questions. Predictably, someone again suggested this might be the beginning of the end of her career.

"That's what they said at last Nationals, and I came back at this Nationals [1995 American Classic] and won it," she responded. "No goodbye for me, not until '96."

Shannon's somber facial expression throughout the American Cup had some wondering why she put herself through the torture of keeping up with the juniors, who had seemingly limitless reserves of energy and talent. Besides, Shannon had already proven herself. Why struggle to hang on just to add a few more medals to the heap?

But Shannon had made a commitment to go all out for the 1996 Olympics, and she intended to keep it. In addition to the pledge to herself, there were other forces compelling her to stick with it.

"I think she is still doing it because she's been pushed from *every* angle," Terri Thomas revealed.

Shannon had expectations of herself, as did her coaches and parents. Although her reasons for continuing may not have been completely her own, she vowed to press on to reach her goal.

Shannon, Steve, and Peggy flew from Seattle to Mar del Plata, Argentina, for the 1995 Pan American Games. Shannon dazzled the spectators, winning the all-around and individual gold medals on bars and floor. She placed second on vault. The U.S. team, with Shannon's help, easily captured the victory as well.

Shannon celebrated her eighteenth birthday in Argentina.

"They brought out a big birthday cake and everyone got to have a piece," she recalled warmly. "It was really neat. I got a big teddy bear from Kathy Kelly at USA Gymnastics, and Peggy gave me a big teddy bear also."

Shortly after the Pan Am Games, a tragedy devastated Shannon's local community and shocked the entire country. On the morning of April 19, 1995, a car bomb exploded next to a government building in Oklahoma City, demolishing much of the building, killing over 150 people, and injuring many others.

"I was walking to my car, getting ready to go to school, and I heard what sounded like a *big* clap of thunder," Shannon said, describing the explosion. "I looked up and it was blue sky, not a cloud in sight. I was thinking, 'That's really strange.' So when I got in my car and started driving to school, all of a sudden all the music went off. On every station they were talking about something that happened in downtown Oklahoma City. They didn't even know what happened.

"When I got to school I asked everyone if they had felt it and they said the glass shook. So we listened to it and watched on TVs around school all day long. It was really hard to get through. A lot of people at our school had family there."

The bomb also shook the gym, which was located just five miles from the blast. Steve was coaching Jennie Thompson at the time, and both ran outside to see what had happened. They figured it had been a bomb because they could see the smoke filling the air. The explosion cracked a window in the gym and damaged a sprinkler.

Neither Shannon nor Steve knew personally any of the bombing victims. However, they were both touched by the devastation that hit so close to home. Both donated time and money to the relief efforts.

"My parents [and I] went out and bought a bunch of food for the rescue workers," Shannon said. "We took it down to the site so they could have stuff as soon as they got off shifts. Over the radio and television they would have a list of everything that they needed. People would rush down with whatever they had to give them."

This was not the first time a tragedy that made national news had affected Shannon. When she was nine years old, a mass murder had occurred at the Edmond post office very close to her home. On August 20, 1986 at 6:45 A.M., a postal worker, Patrick Henry Sherrill, had burst into the Edmond post office and opened fire on his co-workers, killing fourteen people and injuring seven others. Then he had pointed the gun at himself and pulled the trigger.

Shannon remembered: "I was on the way to gym. My dad was taking me and another girl to gym that day. It had already happened when we left. We actually passed by the post office; it's right next to where we live."

Shannon was fortunate in that she did not lose any loved ones in either tragedy.

Shannon did not compete much in the spring. She concentrated on her goal of finishing her senior year on time. She also wanted to enjoy her final year of high school.

She was asked to go to the prom by three different guys, but she decided not to go. She was between boyfriends at the time and was not serious about any of them.

She told her mom, "I really don't think I would feel comfortable with any of them. That's silly to go to something that important as the prom and not really go with someone you really want to go with."

Shannon had begun dating at the end of her junior year. She

had dated one guy for about nine months. However, her schedule made it difficult to have much of a social life. Every spare moment was filled with homework, gymnastics, or sleeping. Still, Shannon had several male friends with whom she occasionally did things.

Andy Brannick, a friend from a nearby rival high school, sometimes asked Shannon out to dinner and a movie. "I'm a gymnast," he said, "and I've missed out on a lot of things that I wished someone had invited me to. Being a teenager, you want to be able to get out."[7]

On May 18, 1995, Shannon graduated from Edmond North High School with the rest of the five hundred students in her class.

"It wasn't anything out of the ordinary for anyone else," Shannon said about graduating, "but I think for me it meant a little more because I was able to continue with gymnastics and still graduate with my class."

Shannon boasted a 3.96 cumulative grade point average. She had earned an A in every course except one: during her sophomore year she had received a B in geometry.

Shannon did not resent the teacher who had given her that grade. In fact, she went out of her way to help him. The teacher, Darrell Allen, was diagnosed with leukemia in the winter of 1995. When his medical bills became unbearable, Shannon organized a fundraiser that was held at Dynamo two days after her graduation. She spent the weekend working instead of celebrating.

"She did a lot of work," Claudia acknowledged. "She did *so* many interviews, because everybody under the sun wanted to interview her about it. . . . It helped to get the word out."

Shannon used her connections to solicit donated items from famous athletes and sports figures: Oksana Baiul, Bonnie Blair, Brian Boitano, Nadia Comaneci, Bart Conner, Steffi Graf, Dan Jansen, Nancy Kerrigan, Greg Louganis, Nolan Ryan, Barry

Switzer, Tiger Woods, Kim Zmeskal, and many others. The auction went well, raising over $5,000 for the Allen family. Unfortunately, Darrell died a week later. This was a very sad moment for Shannon.

"It was really hard for me, because I haven't known any people that were real close [to me] that died," she said reflectively.

Although Shannon mourned the loss of her teacher, she looked forward to the summer. With some extra free time, she began learning golf.

"That's something you can do for the rest of your life," she reasoned. Besides, her agency, ProServ, had given her a set of clubs for graduation. Shannon liked to golf with her friends and her dad. She wanted to be able to play in Bart Conner and Nadia Comaneci's golf tournament in the fall.

Shannon spent most of the summer training and preparing for the U.S. Championships, but she had some fun at the Team USA gymnastics camp in July. It was her fourth visit to the camp. While in New York, she and Peggy even had the chance to see *Phantom of the Opera* in the Big Apple.

During the summer, Shannon also changed her floor music. She felt that the jazz routine was not her style and opted for a Russian-flavored musical piece and a more classical routine.

Shannon traveled to New Orleans in mid-August 1995 to win back the U.S. Championship title she had lost the previous year to Dominique Dawes. After compulsories, Shannon led the entire field. This time, her competition was not coming from Dominique Dawes but from another athlete with the same first name, Dominique Moceanu, Bela Karolyi's newest sensation.

Shannon began the optional round on balance beam. She mounted confidently and hit her opening skills. But on the final layout of her three-layout series, her right leg missed the beam and she stumbled off the apparatus.

"Come on now!" Steve shouted encouragingly from the sidelines. Shannon regained her composure and flawlessly executed the rest of her set. After sticking the dismount, she glumly walked over to her coaches knowing the error would more than likely knock her out of the running.

Meanwhile, Dominique Moceanu started the night on vault, nailing both attempts and taking the initial lead.

Despite the early mishap, Shannon rose to the occasion and battled back with two solid sets on floor and vault. By the end of the evening she found herself challenging for the lead with one event remaining.

On her last event, however, Shannon narrowly avoided a disaster on bars while performing a straddle back to handstand. She arched her back as if doing a reverse planche, but she strained mightily to bring her legs back and keep from falling.

"What is that new move?" Steve laughed after Shannon finished. "You're the fighter tonight. No matter what."

Dominique electrified the crowd on floor to capture her first senior national championship at the age of thirteen, and Shannon finished second for the second year in a row. But finishing in the number-two spot was quite an accomplishment considering her troubles on both bars and beam.

In event finals the next day, Shannon was determined to do better. She won the gold on vault and the bronze on floor.

Three weeks later at the World Team Trials in Austin, Texas, the placements were the same. Shannon was phenomenal in optionals, logging the highest score on bars with a 9.837 and on beam with a 9.912. Although spunky Dominique Moceanu was a tad better and earned the top all-around honors, Shannon proved she was still a force with which to be reckoned.

Shannon had been pacing herself to be at her best by October. "I'm not in top form yet," she said, "so hopefully I'll peak at World Championships."

Unfortunately, during the 1995 Worlds in Sabae, Japan, Shannon badly injured her right foot on a beam dismount. "I've had great workouts up until a couple days ago when I crunched my ankles," she said. Shannon had done well in the team compulsories, posting the third highest individual score, but that had been before her injury.

At the start of the team final, the American squad—without the help of Dominique Dawes, Amanda Borden, or Amy Chow, all of whom had withdrawn because of injuries—was in second behind Romania. It would be difficult for the United States to hold on to its position since Shannon could barely walk and most of the other team members were inexperienced in world-level meets.

Shannon, however, showed incredible toughness. She caught all three of her uneven bar release moves and nailed her dismount, blocking out the burst of pain shooting through her foot as she landed. She smiled briefly then limped off the podium. On beam, again ignoring the throbbing ache in her ankle, she elegantly flowed through her set for the highest U.S. score.

Steve was hesitant to let her compete on the remaining two events because they were so taxing on her leg, but Shannon wanted to continue. "I love competing and I really wanted to be out there," she said. "I've trained for this for a long time and I would hate to miss a chance to compete."

Steve consented but watered down Shannon's tumbling passes, keeping in just enough difficulty for her to earn a good score.

After a wonderful floor routine by Shannon, Kathy Johnson commented, "Let me tell you how important this performance was for the United States: without it I think they could have slipped out of the medals—a gutsy move by Shannon Miller."

Finishing with a solid vault, Shannon helped the team stay barely ahead of the Russians to place third. The Chinese performed admirably for second, and Romania was first.

The next day, October 8, Steve was not sure he wanted Shannon to compete in her fourth and possibly final all-around meet at a World Championship. But Shannon, as in the team competition, said she wanted to compete despite the injury.

She got her wish. But she had trouble right from the start. She stumbled on her front double twist on floor, which dropped her to fifteenth place. She gained some ground on vault, but she had a big break on bars that proved too costly to overcome. Shannon wound up placing twelfth overall, her lowest finish at any major national or international meet. Lilia Podkopayeva from the Ukraine won the all-around. Although Shannon qualified to all four event finals, she only competed on bars and beam, placing seventh and fourth, respectively.

Her injury had been frustrating, but Shannon did not regret her decision to compete. Although she had been unable to defend her title, her presence had earned a medal for the American team, and she had proven her level of difficulty was just as high at the age of eighteen as that of much younger competitors.

Though not in the limelight as much as she had been in previous years, Shannon was not any less serious about her Olympic aspirations. Although the road to the Olympics was sometimes discouraging, as the Games drew nearer it became easier for her to keep at it. A sign hanging in her gym's front window reading "896 Miles to Atlanta" served as a constant reminder of her goal. There were now months—not years—until the torch would burn brightly in Georgia.

Shannon planned to dazzle the world one more time. She was not the tiny youngster who had stepped onto the scene six years prior. She was now a young lady. She had won as a child; it was time to win as a woman.

Chapter 11

Georgia Gold

"I think that Shannon's going to be a two-time Olympian," Steve predicted, "and I believe that she is going to be a two-time Olympic medalist."

Shannon hoped he was right and that all of her hard work would finally pay dividends in Olympic gold. But she had six months and several competitions to get through before then.

Her first appearance of the Olympic year was at the Reno Team Challenge on January 14. This unique professional event was a battle of the sexes. The men competed against the women in individual duels on four events: vault, still rings versus balance beam, high bar versus uneven bars, and floor.

Shannon decided to just do bars because of pain in her left forearm. She executed her normal set, except she ended with the compulsory dismount, a toe on front flip off with a half twist. At the conclusion of a tight race the women were declared the winners, and a donation to the Special Olympics was made on their behalf.

Shannon's arm still had not improved by February, so she pulled out of the Peachtree Classic, the American Cup, and the Three-on-Three Championships. As winter turned to spring, the pain in her forearm settled in her wrist, and she had to bypass the Individual Apparatus World Championships—the same meet she had missed four years ago because of a dislocated elbow.

While Shannon would have liked to compete, one benefit of skipping several meets and keeping a low profile was being able to dodge a lot of the pre-Olympic hype. Strangely, it seemed like 1992 all over again. As the press had been enamored by Karolyi-student Kim Zmeskal then, they were now just as preoccupied with Bela's latest phenom, Dominique Moceanu.

"Sometimes I get a little egotistical and say, 'Shannon, aren't you mad about that? Don't you mind?' "[1] Steve confessed. But Shannon did not object to being in the background. In fact, she preferred it. She had done well as the underdog in 1992 and hoped to do the same this year.

"There's always going to be somebody who comes along and is hot for a little while," Steve told *Newsweek* magazine. "It's the same every year: if Shannon hits, she wins."[2]

Of course, this Olympics would be different in that Shannon could no longer creep in unobtrusively as the unknown underdog and seize a medal. She was not considered the favorite, but she was well known, and people were watching.

"There's a little bit more pressure, I think, now from other people, but I try not to let it bother me," she said. "I try to keep my focus on what I'm doing and just know that the pressure that's on me is from myself—trying to please my coaches and please myself—and that's about it."

When the media did pay attention to Shannon, the same question invariably arose: was she too old for gymnastics? "I didn't feel like I was too old to do it," Shannon said, "so I didn't know why everyone else thought I was too old to do it. When I kept hearing it and hearing it in the media, I think it drove me to really want to accomplish something better at the Olympics."

The repeated line of questioning about her age really tried Shannon's patience. "The one question I don't ever really care to hear again is if nineteen is too old to compete in the Olympics," she told one reporter.

By May, Shannon and her coaches felt she needed a tuneup before Nationals since she had not competed in months. She participated in two compulsory events, vault and bars, at the U.S. Classic. She had problems on bars, falling on a hecht—a transition move from the low bar to the high bar.

Steve was not pleased. "That's why I brought you here," he told Shannon. "Let this be your warning."[3]

At the 1996 U.S. Championships in June, Shannon competed on all four events for the first time since the World Championships. After an excellent compulsory performance, she was ahead of Dominique Moceanu by a little over a tenth. To advance to the Olympic Trials, Shannon merely needed to stay in the top fourteen. Barring a major calamity, she would easily make the cut, but she was also hoping to maintain her lead.

Unfortunately, Shannon's wrist had begun hurting more and more, and her coaches wondered if she should continue. But she was adamant about competing.

"I want to earn my way to Trials just like everybody else,"[4] she told them.

To get through optionals, Shannon tightly taped her wrist and ignored the pain. She had a shaky start on her first event, beam, falling on her two consecutive layouts. The situation seemed eerily similar to last year when she had led after compulsories but had fallen on her first event while executing the same maneuver. The mistake had cost her the championship then, and it looked like it might do so again.

She scored a low 9.30, which opened the door for Dominique, who—like last year—solidly hit her vaults and shot past Shannon. But Jaycie Phelps outdid both stars with a stellar bar set and seized the first-round lead.

"I've had competitions before where I've had to come back," Shannon noted. "The fall woke me up and got me going for the next events."

Shannon was outstanding in the remaining three rotations. She nailed all of her new skills: a double layout somersault on floor, a one-and-a-half-twisting Yurchenko on vault, and a double layout dismount on bars.

"It was fun," Steve said light-heartedly afterwards. "We thought it was going to be a lousy meet here and it wouldn't be any fun. We trained too hard to not have any fun today."

Shannon's efforts paid off as she edged out Jaycie and Dominique to capture her second U.S. title. She did not realize she had won until NBC commentator Beth Ruyak congratulated her.

"That's the first I've heard," she said happily. "I started out pretty rough. I had a rough beam routine. I had a miss, so I had to really come back. Mainly I was trying to focus on doing all my new skills, and they all came out well, so that's good."

Shannon withdrew from the event finals to protect her ailing wrist. With the Olympics only a month away, she needed to give her injury time to heal. She and her coaches decided to avail themselves of a rule that allowed an injured gymnast who had placed among the top seven at the U.S. Championships to skip the Olympic Trials and request that her score from Nationals be used as her Trials score. They submitted a petition to USA Gymnastics with a medical form citing acute and chronic flexor tenosynovitis in the wrist as the reason she could not compete at Trials.

Her petition, along with one submitted by Dominique Moceanu, was accepted the next day. "It's just nice to have it official because it takes the pressure off," Steve remarked. If the petition had not been approved, Shannon would have been barred from competing at Trials and thus disqualified from the selection process.

While the petition's acceptance did not automatically place Shannon on the Olympic team, she and Steve hoped her scores from the U.S. Championships would keep her in the top seven at Trials and earn her a spot on the squad.

"There is certainly a chance they'll be beat," Steve commented, "but it's highly unlikely that they'll be beat by six or seven people."

Although Shannon was not competing, she went to the Trials in Boston to cheer on her teammate Jennie Thompson. She and her mom watched the meet from a skybox.

Not long into the competition, it was evident that Shannon and Dominique's positions on the team were not in jeopardy. The scores being posted were not nearly high enough to unseat them. In fact, some eyebrow-raising low marks caused observers to wonder whether the scores for lesser-known gymnasts were being kept deliberately low.

"It's obviously not the same scoring system that they used at Nationals," Kelli Hill openly charged. "It's being done to protect the two petitioners."

The other athletes battled it out for the remaining five spots. When the chalk cleared, veterans Dominique Dawes and Kerri Strug had clawed their way to the top. Jaycie Phelps, Amy Chow, and Amanda Borden had also earned positions on the team. Unfortunately, Jennie had suffered a few falls and had missed making the squad.

Although Steve was disappointed for Jennie, he felt the team was strong. "We finally have a team that has the opportunity to win the gold," he exclaimed. "If we hit all our routines like the '92 team did in Barcelona, with the home court advantage there's nobody that can beat us."

Shannon had one week to touch up her routines in Oklahoma, then it was off to Greensboro, North Carolina, the site of the training camp for the women's gymnastics team. For several days, the Olympic squad polished their sets at the Greensboro Coliseum on equipment similar to that being used for the Games. Besides adjusting to working as a team, the group adapted to the Eastern time zone and the southern climate.

The training camp concluded Saturday, July 13 with an exhibition at the Coliseum. The team flew to Atlanta the next day. After spending seven hours at accreditation, where they received their Olympic credentials and were measured for USA uniforms, the athletes checked into their secret lodging facility, a fraternity house at Emory University called Connally House. The two-story brick building was protected by round-the-clock security. Inside, the gymnasts enjoyed luxurious furniture, multiple televisions, and individual bedrooms. The private enclave also included such amenities as chefs, nutritionists, and sports psychologists. Although the 1992 Olympic team had stayed in the Olympic Village, problems with noise and distractions had convinced the coaches to board the athletes in a more isolated spot this time.

Besides living in protected seclusion, the team trained in a private club at an undisclosed location while all of the other gymnasts practiced at the Atlanta International Convention Center near the airport. The U.S. women wanted to work out at the same time of day that their meets would be held, and it was not possible to do that at the Convention Center.

This special treatment brought sharp criticism from other

213

countries. "It's not fair," Romanian head coach Octavian Belu protested, noting that the Spanish team had trained with all the other competitors at the 1992 Barcelona Games. "Why don't they train with us?" He felt the opportunity to "train in secret" gave the Americans an unfair advantage.

"It's not meant to be anything of an advantage," maintained Kathy Kelly, women's program director for USA Gymnastics. "We are not training any more hours a day than is set up by the organizing committee."

Just prior to the Games there were two podium work-outs—one for compulsories and one for optionals—in the Georgia Dome, which had been divided in half to accommodate basketball on the other side. The podium practices helped the gymnasts get acquainted with their surroundings and get used to competing on elevated equipment.

Shannon was disappointed that she would again have to miss the opening ceremonies and the lighting of the flame. Since the gymnasts would have had to stand out in the heat and humidity for at least four hours, the U.S. coaches had decided it was better not to go and risk getting sick or worn down. At least Shannon had been able to carry the Olympic torch in Oklahoma during its nationwide tour.

The women's compulsories were Sunday, July 21. After a random draw, the U.S. began on uneven bars in the third of four sessions. This was a good starting position. Romania had the misfortune of drawing the first session, where scores tended to be lower, while Russia and China drew the most advantageous fourth and final session. Since Shannon was used to starting competitions on bars, she was happy with her rotation order.

The U.S. women—faces deadly serious, determination burning fiercely in their eyes—marched into the arena under a barrage of cheers. Armed with hand grips and ready for battle, they started the competition strongly on bars. Shannon was the anchor and came through with an excellent set for a 9.775.

The next event did not go as smoothly. Several wobbly beam routines and a fall from Jaycie put the pressure on Shannon and Dominique Moceanu.

"I saw Jaycie's score and I heard the crowd," Shannon said. "I knew I really needed to help the team."

Shannon performed like the veteran she was, coolly logging the highest score on the event, a 9.737. Dominique followed with a confident routine worth a 9.687.

The Americans danced expressively on floor to earn solid scores. Fifth up, Shannon performed outstandingly well to move the team ahead of the Romanians—who had gone earlier in the day—for the first time.

The final event was vault. Shannon and most of the other Americans stuck their Tsukahara vaults to propel the U.S. well ahead of Romania and into the lead for the moment. However, China and Russia were still to come, and scores tended to rise a little higher with each round.

In the final session, the Chinese had problems on bars and beam that effectively dropped them out of contention. The Russians, however, took full advantage of their fourth-round draw to surpass the United States by a little over a tenth and grab the top spot.

The Romanians, who had been favored to win, were in third after compulsories. Regrettably, several of their strongest athletes had suffered injuries before the Games that kept them from competing. In addition, Gina Gogean had almost decided not to compete because of an emergency appendectomy a few weeks prior, and Lavinia Milosovici was competing on an injured ankle.

"[The U.S.] looked like a very strong army," Octavian Belu remarked after the meet, "and we looked like a commando unit trying to survive."[5]

The Americans looked strong, but they were by no means

free of injuries. Besides Shannon's wrist problem, Dominique Moceanu was recovering from a stress fracture in her right leg and Amy suffered from pain in her lower back.

In the individual standings, Shannon was in second place behind reigning World Champion Lilia Podkopayeva. Three other Americans, Kerri and both Dominiques, were also in the top eleven.

Following the compulsories, Shannon had a day to fine-tune her routines in preparation for optionals. The men, who competed on the alternate days, finished their team competition.

When the Americans emerged for the first time on Tuesday, July 23, fans leaped to their feet waving flags and cheering loudly. It was an inspiring moment for Shannon.

"You could barely hear anything else," she said. "You just heard this *massive* crowd screaming out 'USA!' It almost brought tears to your eyes. "

Jaycie, Kerri, Dominique Moceanu, and Amy got the team off to a great start on bars. Shannon continued the momentum with an impressive set worth a 9.787. Although she had initially received a higher score, the head judge lowered her mark because she thought it was too high.

Steve was furious. "Usually I want to hug someone after a good routine," he said. "I wanted to punch someone."

After waiting a long time for the judges to post Shannon's score, Dominique Dawes was allowed to begin. Her magnificent set was just enough to put the U.S. in the lead for the first time in Olympic history.

The Americans remained invincible on beam. Amanda and Jaycie got the ball rolling. Kerri and Dominique Dawes also earned high marks, leaving Shannon and the other Dominique to put the icing on the cake with scores of 9.862 and 9.85, respectively.

The team's confidence continued to grow on floor. Jaycie,

Amanda, and the Dominiques got the crowd going with personable exercises. Shannon landed her double layout somersault a little low, but the rest of the set was stunning. Kerri was last and further widened the gap between the U.S. and the Russians.

As the Americans marched to vault, they held a firm grip on first place. It looked like victory would be theirs. All they had to do was hit their vaults—for that matter, only *one* vault each, because the best of the two would count.

Jaycie started off well, fidgeting only slightly on her landings. Amy and Shannon played it conservatively by doing an easier vault first. With an adequate score in the bank, each threw a difficult vault on her second attempt. Dominique Dawes followed with a solid vault, but she hopped slightly at the end.

The team's scores were good, but not great, because no one was sticking the landings. Nonetheless, by the time the fifth competitor—Dominique Moceanu—was up, she just needed one decent vault to win it all for the U.S. The largely-American audience waited anxiously to begin the celebration, believing one of Dominique's vaults would surely clinch the gold. But all they could do was gasp in disbelief as she sat down on *both* attempts.

Kerri, the final vaulter, stepped on the podium needing at least a 9.493 to clinch the victory. With that score, the Russians would not be able to surpass the U.S. no matter how well their final two athletes did on floor.

On her first try, Kerri buckled under the pressure and sat down like her teammate had done moments earlier. The spirited crowd became suddenly subdued. The gold, which had seemed so solidly within their grasp, was no longer a lock.

Upon landing, Kerri had heard a pop from her ankle. When she stood up, severe pain shot through her left foot. She gingerly walked back to her starting marker, shaking her foot and trying not to limp.

"We weren't really sure if she was really hurt," Shannon later remarked, "or if it was something that she could work through and that we should support her and say, 'Come on Kerri, you can do it.' "

Kerri raised her arms to the judges, and a hush fell over the spectators. She bolted forward and her feet pounded down the narrow blue runway, then she hit the springboard and her hands pushed off the vault. She launched herself through the air as 32,620 fans simultaneously held their breaths.

In a brief moment that came to epitomize the 1996 Olympic Games like no other, Kerri pulled out the vault of her life.

The roof was nearly blown off the Georgia Dome as the American fans erupted in a collective shout of triumph. The U.S. had won the gold medal for the first time in history!

But something about the scene did not look quite right. "We saw her arms go up and so we thought, 'Oh, she landed,' " Shannon recalled. "But then she didn't come off the floor."

Kerri finished the vault holding her left foot in the air, and she turned to acknowledge the judges by hopping on one leg. Then her face contorted in pain and she collapsed, crawling on all fours off the mat.

Sensing something was seriously wrong, Shannon closed her eyes and silently prayed for her injured teammate. Martha Karolyi was quickly at Kerri's side.

"I can't walk!" she cried. "Please help me!" Martha and trainer Barb Pearson helped her off the podium, and she was carried to a nearby stretcher.

Racked with pain, Kerri hardly noticed the thunderous applause brought on by the posting of her score, a 9.712. The score clinched the victory for the United States. The rest of the team, still in shock and afraid to believe they had really won, did not know if they should celebrate or worry about their fallen teammate.

Over near the floor, the Russians cried openly, unable to

conceal their disappointment. The Romanians were equally dejected and sat by the bars looking stunned. They had been favored to win but had only placed third. The Russians, at least, could be proud to have clinched the silver even after finishing fourth at the 1995 World Championships.

As it turned out, Kerri's second vault had not been the deciding factor. Because of the United States' considerable lead going into the last event, the scores of the first five vaulters had been enough to win the gold. But at the time, no one could have predicted how well the last two Russians would do on floor.

The applause was deafening as the U.S. team marched onto the floor podium smiling and waving. Bela carried Kerri in his arms and gently placed her at the base of the awards stand. Together, Shannon and Dominique Moceanu helped their injured teammate hop up the steps when the announcer proclaimed them the gold medalists. The frenzied crowd began chanting "U-S-A! U-S-A!" as, one by one, the seven women accepted their hard-won medals. Standing at the end of the line, it was fitting that Shannon received hers last, for *at last* she had struck Olympic gold. After coming so close in 1992, she had finally done it. The shiny medal was draped around her neck, and she accepted a bouquet of flowers. Then the whole team lifted their flowers and smiled before a sea of camera flashes that sparkled across the arena like a thousand fireflies on a summer night.

The boisterous crowd quieted as the announcer's voice boomed, "Would you please rise for the national anthem of the United States of America." Shannon placed her hand over her heart as the national anthem began to play. She sang quietly and stared at the flag as it slowly rose before her. This brief, exhilarating moment made the four long years of training since Barcelona worth every second.

The anthem ended, and the "Magnificent Seven"—as the team would come to be known—huddled together one last time to share this moment of victory. Again, Shannon and Dominique helped Kerri off the stand and into the arms of Bela, who carried her back to the stretcher while the rest of the team took a victory lap around the arena.

The group was ushered to a press room to answer questions. "I know it's important and I know it's extremely exciting for us," Shannon said about the victory, "but I don't think it'll sink in for another few months, or years, to actually know what we accomplished."

The Magnificent Seven were inaugurated as new national celebrities at a party given in their honor by movie-star couple Bruce Willis and Demi Moore at the Planet Hollywood restaurant. Security guards had to hold back the exuberant fans from closing in on the team. The group enjoyed a specially-prepared spaghetti dinner, and each was given a Planet Hollywood jean jacket.

After hobnobbing with Bruce and Demi, Shannon returned to Connally House for a few hours of sleep. She arose at 5:30 A.M. the next morning to get ready for a team interview on the *Today* show, which was followed by an appearance on CBS's *This Morning* and other interviews throughout the day.

Shannon had to break away from the media attention to squeeze in a workout. This was her last chance to fix up any problem spots before the all-around final.

"It was hard to walk into the gym the next day and have to train for another whole competition," Shannon admitted.

On Thursday, Shannon began her second attempt at becoming the best female gymnast on the planet. As in most of her previous major competitions, the random draw had her starting on bars, which meant she would finish on vault. It seemed like shades of Barcelona all over again.

Steve watched for the starting signal. "Okay, it's green," he said. "Be aggressive now!"

Shannon nodded and saluted the judges. She ran, punched the springboard, vaulted over the low bar, and swung up to the high bar. Flowing easily from one move to the next, she caught all three of her releases before transitioning to the low bar. Seconds later she was back on the high bar circling for her dismount. After two flips, she firmly planted her feet on the mat.

Surprisingly, the routine earned only a 9.75 and put Shannon in eighth place. Needing to make up a little ground, she was crisp and focused on beam. When her left heel missed the beam after her second layout, she avoided disaster by immediately shifting her weight to her back leg. Amazingly, she continued without wobbling or breaking the rhythm of the sequence.

After nailing her full-twisting double back dismount, she ran grinning to Peggy, who put her arm around Shannon and told her what an excellent job she had done. Steve, who was behind the barrier for this event since only one of her coaches was allowed on the floor at a time, cupped his hands around her face and exclaimed, "That was great! That was beautiful! Nice job." She scored a 9.862 and catapulted into second place behind Dominique Dawes.

In the third rotation, Shannon looked uneasy during her floor warmup, clutching her wrist after each tumbling pass. When it was her turn to compete, she took her place in the corner. The music began, and she ran hard for her double layout. But she did not get enough height and landed with her head down, which caused her to take a big lunge forward. While she danced elegantly, her problems continued with a low third pass and a step out of bounds on her last pass.

Shannon emotionlessly waved to the crowd then jogged to the edge of the podium and hopped off. Steve tried to console her, but she was unable to fight back the tears when he said, "That step out, did you see it?" Overwhelmed with disappointment, Shannon stopped and bent over to cry for a few moments. Steve kept his arm around her and continued to talk through the routine. "It was a little better double layout in the beginning, but you had a little trouble on every pass. Just a little slow. We're really going to have to get going on vault."

Steve stayed with Shannon as she tried to pull herself together, then she walked over to her bag. As she sat down, the tears started flowing anew. Steve, who was accustomed to Shannon's episodes, came over to talk with her.

"Are you all right?" he questioned. She nodded through the sobs. "Stop crying," he continued softly. "There are people everywhere. Just suck it up. Let's go. You've got vault to go."

Steve's words may have seemed harsh, but after so many years in the gym with Shannon, he knew what it took to motivate her. She needed to finish the meet, and he did not want her to get injured because she was not concentrating.

Shannon scored a 9.475 and dropped to tenth place. Dominique Dawes also had problems on floor that knocked her out of the running.

On her last event, with no possibility of winning a medal, Shannon chose to do an easier vault, a Yurchenko Arabian. Her first one was solid and earned a 9.687. Although she looked as if she might burst into tears at any moment, she made herself vault again. She stuck her second attempt cold, and at last a brief smile flickered across her face. Shannon waved to the crowd, who honored her with the only standing ovation of the night. Her vaults averaged 9.724, which put her in eighth place.

Steve was pleased with her effort and gave her a warm hug. "You're still the champ in my book," he said. "That was a great job."

Several gymnasts—Svetlana Khorkina, Dina Kochetkova, and Mo Huilan—had significant errors in the last round, making it easy for Lilia Podkopayeva to step in and win the meet. Gina Gogean clinched second, and her teammates Simona Amanar and

Lavinia Milosovici tied for third.

"There was a lot of emotion the last few days," Shannon said at the press conference afterwards. "From being on a high winning a gold, to making a mistake and hitting kind of a low."

Following the competition, the U.S. team was invited to meet President Bill Clinton, First Lady Hilary, and their daughter Chelsea. The gymnasts had a few souvenir photographs taken with the Clintons.

A tragedy devastated Atlanta and shocked the entire world two days after the all-around final. Early in the morning on July 27, a bomb exploded next to a speaker tower in the Olympic Park, killing two people and injuring over one hundred others. After learning about the blast, the U.S. women's gymnastics coaches were thankful they had taken so many precautions to safeguard their athletes.

"Everyone was talking about our secret training site and our secret house, but now those same people are probably asking why they didn't do the same," remarked Steve, who could not help but be reminded of the Oklahoma City bombing.

Shannon and her teammates were in the middle of a much-needed break from competition when the incident occurred. The coaches tried to shelter the team from the commotion and exhaustive media coverage of the bombing so they would not lose their focus.

Despite the cowardly act of terrorism, the Games continued. Shannon had qualified to one event final, beam, and she was hoping to give the performance of her life in possibly her final Olympic appearance.

Because Kerri's ankle was severely sprained, Shannon replaced her in the vault final at the last minute. She started with a Yurchenko Arabian and landed with a big hop. On her second attempt, a Phelps, Shannon's steps were off as she approached the springboard, which threw off the entire vault. Her right hand slid off the back of the horse. Lacking the power to complete the skill, she flipped too slowly and sat down with a thud.

As in the all-around, she began to cry after leaving the podium. She finished last of the eight finalists.

"I really had to work hard with putting that out of my mind," she said later. "There wasn't anything I could do about it. But there was something I could do about it the next day on balance beam, and that was probably going to be my best shot at a medal."

Monday was the last day of gymnastics competition. Shannon entered the beam final in first place, and Steve hoped she would remain there.

"She was denied a gold medal on the balance beam [at the 1992 Olympics]," he observed, "which I thought was probably her best event to win a gold on. I would love to see that happen for Shannon here in Atlanta."

Early missteps by Alexandra Marinescu and Dominique Moceanu left the door wide open for Shannon. When it was her turn, she pressed up to a handstand and stepped down on the beam. She maneuvered through her opening sequences flawlessly.

Although Shannon was normally able to mentally block out the crowd noise while performing, part way through her set she was distracted. "I heard some guy way up in the stands go, 'Hey buddy, turn your camera off,' " she later explained. "It was way up in the stands. Then I was like, 'Don't think about that. This is the *Olympics*. This is your beam routine.' "

Shannon forced herself to concentrate. Her front flip was solid as were her two layouts. She hit her Miller move perfectly and prepared for her full-twisting double back dismount.

She nailed it.

Shannon raised her arms in triumph. She had done the best

routine of her life! She smiled broadly and waved to the screaming fans.

"It's so amazing realizing that all those people are there
cheering for you," Shannon said, "and you just hit one of the best
beam routines of your life. And you hit it at the right time."

Steve exclaimed, "That was wonderful! You even did the
Miller right!"

Her set had been *almost* perfect. "She did make a little
mistake and only she and I know where it is," Peggy admitted,
"and we're not telling."

After big hugs from her coaches, Shannon anxiously awaited
her score. When a 9.862 was posted, Peggy gave the new leader
another embrace. Shannon had succeeded in placing pressure on
the remaining four gymnasts. All she could do now was sit back
and watch the others try to outdo her mark.

Lilia was next—certainly a serious threat. She mounted
confidently and hit her tumbling series. Her dance and leaps were
superb, but she had slight wobbles on her front flip and her
dismount. Steve noted the errors and assured Shannon the routine
would not be good enough to surpass her.

When Lilia's score was posted, Shannon and her coaches
nonchalantly looked over and smiled at the 9.825. She could
breath a little easier since Lilia was probably her toughest competitor. But anything could happen with three strong athletes still
to come.

Olga Teslenko of the Ukraine and Gina Gogean followed
with solid but conservative routines that did not measure up,
leaving only one athlete between Shannon and the gold. She
hoped she would not have to relive the heartache of the 1992
Olympics, where last up Tatiana Lisenko had been the one to beat
her.

Roza Galieva started strongly, hitting her roundoff layout
mount and her four-trick tumbling sequence. She moved effort-

lessly through the required leaps and turns. With each perfectly-executed skill, the disheartening prospect of narrowly losing the gold—*again*—loomed ever larger for Shannon. Would she *never* receive the individual Olympic gold medal for which she had worked all her life?

On her second to last skill, a front flip, Roza answered that question. Suddenly losing her balance, she toppled off the side of the beam.

The gold belonged to Shannon.

Steve embraced his star pupil and declared, "Good things happen to good people, I'm telling you."

Moments later, under a volley of thunderous applause, Shannon marched to the awards stand to receive her very first individual Olympic gold medal. A voice boomed over the loudspeakers: "Now, ladies and gentlemen, would you please welcome the gold medalist from the United States of America, Shannon Miller!"

Shannon waved and stepped up to the first-place podium. She accepted her medal with a smile that spoke volumes, then she turned to face the flag as the *"Star-Spangled Banner"* played for her once again.

"It's really hard not to cry when your national anthem is playing, and you just realize what you've done," Shannon said. "It's such a great feeling of pride for your country. It was a lot greater than I had ever expected."

This was in all likelihood the final Olympic performance for America's most decorated gymnast. After so many years in the sport, it was the perfect way to finish.

"You always think a little bit about how you want to end your career," Shannon said afterwards. "This is it. It was one of the best routines I have ever done."

The next and final day of gymnastics was the Champions

Gala. For the show, Shannon performed her award-winning beam set. In the finale, she and her teammates did a stirring group exercise. One by one they danced out on the mat to the inspiring instrumental *"On American Shores"* by John Tesh, who was honored they had chosen his music. Together, the women performed a dance segment from the compulsory floor routine as *"Georgia"* echoed sentimentally throughout the arena. Switching gears, they got the crowd going with *"YMCA"* and *"Macarena"* as they did the obligatory hand motions and danced playfully around the floor. They finished their upbeat presentation to the patriotic song *"God Bless the USA."* The crowd went wild, snapping pictures and screaming for their heroes.

After all the Olympic gymnastics was over, it was time for Shannon to have some fun. She took in some shopping at the Athlete's Village and went to see the U.S. Dream Team play basketball. She even got to meet the NBA superstars at an informal meeting that was set up between them and the gymnasts. Shannon had photos taken of her with these giant athletes and got their autographs.

When she asked Reggie Miller for his, he pulled off his Team USA jersey and put it on her. After reporters took pictures of the exchange, he joked, "I'm going to make sure it's in all the papers tomorrow that Shannon stole Reggie's jersey."[6]

The Magnificent Seven were in demand. Before leaving Atlanta, Shannon appeared on the *Today* show for a second time and with her teammates on *Good Morning America*. The team could be found everywhere from the Wheaties cereal box to the *Late Show with David Letterman*. Shannon was also invited to the *Late Night with Conan O'Brien* show. She had to decline an invitation to the White House so as not to miss a hometown parade given in her honor. She did not want to disappoint her many local supporters.

Back in Edmond, thousands of people turned out to celebrate

Shannon's success. She rode through town in the back of a red convertible and waved to the cheering crowd. As in 1992, she was given a new car, this time a hunter-green Camaro. A local sculptor, Shan Gray, planned to create a bronze statue of Shannon to be placed a short distance from the Edmond Library in Liberty Park.

Shannon was overwhelmed by the outpouring of support from the local community. "I don't think we really knew what we had done," she observed, "even when we were standing up there on the medal stand. I didn't know for me how big an accomplishment it was until I got back home and saw all the reaction from everyone in Oklahoma. . . . It just kind of amazes you that that many people were watching and now recognize me."

She had become a national hero. Even so, some things in her life did not change. Before she knew it, she and Steve were back in the gym preparing for some professional meets and the post-Olympic tour.

"Professional gymnastics has really opened a lot of opportunities for us," Shannon said. "Now we can actually get paid for doing a sport we love to do, so that's exciting. I hope to keep doing the pro competitions and the tours for at least two more years."

On September 2, Shannon participated in a meet at the Summit in Houston billed as "U.S. Versus the World: The Ultimate Gymnastics Competition." This professional meet pitted the gold-medal-winning team—minus Kerri—against six of the world's best female gymnasts on bars, beam, and floor.

Shannon was steady on bars and graceful on beam but opted not to do floor because of her ailing wrist. She had only begun tumbling again two days prior to the meet and was not fully prepared. Even without Shannon on floor, the United States handily beat the world team, which had a few falls.

Two weeks later, Shannon entered the Professional World

Team Championships held at the Riverfront Coliseum in Cincinnati. This two-day event featured four teams: two from the United States, one from China, and one from Russia. Each team consisted of two men and three women. Shannon was on the USA-1 squad along with Dominique Moceanu, Amy Chow, John Macready, and Chainey Umphrey.

After the men performed for three hours, the women took to the mat at 10 P.M. Despite pain in her wrist every time she put pressure on it, Shannon turned in stellar sets on floor and beam. She had a little trouble on bars but recovered nicely. The meet ended at midnight with Shannon and her teammates trailing USA-2 by less than a tenth.

The finals were the next day. This time the men and women performed together on three events apiece, and the lowest score in each round was dropped. Shannon was clean on floor, bars, and beam. Despite Chainey's withdrawal from the meet after striking his head on the high bar, the USA-1 squad still managed to win.

"It was great," Shannon said afterwards. "We've never done something like this before and it was a lot of fun."

Following the Professional Worlds, Shannon began the thirty-four-city John Hancock Tour of World Gymnastics Champions. During most exhibitions, she performed on bars and beam. She also did a group floor routine with five of the other gold-medal-winning women's team members.

Kerri was the only member of the Olympic squad not to go on this tour. Instead, she opted for another tour sponsored by Magic Productions and the International Management Group that offered the gymnasts substantially more money. Although Shannon and the others had already signed contracts and were obligated to participate in the John Hancock tour, receiving this other offer proved beneficial. Originally, Shannon was to earn $4,500 for every stop on the tour, but after the tour's promoters—John Hancock, Bill Graham Presents, and Jefferson-Pilot Sports—were accused of ripping off the athletes, they increased the rate to $6,000 per exhibition and at least $10,000 for each of several made-for-television professional competitions.

"It has been very confusing," Shannon admitted. "We were getting all kinds of advice from all areas. The bottom line, though, is that we love Kerri and hope we can work something out. We want to be a team again."[7]

After enjoying such tremendous success over the years, Shannon had become a millionaire from her involvement with gymnastics. Numerous appearance and endorsement contracts, like the one for her workout collection that brought in close to $75,000 annually, had proven quite lucrative. Fees for appearing on a Wheaties box and royalties from a couple book deals also helped. In addition, as a gold medalist she received $15,000 from the U.S. Olympic Committee to help offset expenses incurred training for the Games.

Shannon conceded that 1996 was probably her last Olympics, although she refused to rule out competing at the Games a third time. She left the door open to the possibility, noting that Svetlana had been twenty-three at the Atlanta Games, the same age she would be in the year 2000.

"You never know," Shannon stated, "because I don't see how I'm going to give up competing at this high level cold turkey."

Epilogue

Looking back on Shannon's illustrious career, Steve realized how the 1992 Olympics had propelled her to the forefront of elite gymnastics. "Today I don't believe there's a handful of people in this country that could even tell you who won those Olympic Games," he observed. "But they know Shannon Miller. And that's a great reward."

Despite narrowly missing a gold medal at the 1992 Olympics, Shannon did not spend time wondering how those Games could have been different if she had only done *this* skill better or stuck *that* landing. "It doesn't help to look back and think, 'What if?' " Shannon said. "It was so close. I don't look at it as a loss. I won a silver."[1]

Steve considered the 1992 Games a stepping stone to a long and prosperous career in gymnastics. "I never based Shannon's whole career on the Olympics," he said. "I always felt that Shannon Miller's career was going to be a plan, and it was going to be one of longevity."

The Barcelona Games had helped motivate her to continue training to become an Olympic Champion. When she accomplished her goals of winning both team and individual gold medals in Atlanta, Shannon felt that all the sacrifice, all the hard work, and all the agony had been worth it.

"A lot of times I get asked: if I had to choose, would I choose the two gold or the five medals I won in '92?" she said. "I don't think I possibly could. In '92 it just kind of started me out realizing it could happen. I could actually win a gold with the team and possibly a gold individually."

Shannon had impacted Steve's coaching career the way Nadia Comaneci had impacted Bela Karolyi's. Like Bela, Steve had succeeded in bringing out the best from his athlete.

"The highlight of my coaching career was to bring an athlete to attain her full potential and all the goals that she's ever wanted," Steve said. "To build a career out of an athlete—instead of just a couple of years—that has been second to none."

Over the decade of her competitive career, Shannon had become a better person because of her involvement in high-level gymnastics. "Certainly I go into every meet to win," she explained. "However, long ago I realized winning doesn't always mean bringing home the gold medal. Gymnastics makes me feel good about myself—knowing I can set goals and accomplish them, organize my time, and please lots of people. Some athletes today do not believe they should be considered role models, but I believe you don't really have a choice if you are a 'celebrity,' so I try to set the best example I can. I'm lucky. I've had good role models in my parents, teachers, coaches, and older sister."[2]

In the spring of 1997, Shannon plans to enroll as a full-time student at the University of Oklahoma, where she will live in the dorms. With her excellent grades, she hopes an academic scholarship will pay for part of her tuition. She has always enjoyed science and math and may consider a career in sports medicine or business.

Shannon cannot do gymnastics in college since she has accepted prize money in various competitions and is considered a professional by the NCAA. But she plans to stay involved in gymnastics through clinics, exhibitions, and professional competitions. She does not think coaching is for her, but she may consider being a commentator. The governor of Oklahoma asked her in 1995 to serve on the council for physical fitness, and Shannon is interested in being involved with such things after retiring.

Shannon likes Edmond and says she could live there her whole life. She looks forward to someday being married and having children of her own.

Does she want her kids to be gymnasts? "I'd like them to be able to pick and do what they would want to do," Shannon says. "I don't want to force them into anything. If they weren't sure of what they wanted to do, I would start them in a recreational gymnastics class because it gives you a lot of coordination to do other sports as well."

★ ★ ★

Shannon Miller. From underdog to Olympic Champion, she showed the world how to compete to the fullest of one's ability. She demonstrated how to win—and lose—with style and grace and class. She became the most decorated gymnast in American history by displaying poise and character no matter what the situation.

Will Shannon be remembered only by her first name like her predecessors Olga, Nadia, and Mary Lou? "It's not my place to say who's in that line," Shannon remarked. "It's up to the people that watch gymnastics. It's who they choose and who they like."

"No one will consider Shannon in that group until she's gone," Steve said. "When Shannon's gone, her record will stand brighter than anyone else's. She wasn't a flash in the pan that came in and took the world by storm."

The future likely holds more accolades for the Queen of Gymnastics. Regardless, Shannon Miller will always be a winner. She has forever left her mark of elegance on the sport of gymnastics.

SHANNON MILLER

1988 U.S. Classic Winner, Children's Division
1989 American Classic Winner, Junior Division
1990 Catania Cup Champion
1991 U.S. Champion: Balance Beam
Swiss Cup Champion
Arthur Gander Memorial Winner
1992 Dragon Invitational Winner
International Mixed Pairs Champion
U.S. Olympic Trials Winner
Olympic Silver: All-Around, Beam
Olympic Bronze: Team, Bars, Floor
1993 American Cup Champion
World Champion: All-Around, Bars, Floor
USA vs. Ukraine and Belarus Winner
U.S. Olympic Sports Festival Winner
U.S. Champion: All-Around, Bars, Floor
1994 Peachtree Classic Winner
World Champion: All-Around, Beam
USA vs. Romania Winner
Goodwill Games Champion: Beam, Floor
1995 Peachtree Classic Winner
American Classic Winner
Pan American Games Champion
U.S. Champion: Vault
World Bronze Medalist: Team
1996 U.S. Champion
Olympic Gold Medalist: Team, Beam

The *first* American to win back-to-back World Championships.

Member of the *first* U.S. women's gymnastics team to win Olympic gold.

GLOSSARY

Aerial: any move like a front walkover or cartwheel in which the hands are not used.

Arabian: a one-half twist into a front flip.

Double Back: two consecutive back flips; can be done in a tuck, pike, or layout position.

Double Twist: a single layout flip with two twists. Likewise, a triple twist is a single layout flip with three twists.

Flyaway: a bar dismount in which the gymnast swings down from the high bar and lets go to do a flip backwards before landing.

Full-Twisting Double Back: a double back with a full twist on either the first (full-in) or the second (full-out) flip.

Giant Swing: a move in which the gymnast swings all the way around the high bar with a completely outstretched body.

Gienger: a bar release move in which the gymnast does a flyaway with a one-half twist and regrasps the bar. Invented by Eberhard Gienger (Germany).

Layout: a position in which the body is completely outstretched and straight.

Miller: a beam maneuver in which the gymnast does a back dive with a quarter twist to handstand followed by a half pirouette. Invented by Shannon Miller (United States).

Glossary

Pike: a position in which the legs are straight and together with a bend at the waist.

Rudi: a one-and-a-half-twisting front flip.

Straddle: a position in which the legs are straight but split out to the sides.

Thomas: an uneven bar release move in which the gymnast swings around the bar, lets go on top in the handstand, performs a full twist, and regrasps the bar. Invented by Kurt Thomas (United States).

Tkatchev (or reverse hecht): a bar release move in which the gymnast swings around the bar, lets go just before reaching a handstand, straddles his or her legs while flying over the bar, then leans forward to regrasp the bar. Invented by Alexander Tkatchev (USSR).

Tsukahara: a vault in which the gymnast does a half turn onto the vault followed by a back flip. Invented by Mitsuo Tsukahara (Japan).

Tuck: a position in which both knees are bent and brought up to the chest, forming a ball with the body.

Whip Back: a back handspring without the hands touching the floor.

Yurchenko: a vault in which a roundoff is done onto the springboard followed by a back handspring onto the vault and a back flip. Invented by Natalia Yurchenko (USSR).

NOTES

Chapter 1 MOSCOW SENSATION

1. Shannon Miller, *Shannon's News*, Vol. 2, No. 2, p. 3.
2. Dwight Normile, "Shannon Miller: Emerging from the Pack and Into the Spotlight," *International Gymnast*, March 1992, p. 32.
3. Dwight Normile, "Shannon Miller: Emerging from the Pack and Into the Spotlight," *International Gymnast*, March 1992, p. 32.
4. "Shannon Miller: All-Star Attitude," *'Teen*, April 1993, p. 78.
5. "Edmond Gymnast Highlights Olympic Festival '89 Finish," *Edmond Evening Sun*, August 1, 1989, p. 8A.

Chapter 2 IN THE SHADOW

1. Dwight Normile, "Shannon Miller: Emerging from the Pack and Into the Spotlight," *International Gymnast*, March 1992, pp. 25, 33. This note applies to the immediately preceding quote as well.

Chapter 3 PINS AND NEEDLES

1. Dwight Normile, "Shannon Miller: Emerging from the Pack and into the Spotlight," *International Gymnast*, March 1992, p. 32.
2. Karen Rosen, " 'Our Turn' in Games, Nunno Says," *Atlanta Constitution*, November 17, 1992, p. 5E.
3. Jan Farrington, "No Stopping Her: The Case of Shannon Miller," *Current Health 2*, May 1993, p. 11.

Chapter 4 NUMBER ONE

1. Bobby Rockel, "Miller, Nunno Put Shine on Routine," *Edmond Evening Sun*, July 19, 1992, p. 5D.
2. Luan Peszek, "Zmeskal & Roethlisberger Rise to the Occasion," *USA Gymnastics*, July/August 1992, p. 23.
3. Bobby Rockel, "Parents Help Pave Shannon's Success," *Edmond Evening Sun*, July 19, 1992, p. 5D.
4. Dwight Normile, "Barcelona Bound?" *International Gymnast*, August/September 1992, p. 24.
5. "Tiny but Mighty," *The Sporting News*, July 20, 1992, p. 12S.
6. Dwight Normile, "Barcelona Bound?" *International Gymnast*, August/September 1992, p. 27.
7. Steve Wieberg, "Gymnastics Rivalry Full of Twists," *USA Today*, July

24, 1992, p. 2C.
8. Dwight Normile, "Barcelona Bound?" *International Gymnast*, August/ September 1992, pp. 27, 59.
9. Bobby Rockel, "Parents Help Pave Shannon's Success," *Edmond Evening Sun*, July 19, 1992, p. 5D.
10. Jill Smolowe, "Don't Call Them Pixies," *Time*, July 27, 1992, p. 59.
11. Karen Rosen, "Attack Makes U.S. Gym Coach Feel Vindicated," *Atlanta Constitution*, January 16, 1994, p. 14E.

Chapter 5 BARCELONA
1. Christine Brennan, "Miller's Up, Zmeskal Vows Not to Stay Down," *The Washington Post*, July 28, 1992, p. 7D.
2. E.M. Swift, "Amity Beats Enmity," *Sports Illustrated*, August 10, 1992, p. 76.
3. Steve Wieberg, "Miller Showing the World She's Back in Charge," *USA Today*, July 29, 1992, p. 3E.
4. "Boginskaya Sets Tone for Unified Team Victory," *International Gymnast*, October 1992, p. 12.
5. Steve Wieberg, "Miller Showing the World She's Back in Charge," *USA Today*, July 29, 1992, p. 3E.
6. Jerry Adler and Mark Starr, "Flying High Now," *Newsweek*, August 10, 1992, p. 20.
7. "Shannon Miller: All-Star Attitude," *'Teen*, April 1993, p. 78.
8. Mary Ann Hudson, "She's Best in U.S.," *The Los Angeles Times*, July 15, 1992, p. 14C.
9. Minot Simons, "New Life? Kill It," *International Gymnast*, April 1993, p. 30.
10. E.M. Swift, "Amity Beats Enmity," *Sports Illustrated*, August 10, 1992, p. 78.

Chapter 6 AWARDS AND AUTOGRAPHS
1. E.M. Swift, "Amity Beats Enmity," *Sports Illustrated*, August 10, 1992, p. 81.
2. E.M. Swift, "All that Glitters," *Sports Illustrated*, December 14, 1992, p. 78.
3. Dwight Normile, "Dominique Dawes," *International Gymnast*, February 1993, p. 50.
4. Karen Rosen, "Vision of '96 Encore Drives Miller," *Atlanta Constitution*, March 10, 1993, p. 2E.

5. Kevin Paul Dupont, "Miller Winds Up with a High Five," *Boston Globe*, August 2, 1992, p. 53.
6. Joel Achenbach, "Shannon Miller's Silver Silence," *The Washington Post*, August 5, 1992, p. 6C.
7. Mary Ann Hudson, "She's Best in U.S.," *Los Angeles Times*, July 15, 1992, p. 14C.
8. Jere Longman, "A Gymnast's Toughest Balancing Act," *The New York Times*, December 16, 1994, p. 14B.
9. Kirsten A. Conover, "Sitting Down with Shannon Miller," *The Christian Science Monitor*, October 2, 1992, p. 14.
10. *USA Gymnastics*, November/December 1992, p. 20.
11. Carolanne Griffith-Roberts, "The Road to Atlanta," *Southern Living*, October 1995, p. 32.
12. Phil Hersch, "No Time is Free Time for Mighty Mite Miller," *The Chicago Tribune*, September 13, 1991, p. 1, sec. 4.
13. "Miller Joins Parents, Friends to Celebrate 'Sweet Sixteen,' " *Edmond Evening Sun*, March 14, 1993, p. 6A.
14. Karen Rosen, "Vision of '96 Encore Drives Miller," *Atlanta Constitution*, March 10, 1993, p. 2E.
15. E.M. Swift, "All that Glitters," *Sports Illustrated*, December 14, 1992, p. 76.

Chapter 7 WINNING OVER THE WORLD

1. "Miller Joins Parents, Friends to Celebrate 'Sweet Sixteen,' " *Edmond Evening Sun*, March 14, 1993, p. 6A.
2. Steve Woodward, "Competing Really a Pain in the Back for Miller," *USA Today*, July 30, 1993, p. 10C.
3. Dwight Normile, "1993 World Championships," *International Gymnast*, August/September 1993, p. 14.
4. Karen Rosen, "U.S. Gymnastics Looks Fantastic," *Atlanta Constitution*, April 25, 1993, p. 6F.
5. Karen Rosen, "U.S. Gymnastics Looks Fantastic," *Atlanta Constitution*, April 25, 1993, p. 6F.

Chapter 8 UNBEATABLE

1. Oscar Dixon, "Grandparents' Royal Welcome," *USA Today*, July 30, 1993, p. 10C.
2. *USA Gymnastics*, November/December 1993, p. 25.
3. *USA Gymnastics*, November/December 1993, p. 25.

Notes

Chapter 9 A REPEAT DOWN UNDER

1. "Shannon Miller: Gymnastics Legend," *USA Gymnastics*, July/August 1994, p. 25.
2. "Shannon Backs Out at Reese's," *Edmond Evening Sun*, January 25, 1994, p. 6.
3. Karen Rosen, "Attack Makes U.S. Gym Coach Feel Vindicated," *Atlanta Constitution*, January 16, 1994, p. 14E.
4. Terry Tush, "Performing at Personal Best Most Important, Mother Says," *Edmond Evening Sun*, April 22, 1994, p. 1A.
5. Kirsten A. Conover, "Sitting Down with Shannon Miller," *The Christian Science Monitor*, p. 14.
6. Shannon Miller, *Shannon's News*, Vol. 1, No. 4, p. 1.
7. Jeff Lowe, "Shannon Miller and Dusty," *Sports Illustrated for Kids*, July 1994, p. 48.

Chapter 10 HANGING ON

1. Steve Woodward, "Russian Derails Miller's Run of All-Around Championships," *USA Today*, August 1, 1994, p. 7C.
2. Thomas Stinson, "Miller's Streak Ends with All-Around Silver," *Atlanta Constitution*, August 1, 1994, p. 7D.
3. Suzanne Possehl, "Miller Again Proves That She's Just Golden," *The New York Times*, August 2, 1994, p. 13B.
4. Terry Tush, "No More Fear," *Edmond Evening Sun*, August 20, 1995, p. 1B.
5. "Holiday Spirit," *USA Gymnastics*, November/December 1994, p. 44.
6. Thomas Stinson, "A New Shannon Miller Arrives," *Atlanta Constitution*, February 3, 1995, p. 1D.
7. Jere Longman, "A Gymnast's Toughest Balancing Act," *The New York Times*, December 16, 1994, p. 14B.

Chapter 11 GEORGIA GOLD

1. Terry Tush, "Miller's Shoulders Carrying Load," *Edmond Evening Sun*, July 23, 1996.
2. Mark Starr, "Hands Together, Feet Apart," *Newsweek*, June 10, 1996, p. 80.
3. Terry Tush, "Preparing for the 1996 Olympics," *Edmond Evening Sun*, June 5, 1996.
4. Susan Vinella, "Miller Leads U.S. Championships After Compulsories," *Atlanta Constitution*, June 6, 1996, p. 8G.

5. E.M. Swift, "Profile in Courage," *Sports Illustrated*, August 5, 1996, p. 61.

6. Fran Blinebury, "Golden Girls Meet Their Dreams," *The Houston Chronicle*, August 2, 1996, sec. B, p. 3.

7. Jack McCallum and Kostya Kennedy, "A Team Torn Apart," *Sports Illustrated*, September 9, 1996, p. 10.

EPILOGUE

1. Suzanne Possehl, "Miller Again Proves That She's Just Golden," *The New York Times*, August 2, 1994, p. 13B.

2. Shannon Miller, *Shannon's News*, Vol. 2, No. 1, p. 2.

ABOUT THE AUTHOR

When not researching or writing about the sport, Krista Quiner coaches gymnastics at Shields Gymnastics in Mount Freedom, New Jersey. She grew up in Medina, Ohio, and now resides in New Jersey with her husband. Formerly known as Krista Bailey, she was a competitive gymnast for fifteen years. She began her gymnastics career at Gymnastics World in Broadview Heights, Ohio. She competed as a class I gymnast at Gymnastics of Ohio in North Canton throughout high school and received a gymnastics scholarship to the University of Denver, an NCAA Division I school, where she set a school record on floor exercise. Krista holds a Bachelor's degree from the University of Denver in International Studies and French.

FOR FURTHER READING:

Dominique Moceanu: A Gymnastics Sensation
Written by Krista Quiner
Published by The Bradford Book Company in 1997

Kim Zmeskal: Determination to Win
Written by Krista Quiner
Published by The Bradford Book Company in 1995

Dare to Dream
Written by Tim Daggett with Jean Stone
Published by Wynwood Press in 1992

FOR CHILDREN'S READING:

Mary Lou Retton: Gold Medal Gymnast*
Written by Hal Lundgren
Published by Children's Press in 1985

A Very Young Gymnast*
Written by Jill Krementz
Published by Alfred A. Knopf in 1978

Sports Star: Nadia Comaneci*
Written by S.H. Burchard
Published by Harcourt Brace Jovanovich in 1977

Olga Korbut: Tears and Triumph*
Written by Linda Jacobs
Published by EMC Corporation in 1974

These books are out of print but are available in libraries.